AF614865

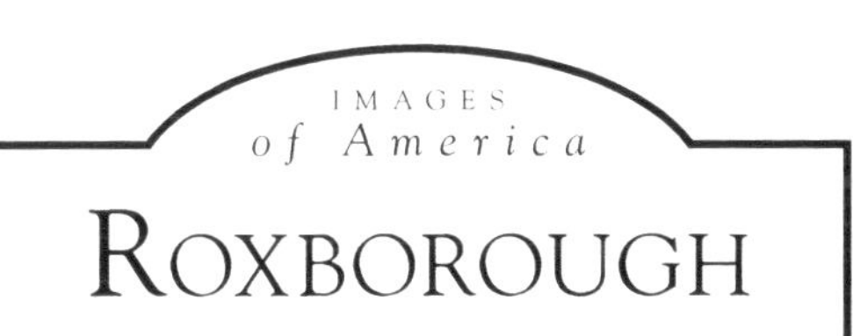
IMAGES
of America
ROXBOROUGH

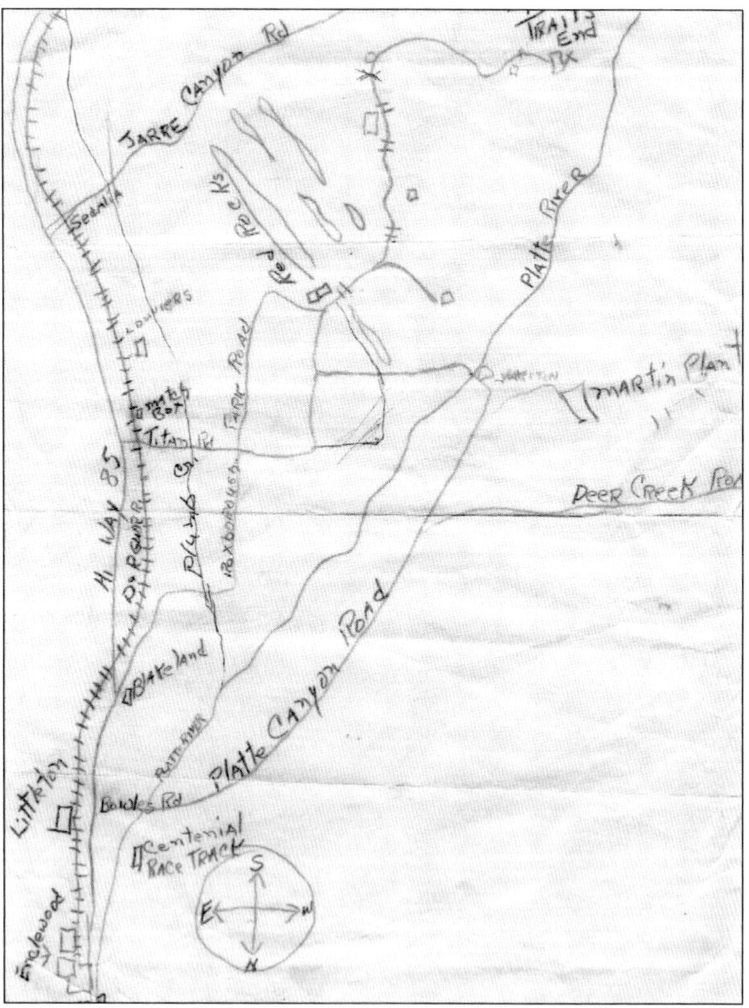

Mountain Jeannie's Map, 1950s. This map was drawn more than 50 years ago by Ada Jean (Slaton) Thiele. Those who knew her called her "Mountain Jeannie," and stories about her adventures are legendary in Roxborough. She was born in 1906 in what was then Indian Territory (later Oklahoma), married at 15, and had three children. After an unsuccessful marriage, she became a drifter, worked at poor-paying jobs across the West, and settled in Roxborough in the early 1940s. This map includes her favorite watering hole, the Matchbox. Jeannie became a local legend when she lived alone in the foothills west of Roxborough. She was known to be a good shot and proved it by displaying hides from a mountain lion that attacked her livestock and a bear that relentlessly went through her food storage. She was also known for her home-brewed liquid refreshments and naughty tales. This map is a detailed drawing of a part of Roxborough after the Glenn L. Martin missile plant was built, before the Army Corps of Engineers built Chatfield Dam and developers constructed hundreds of homes within Roxborough's majestic red rocks. The map was donated to the Roxborough Area Historical Society by Roy and Janet White, who visited Jeannie in her Trails End home in June 1965. (Roy White family.)

On the Cover: In 1870, Ferdinand Hayden invited photographer William Henry Jackson to join the 1870 federal government survey of the Yellowstone River and Rocky Mountains. One of the photographs he took was *Red Sandstones near Platte Canon*. This is now Roxborough's Arrowhead Golf Club's 15th fairway. (History Colorado.)

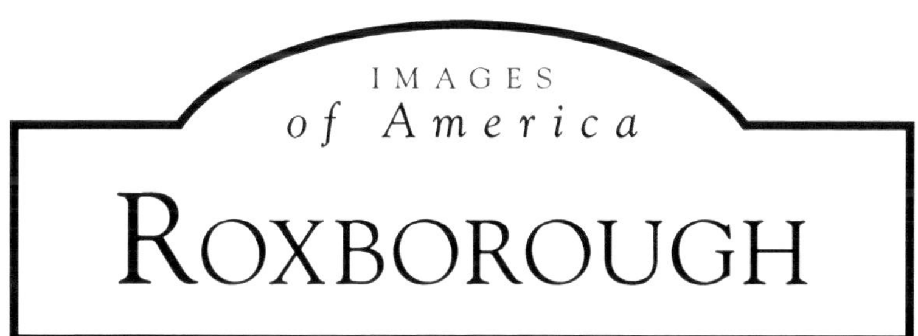

Flo Tonelli and Char Nauman

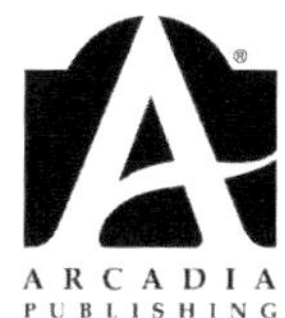

ISBN 978-1-4671-1636-7

Published by Arcadia Publishing
Charleston, South Carolina

Printed in the United States of America

Library of Congress Control Number: 2016931070

For all general information, please contact Arcadia Publishing:
Telephone 843-853-2070
Fax 843-853-0044
E-mail sales@arcadiapublishing.com
For customer service and orders:
Toll-Free 1-888-313-2665

Visit us on the Internet at www.arcadiapublishing.com

To those early pioneers, those who followed, and those who continue to work to preserve Roxborough's rich Western history, and to our fellow Roxborough Area Historical Society members who encouraged us along the way

Contents

Acknowledgments 6

Introduction 7

1. Roxborough's Dinosaur Highway 11
2. "Made by Nature Alone" 23
3. Water! 33
4. The Helmers 47
5. Mining Roxborough's Hogback 61
6. Tourists, Farmers, Ranchers, and Space Cowboys 71
7. Living the Roxborough Dream 87
8. Surrounded by Natural Beauty 111

ACKNOWLEDGMENTS

There is no museum in Roxborough where historical information is collected, so in writing this book, the authors had to contact dozens of sources. Thankfully, we acquired stories, materials, and images from some whose personal histories in Roxborough went back for generations. We are especially grateful to Mary Lou and Kenneth Shields, Sylvia Hill, Rusty Simon, Bob Swan, and so many others who shared photographs and their families' stories.

We were also fortunate to gather information from several organizations. Special thanks go to Heidi Geist of Denver Water; Shaun Boyd and Blake Graham at Douglas County History Research Center; Jenny Hankinson of the Littleton Museum; Angel Tobin, Betsy Healey, and Todd Farrow at Roxborough State Park; Melissa VanOtterloo at History Colorado, Denver; the Stephen H. Hart Library; and the Roxborough Park Foundation.

To our wonderful and generous local historian Ed Bathke, thank you. Ed supplied us with valuable information and historic photographs he and his late wife, Nancy—both charter members of the Roxborough Area Historical Society—collected over many years.

Thanks go to former Roxborough State Park manager Susie Trumble, who is an expert in all things Roxborough. We turned to Susie for information and advice many times.

The authors are not illiterate in computer technology, but photography technicalities are beyond our capabilities. Thankfully, Cathy Rapp came to our rescue and spent many hours helping us prepare images for publication. During the final stretch, Greg Akiyama and Jan Berger pitched in to offer technical assistance, which helped us finalize some of our numerous images.

We turned to Tom Olkowski, Lance W. Moreland, and Ed Yeats for photographs that depict Roxborough as it appears today. Remarkably, much of Roxborough's natural beauty looks the same as it did to those early pioneers. Geology is slow to change. But in the next few years, large planned residential developments will erase some of the vistas we have come to love. Tom is preserving those scenes in his Vanishing Prairie project.

And, finally, we would like to acknowledge the books and authors from which we drew valuable information: *Chronicles of Douglas County, Colorado*, and *A Photographic Journey*, compiled by Douglas County's Castle Rock Writers; *Roxborough State Park: Hogbacks and History*, by Dale Cavanagh; *Fading Past: The Story of Douglas County, Colorado*, by Susan Consola Appleby; *History of Douglas County: In the Beginning*, edited by Bob Rotruck; and *Report on the Hildebrand Ranch House and Family*, by Art Cornell.

Introduction

Roxborough is located in Colorado's northwest Douglas County, 25 miles south of the mile-high city of Denver. High grassy plains are to Roxborough's east, while Pike National Forest and the Rocky Mountains are to the west.

Roxborough's slanted 200-foot-tall red rocks rose up about 68 million years ago to form a natural barrier between plains and mountains. They reach skyward toward mountains covered in scrub oak, pine, juniper, and fir forests. Surrounded by natural beauty, the ancient monoliths stand tall as Roxborough's signature natural splendor.

It was in this remote frontier wilderness that men in Stephen H. Long's 1820 expedition searched for the headwaters of the Platte River near present-day Waterton.

According to Dr. Edwin James, botanist and geologist for the expedition, members scattered in various directions, "being eager to commence the examination of that interesting region . . . The woodless plain is terminated by a range of naked and almost perpendicular rocks, visible at a distance of several miles, and resembling a vast wall, parallel to the base of the mountain . . . the whole scenery truly picturesque and romantic."

Archaeologists think this spectacular geology, location, and availability of food and water made a desirable setting for Ice Age animals and humans, who lived here thousands of years before the Long Expedition happened upon the scene. An accidental archaeological discovery made in 1961 occurred when Roxborough rancher Charles Lamb enlarged a pond for his stock. As equipment dug deeper into the earth, large bones were uncovered. During the next few decades, archaeologists discovered the remains of more than 30 mammals, including Columbian mammoths, camels, ground sloths the size of an ox, and other animals estimated to have lived in the area as long as 13,000 years ago.

Much more recently, trappers, gold-seekers, and adventurists preceded the main onslaught of pioneers, and by 1860, settlers were arriving on foot, horseback, and wagons. By the 1870s, railroads built settlements and laid tracks. More people arrived; many were of German, British, and Irish heritage and were looking for opportunities to attain land for homesteads, farms, and ranches.

Although the area was too remote for many, a few quickly claimed, exchanged, and sold land throughout Roxborough. Civil War veteran Amos Miksch built his homestead around 1868. It was occupied until 2005 and is still standing in the heart of Roxborough.

From 1872 through 1876, the Hayden Survey Party mapped parts of Colorado. Noted photographer William Henry Jackson took pictures of the red sandstones of Roxborough for the survey party. By the 1870s, hundreds of homesteads were scattered throughout the area that was called Platte River Valley, Plum Creek, Waterton, Kassler, or Washington Park. Small communities began springing up along the South Platte River and creeks to support miners, loggers, farmers, ranchers, and others in the valley.

For those who were rugged, resourceful, adventurous, and hardworking, opportunities were plentiful for finding work in farming, mining, and lumber mills, or on the railroad. Workers were needed to build reservoirs, dams, and waterways. Denver's population needed more of the liquid gold, which became so valuable that a popular saying emerged: "Whiskey is for drinking. Water is for fighting."

Entrepreneur Henry S. Persse literally put Roxborough on the map. Persse purchased land called Washington Park from homesteaders in 1889. He built a small cabin and, in 1903, a solid stone house that was frequented by wealthy Denver citizens and government officials. To eliminate confusion with Denver's Washington Park, Persse is said to have renamed the area Roxborough after his family's estate in Galway, Ireland. Persse's love for Roxborough is evident in his printed postcards, on which he proclaimed its serenity and beauty in verse.

Persse created the Roxborough Land Company and purchased more land from homesteaders. Like many others who discovered Roxborough years later, he made elaborate plans to build an extraordinary resort. None of his grand plans came to fruition, and in 1918, while crossing a Denver street, he was struck and killed by a trolley. The land company was dissolved a few years later.

Near where the South Platte River opened to the plains, trains stopped in Waterton to service their steam engines. A few homes, a boardinghouse, and a small store were located nearby. In 1917, when LeRoy Russell Berens was seven years old, his father, Herman Berens, was hired to fire boilers in the Kassler Waterton plant. The Berens family lived in a frame home in Waterton Canyon "around the first bend past Kassler." LeRoy began working with the company when he was 20 and eventually became superintendent. Signage in Waterton Canyon tells the history of the Berens family, a father-and-son team that was typical of those generations who worked for the "water department."

Trains supplied necessities to towns along the river, and a spur was built to Kassler (and then Silica), where cars were unloaded of supplies and then loaded with sand, clay, and white bricks to be delivered to foundries and construction sites in Denver.

Glenn L. Martin, a pioneer in American aviation, started an airplane company in 1912 that provided World War I and World War II aircraft for the United States military. During the mid-1950s, Martin Company executives entered a new age and began searching for large tracts of land in a remote area where engineers could design and test rocket engines for missiles. The search brought the Martin Company to Colorado where it found an ideal place between the hogbacks and foothills about 17 miles southwest of Littleton. Thousands of acres near the South Platte River were purchased by the company from local ranchers and, according to longtime resident Rusty Simon, "everything changed after that." Instead of farmers, miners, cowboys, and ranch hands, space-age workers entered the community. Country roads became two- and then four-lane highways. One road's name was changed from Jones Road, named after a local dairy farmer, to Titan Road, after Martin's famous Titan rocket.

Despite Roxborough's location, 15 miles from Littleton and 25 miles from Denver, it has retained a rural feeling and serves as a reminder of the Old West. On its high plains, cowboys can still be seen branding cattle. Small hobby farms, large ranches, and bountiful recreational areas provide opportunities for visitors to view some of the most beautiful scenery in Colorado. Local wildlife includes turkeys, foxes, mule deer, and elk. Rattlesnakes, bears, and mountain lions are occasionally spotted, too.

Along Waterton Road, several popular recreational areas can be accessed—Chatfield State Park, High Line Canal, and Platte Canyon Reservoir. Denver Botanic Gardens Chatfield Farms is a few miles north. The hogback, foothills, Sharptail Ridge, Roxborough State Park, Colorado Trail, Waterton Canyon, and High Line Canal Trail are within a few miles of each other. The nationally recognized Arrowhead Golf Club is visited by people from around the globe. All of these are within or near the boundaries of Roxborough's 80125 zip code.

If you hike the hundreds of trails weaving along soaring peaks of ancient red sandstones in Roxborough State Park, you will hear the silent whisperings of Roxborough's history—it will remain a time and place you will not forget.

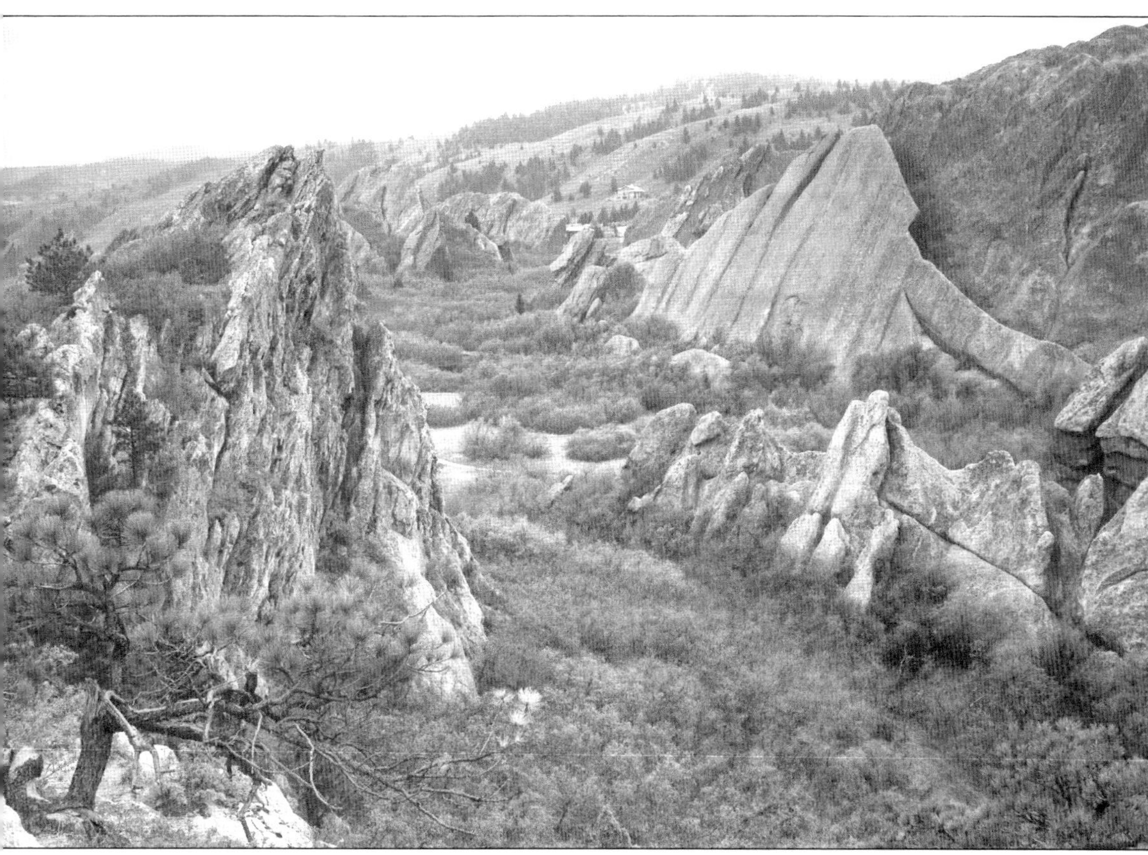

Roxborough State Park. From an overlook in Roxborough State Park, one can see the soaring red sandstone monoliths that rose from a horizontal position 68 million years ago. The close-to-4,000 acre park has been designated a Colorado National Area and a National Natural Landmark. Because of its unique geology, wildlife, and vegetation, the park prohibits camping, mountain biking, pets, and horses. The serene milieu throughout the park provides visitors with an exceptional opportunity to feel nature's silent energy. A home in adjacent Roxborough Park (a residential community) can be seen in the image. (Lance W. Moreland.)

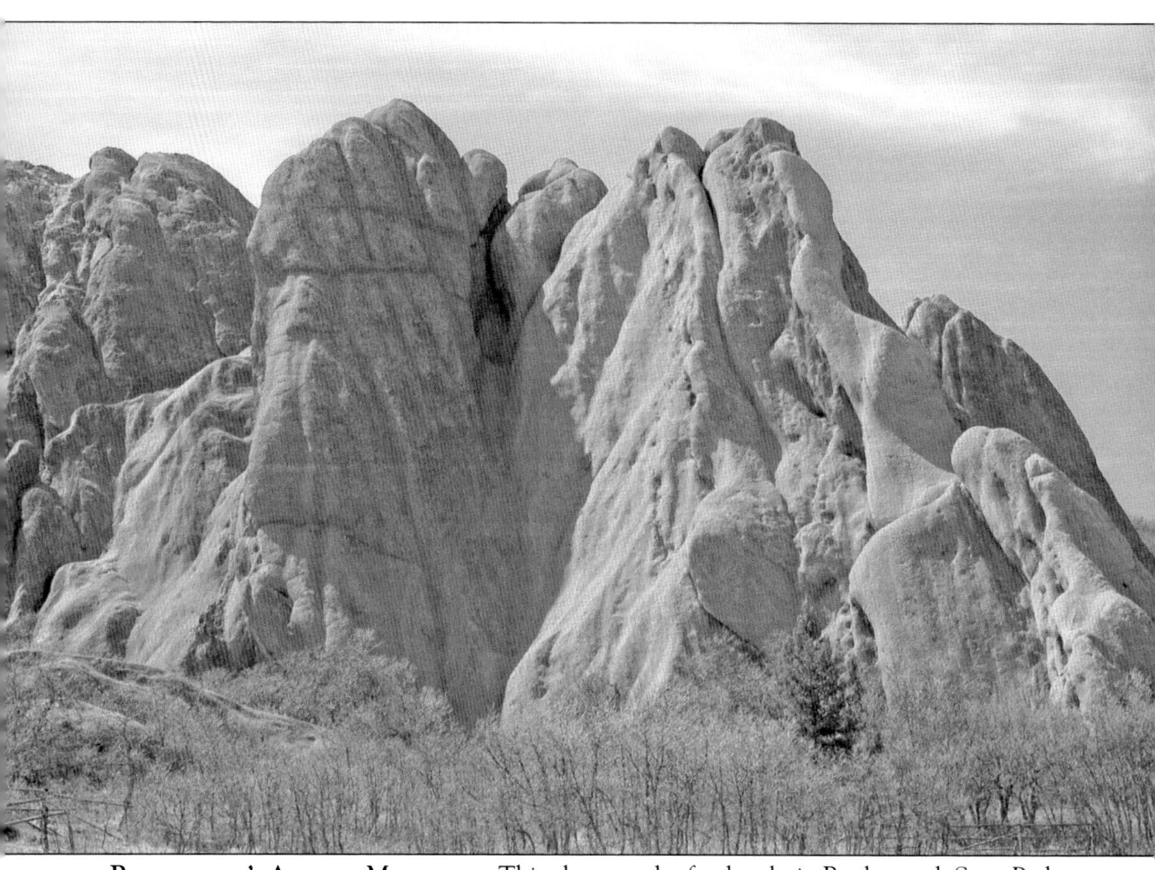

Roxborough's Ancient Monoliths. This photograph of red rocks in Roxborough State Park was taken in 2015, but the view is largely unchanged from one that might have been seen 150 years ago. The prominent soaring sandstone red rocks in Roxborough are found in the same Fountain Formation as those in Denver's celebrated Red Rocks Amphitheatre several miles to the north and those in renowned Garden of the Gods in Colorado Springs about 70 miles away. Formed by the erosion of the Ancestral Rocky Mountains, the formation runs along the east side of the younger Rocky Mountains that exist today. (Tom Olkowski.)

One

Roxborough's Dinosaur Highway

It can be difficult to grasp the massive geologic changes that created Roxborough. One million years ago was only yesterday when considering the life span of the universe. Roxborough's geologic wonders reflect the ever-changing, diverse events that occurred on this planet over millions of years.

Fortunately, there are those who can explain its marvelous creation, although scientific explanations are not always necessary. In Roxborough's vast natural surroundings, people can see, smell, hear, and touch its agelessness. There is the unexpected wonder of seeing soaring red sandstone spears bathed in sunlight as the breath of a clean, soft wind fills nostrils and lungs, and there is the silence that engulfs one when stumbling upon wildlife surprised to see humans. All is beautiful—and mysterious. This is Roxborough.

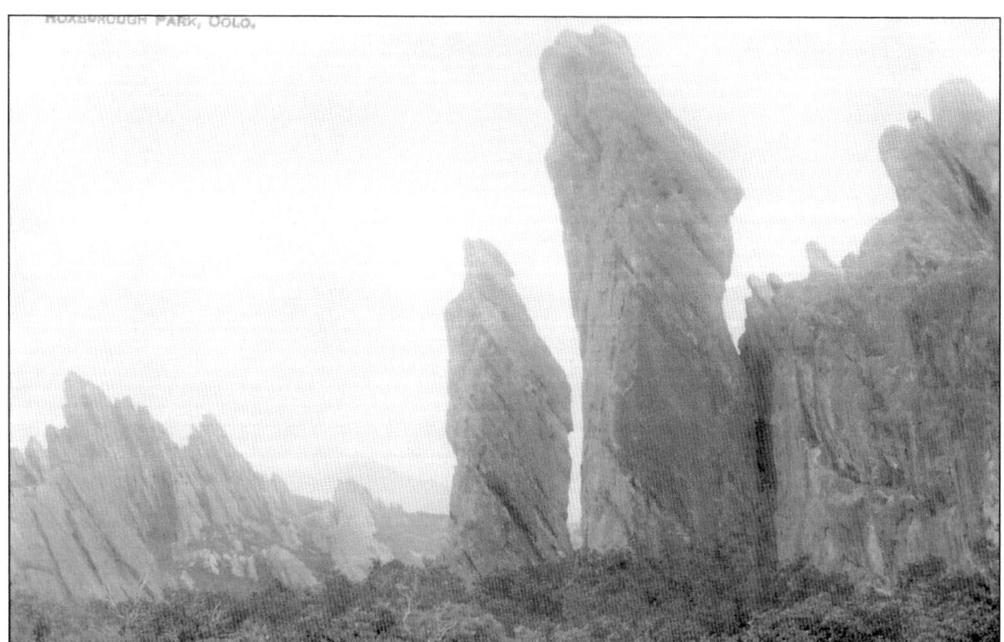

Roxborough's Geology. Roxborough's jagged red rock monoliths were formed 300 million years ago. They remained under the earth until about 68 million years ago, when a major upheaval, which lasted millions of years, triggered the land's rise and caused the sandstone slabs to rise at a 60-degree angle. (Ed and Nancy Bathke Collection.)

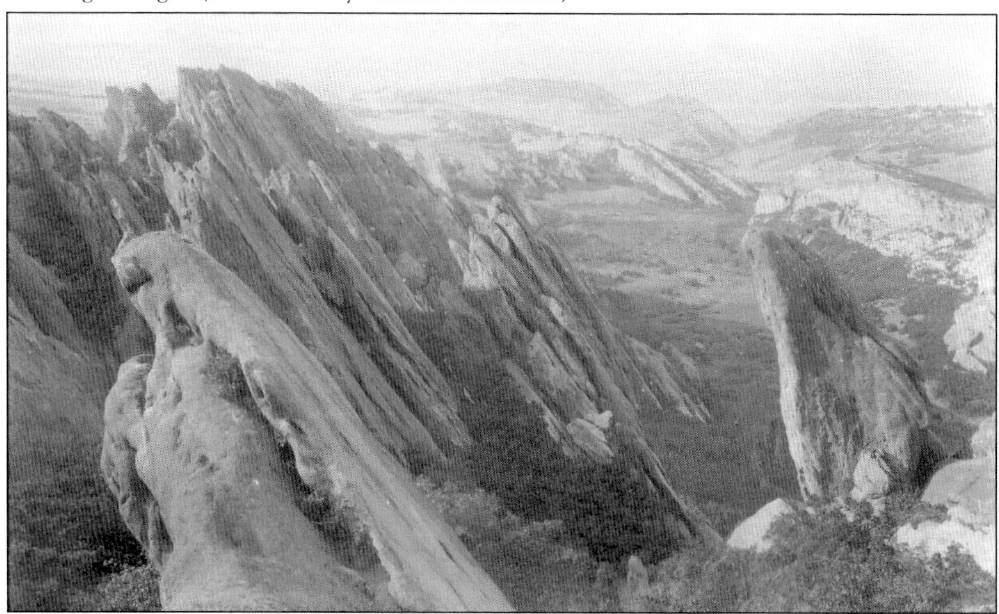

Roxborough's Three Hogbacks. Roxborough's three ridges, called "hogbacks," are made of tilted rocky layers. Each was formed during a different geological period. They are named Dakota Hogback, Lyons Formation, and Fountain Formation. Roxborough's signature red rocks in the foreground are in the Fountain Formation. The Dakota Hogback is just one mile from Carpenter Peak, Roxborough's highest foothill, but in geological time, there is nearly 1.5 billion years' difference between them. (Ed and Nancy Bathke Collection.)

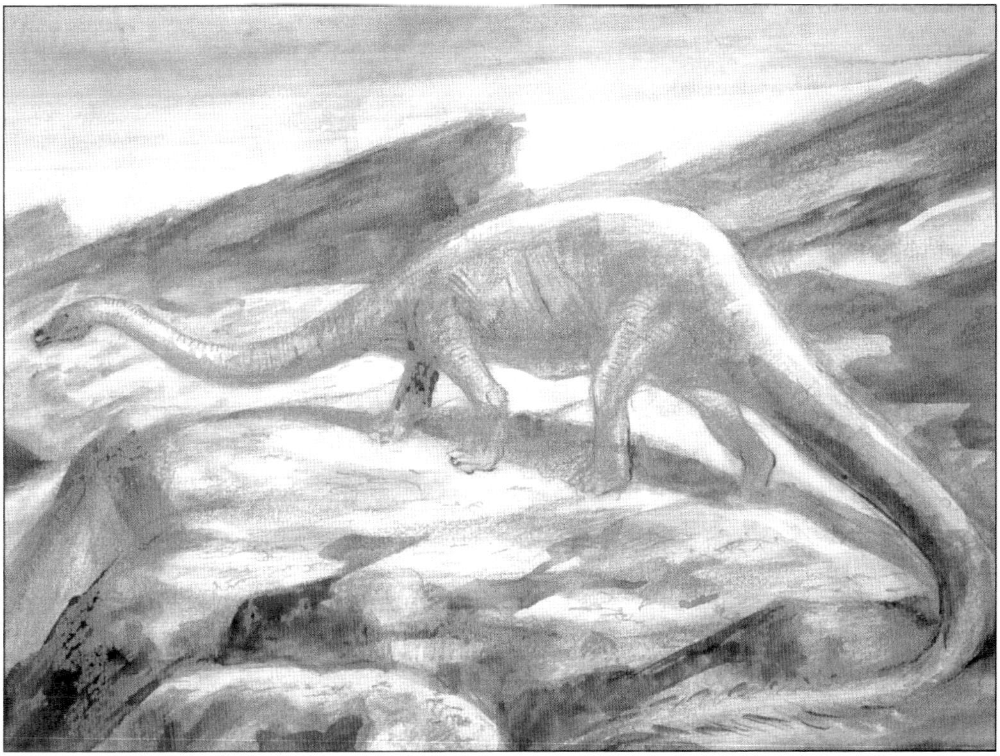

Dinosaur Highway. In this drawing, a long-necked sauropod dinosaur roams the land. In the book *Chronicles of Douglas County, Colorado*, Derald Hoffman states: "150 million years ago, during the late Jurassic era, dinosaurs lived in Douglas County with many racing along in Roxborough State Park, called the 'Dinosaur Freeway.'" Fossilized dinosaur footprints made eons ago have been found in the Dakota Hogback. (Denver Public Library Western History Collection.)

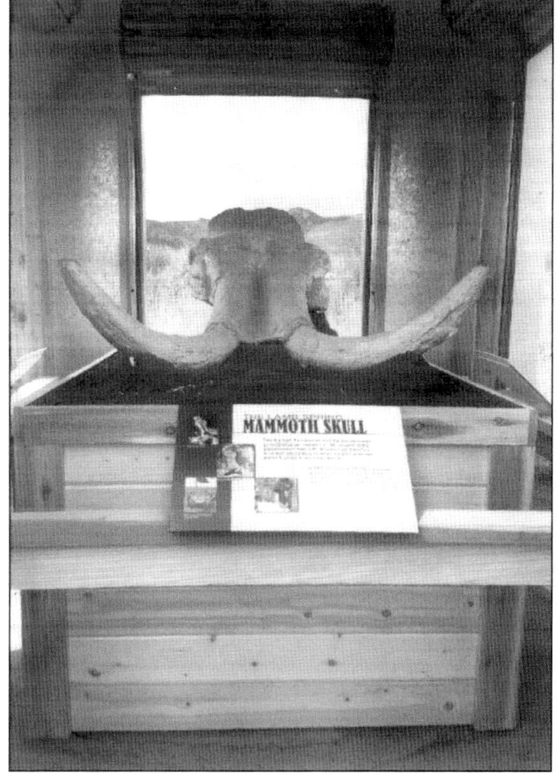

Signs of Prehistoric Life. Shown in this image is a replica of a Columbian mammoth skull found at Lamb Spring. The skull itself can be viewed at the National Museum of Natural History in Washington, DC. It is not difficult to discover fossilized sea shells, shark teeth, and animal and human relics throughout Roxborough. Archaeologists designated Roxborough State Park as "significant for its unusually high site density and broad range of prehistoric types." (Char Nauman.)

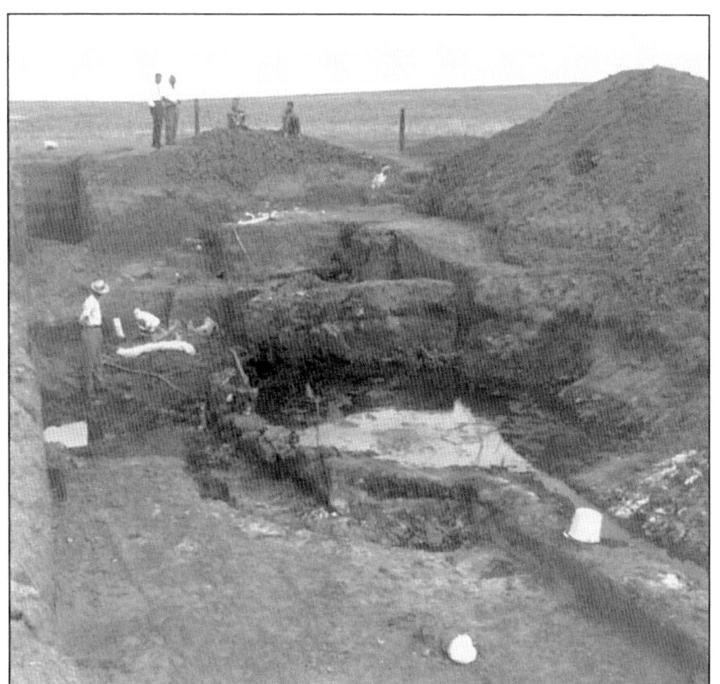

Ancient Animals. In 1960, Roxborough rancher Charles Lamb was enlarging a stock pond at the site of a natural spring when he uncovered a large tusk and several bone fragments. US Geological Survey (USGS) scientists identified the bones as the remains of ancient mammoths, horses, camels, and bison. (US Department of Interior.)

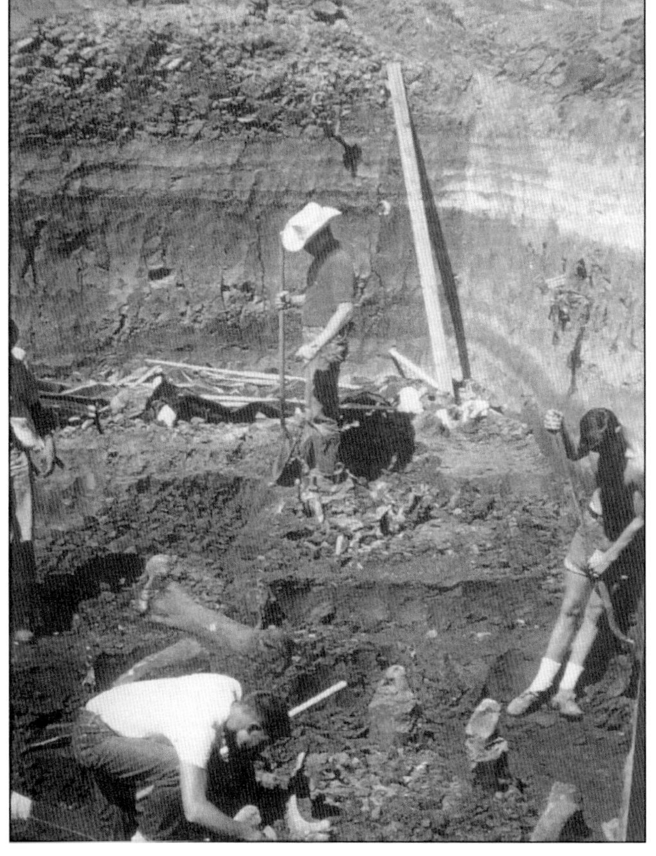

Ice Age Animals. In this photograph, unidentified scientists examine the earth once under Charles Lamb's pond. In 1961–1962, Smithsonian Institution archaeologists and USGS geologists found bones of at least five mammoths, one of which was radiocarbon-dated to the end of the Ice Age. In 1980–1981, more excavations were conducted, and Smithsonian archaeologists found more than 30 mammoths, the largest number found at any site in Colorado. (Jack Warner.)

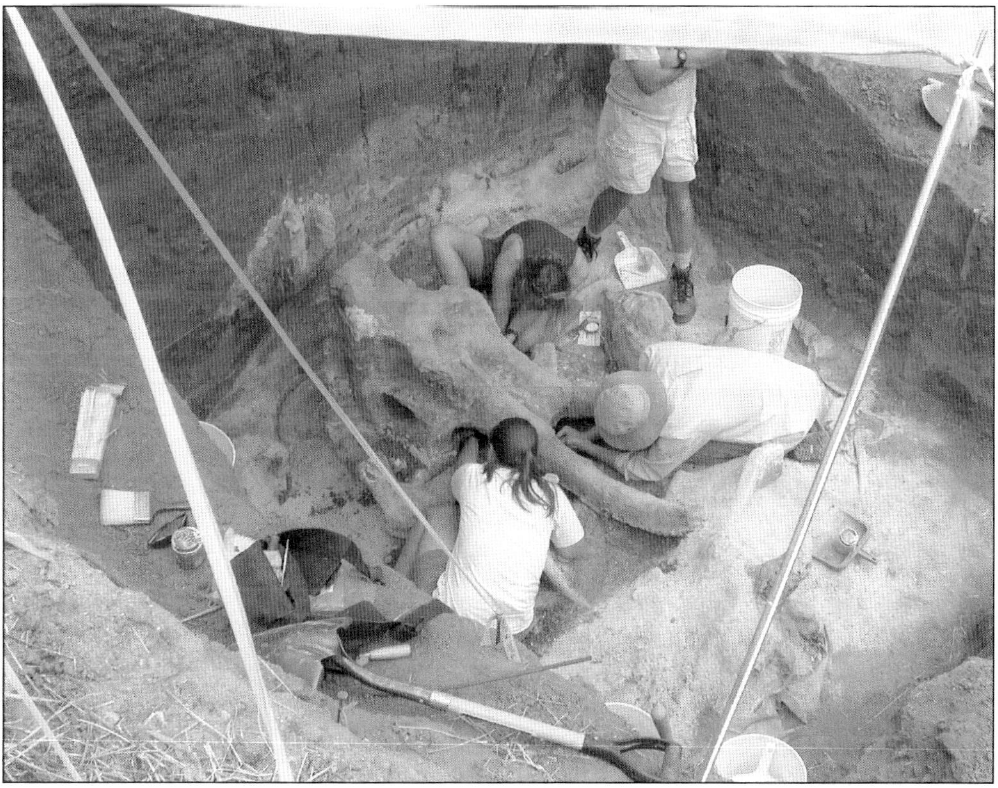

LAMB SPRING ARCHAEOLOGICAL PRESERVE. In this photograph, archaeologists uncover the skull of a large mammoth. In 1995, the Archaeological Conservancy—with the help of the Denver Museum of Nature and Science, Smithsonian Institution, and Douglas County—purchased 35 acres, including the land containing Lamb Spring. According to the Lamb Spring Archaeological Preserve website, artifacts left by humans indicate that people hunted and camped around the spring during the past 9,000 years—and possibly much longer ago than that. (Jack Warner.)

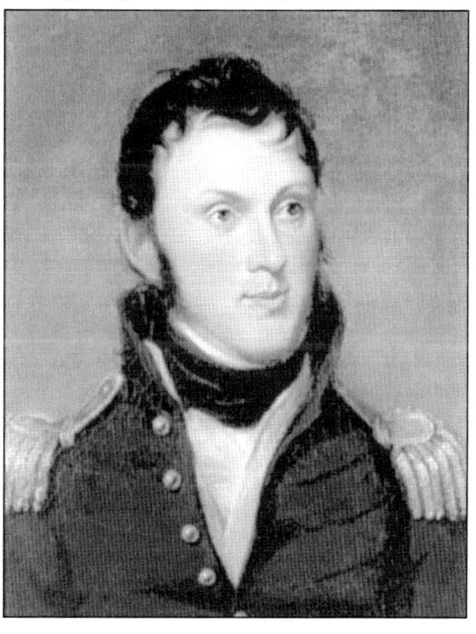

STEPHEN LONG EXPEDITION. In the early 19th century, Maj. Stephen Long (pictured) was commissioned to survey the American West. Long and his men entered the area in 1820 and camped along the South Platte River near present-day Kassler/Waterton. Dr. Edwin James, the survey's geologist-botanist, wrote in his journal that "the whole scenery with its almost perpendicular rocks . . . was truly picturesque and romantic."

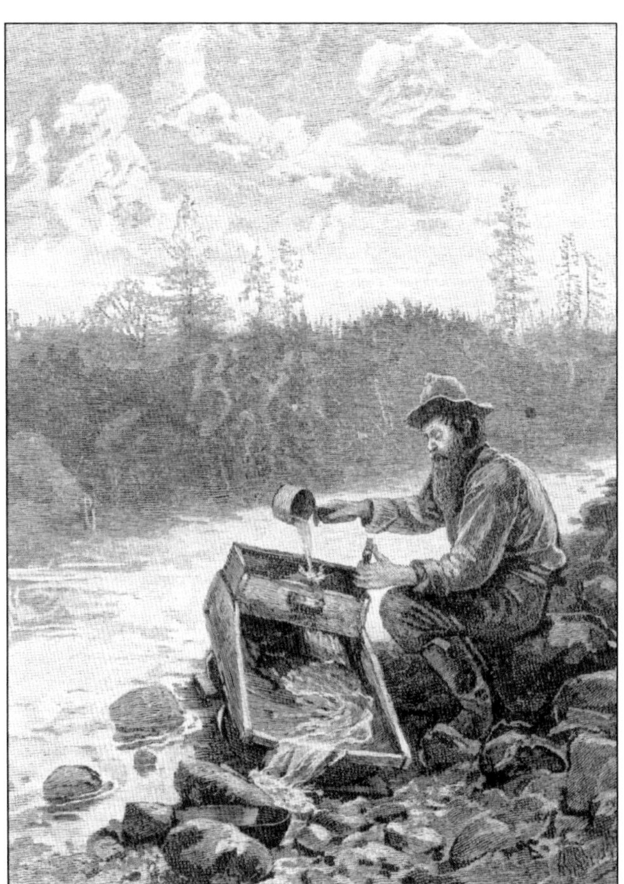

Early Miners. Placer mining was common along the area's rivers, creeks, and streams, but little gold was found in the Roxborough area. In her book *Douglas County, A Historical Journey*, Josephine Lowell quotes an 1850s news journal: "several men who were too lazy to mine and too poor to return home last summer . . . settled on a nice claim along the Platte."

An Act of Congress. This structure rests on an old homestead owned in the 1850s by Ramona Moreno, widow of Rafael Moreno, a veteran of the Navajo Indian War who obtained it through an act of Congress. Pictured is the ranch house built in the 1940s by the Atchinson family, who owned a 5,000-acre ranch. Their ranch was purchased by the Martin Company in the mid-1950s and is presently leased from the Army Corps of Engineers by the Audubon Society. (Prysby family.)

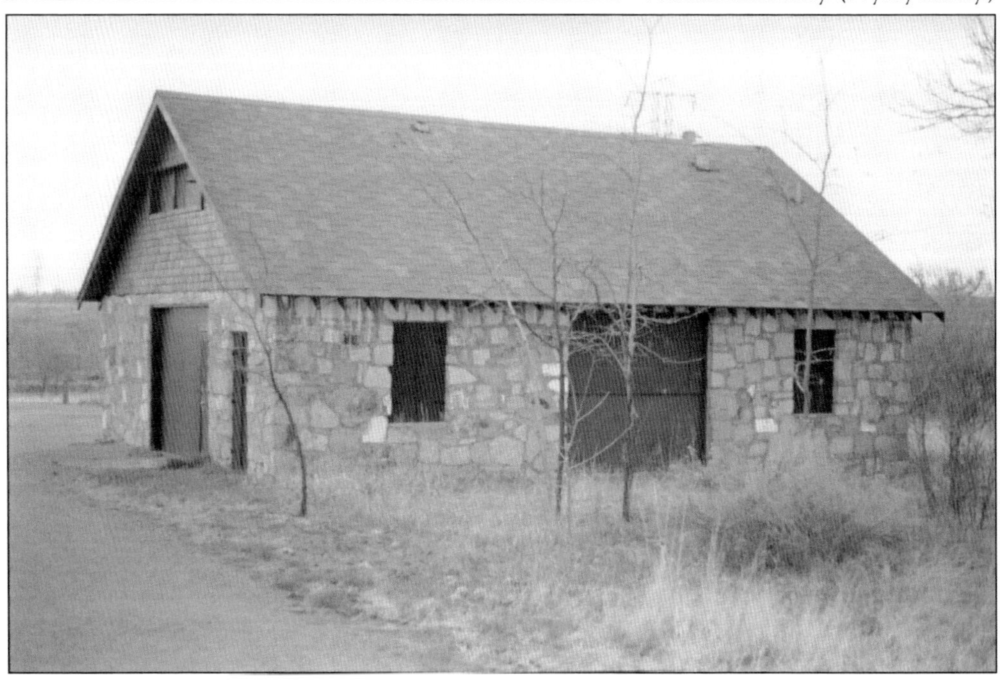

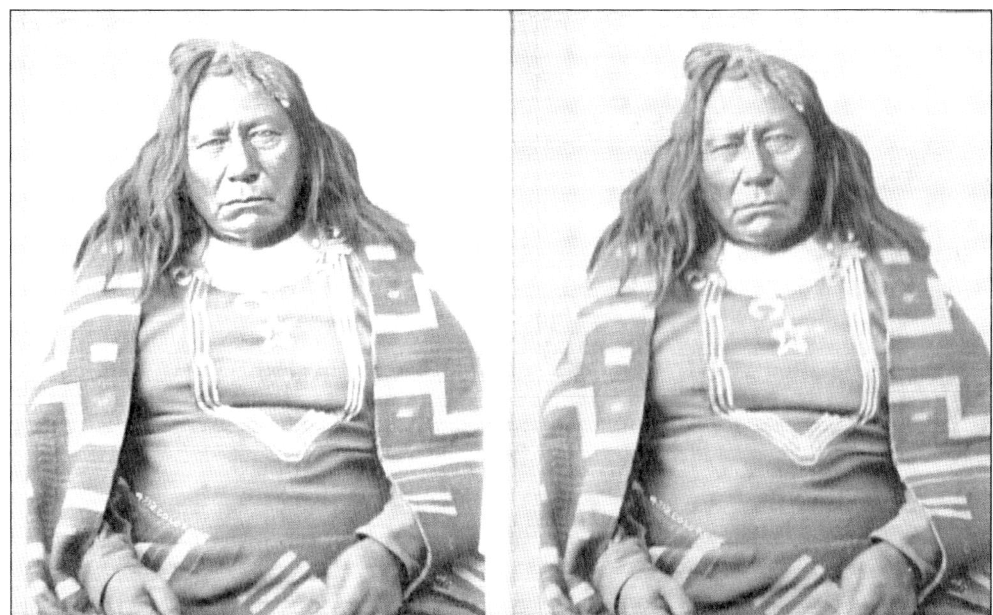

Indigenous and Native Americans. Fire pits dating to about 1000 BC have been found in Roxborough. More than 500 years ago, various Native American tribes inhabited Roxborough and lived in the area until about the 1870s. Ute leader Colorow (pictured in this stereograph) often traveled through the area and visited homesteads in the red rocks. He was known for his love of ranchers' biscuits. (Ed and Nancy Bathke Collection.)

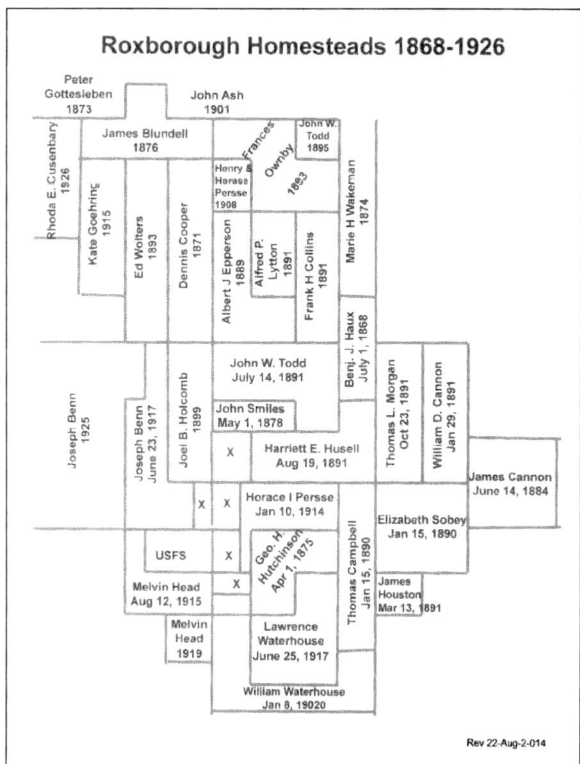

Early Homesteads. Many settlers waited until Native Americans were moved to reservations and the Civil War ended. Entrepreneurs and pioneers began acquiring land throughout the Plum Creek region and Platte River Valley. Edward M. Griffith is said to have established one of the earliest homesteads and is sometimes given credit for naming the area Roxborough, although most evidence indicates Henry S. Persse named the area Roxborough. (Roxborough State Park.)

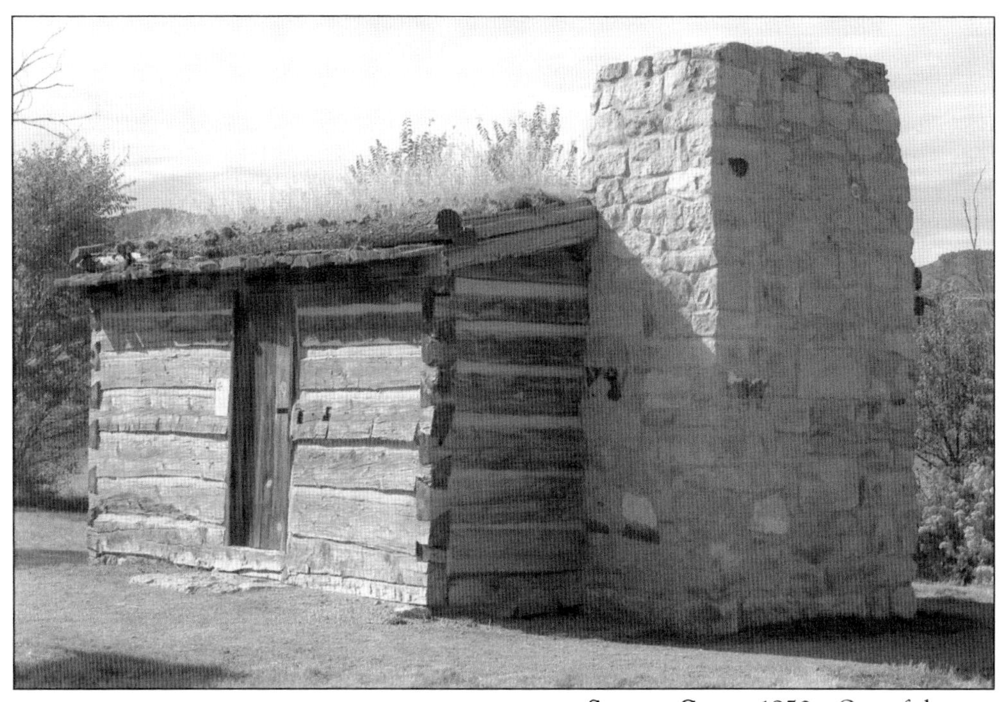

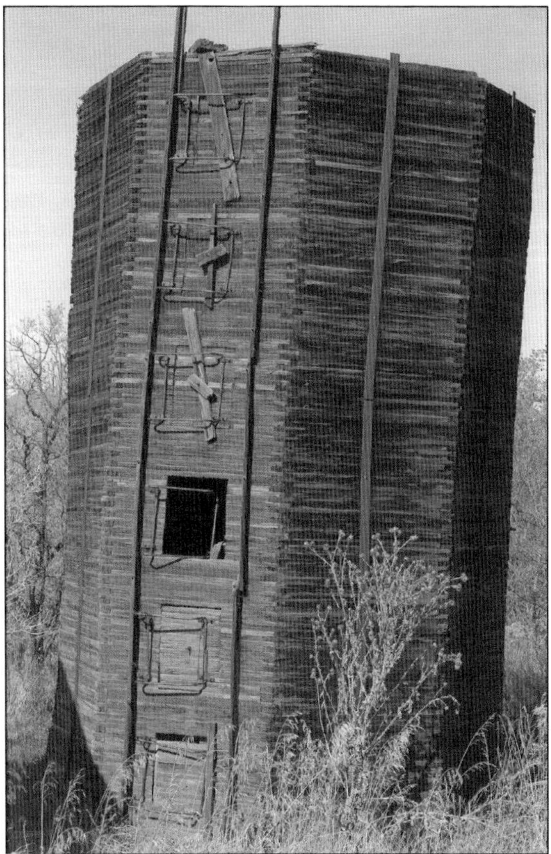

Slocum Cabin, 1850s. One of the oldest structures in Colorado, this 10-by-12-foot home was most likely built by a trapper and sold to Thomas Truxton Slocum. Thomas and his wife, Ann, were among the earliest pioneer families in the area and developed a large cattle ranch. The cabin was moved to nearby Chatfield State Park, where a Slocum Day celebration is held each summer. (Tom Olkowski.)

Slocum Silo. In the early 1900s, this silo was built by brothers Welding, Fred, and Emmitt Slocum, descendants of Thomas Truxton and Ann Slocum. The unusual silo is made of wood. (Tom Olkowski.)

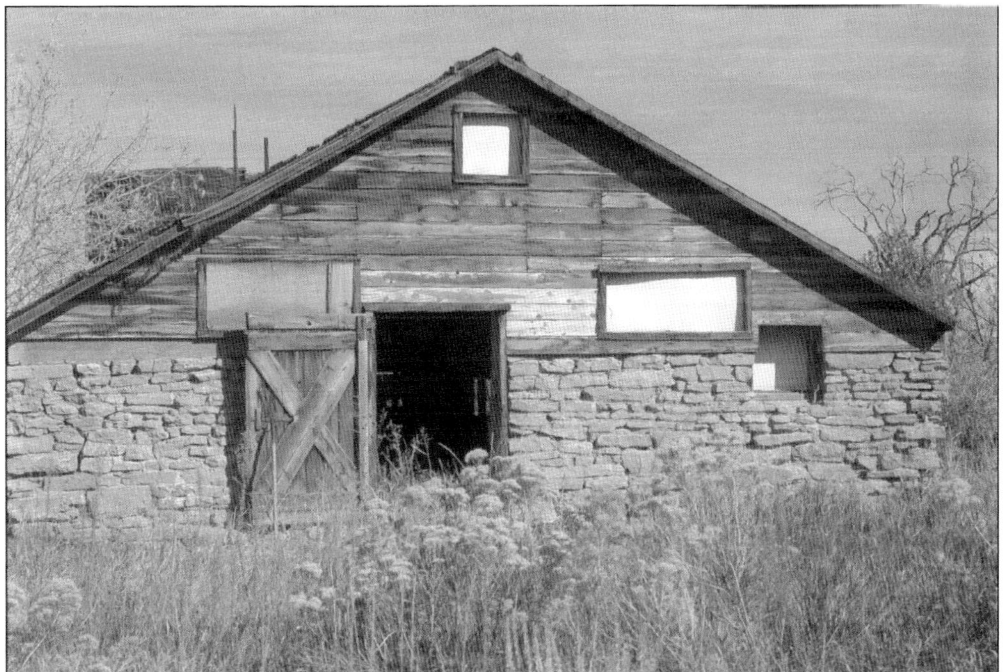

Slocum Barn. Welding Slocum and his two brothers, Fred and Emmitt, built the stone and wooden barn at the beginning of the 20th century. When the ranch was sold to Ravenna developers, Welding's daughter, Margery Slocum Wogan, requested the barn and silo remain intact. Both structures are located at Ravenna's entrance as a reminder of the Slocum family's early pioneers. (Tom Olkowski.)

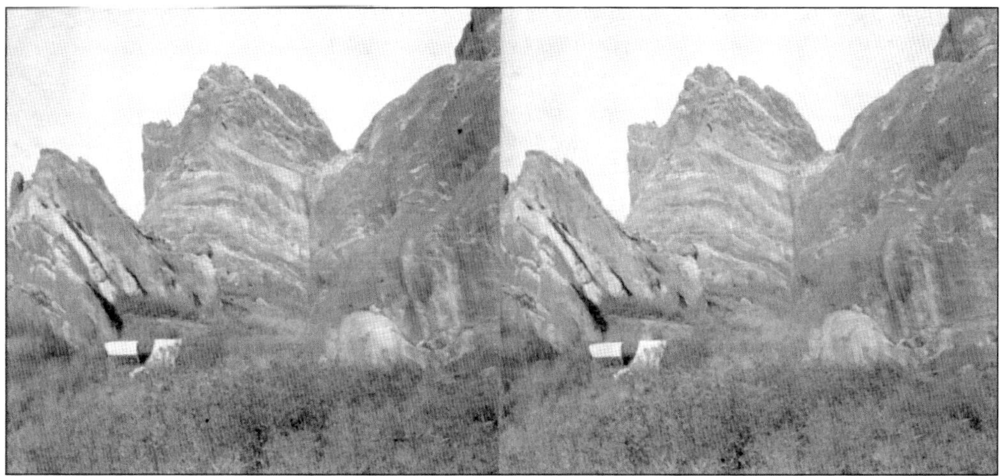

Stereograph of Roxborough Park. The stereograph was popular in the 1870s. Pioneer photographer William G. Chamberlain was a prolific Colorado lensman from 1861 to 1889. He published at least four images of Roxborough Park. In this photograph, Chamberlain's wagon sits in scrub oak at the base of Roxborough's red monoliths. (Ed and Nancy Bathke Collection.)

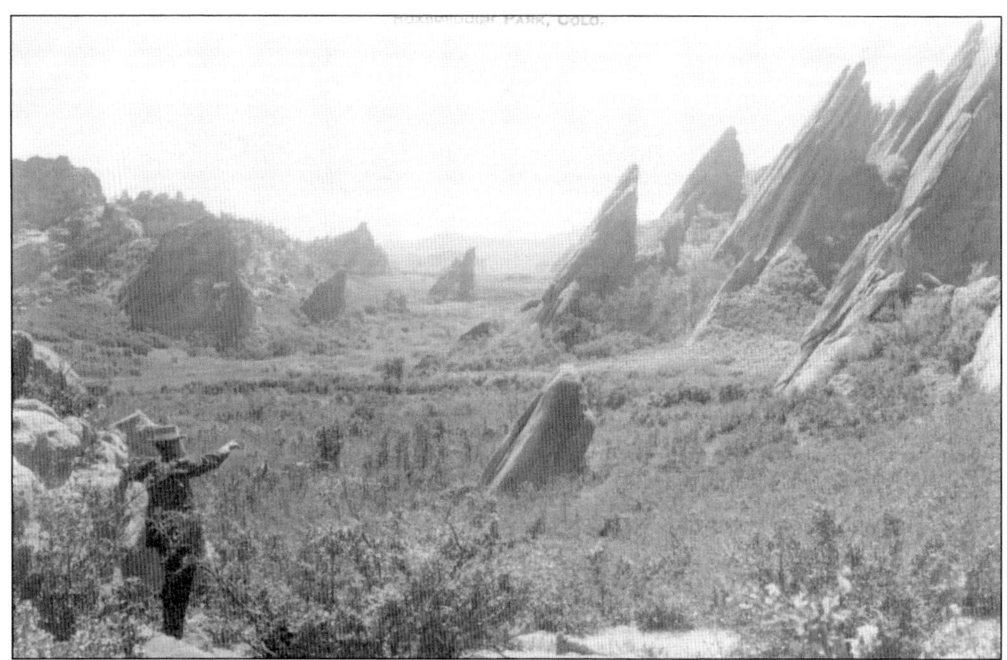

Roxborough's Pristine Beauty. In this image, an unidentified photographer captured the prehistoric beauty of Roxborough and placed the scene on a postcard. This unique landscape remains unchanged in Roxborough State Park. (Ed and Nancy Bathke Collection.)

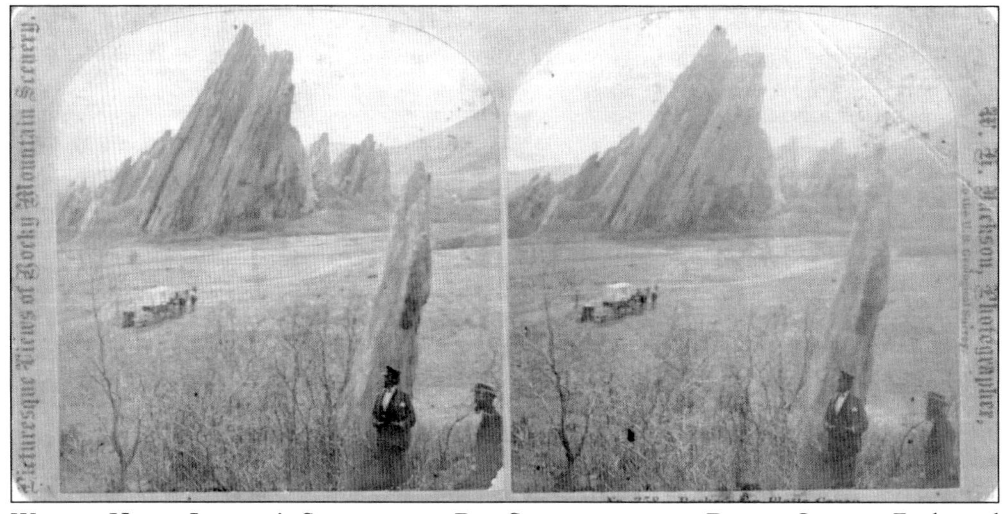

William Henry Jackson's Stereograph *Red Sandstones near Platte Canyon.* Ferdinand Hayden led several surveys into Colorado Territory between 1868 and 1876. In 1870, official photographer William Henry Jackson accompanied the group and produced three images of Roxborough Park. His photography wagon is pictured in the foreground. The view is the same as that of present-day Arrowhead Golf Club's 15th fairway, seen by thousands of Roxborough residents, tourists, and golfers each year. (Ed and Nancy Bathke Collection.)

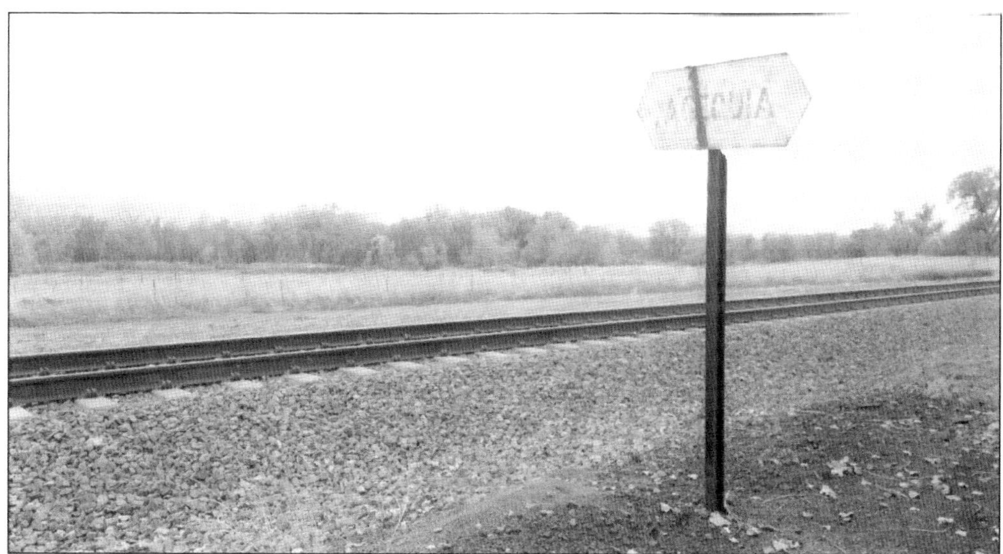

Acequia, an Early Settlement. The 1870s became a period of rapid expansion in Douglas County. In 1871, Acequia was platted by the development arm of the Denver & Rio Grande Railroad. In 1874, Acequia was the site of the first post office in the area. Although the rusty sign along the railroad track remains, Acequia disappeared decades ago. (Kimberleigh and Kyler Anders.)

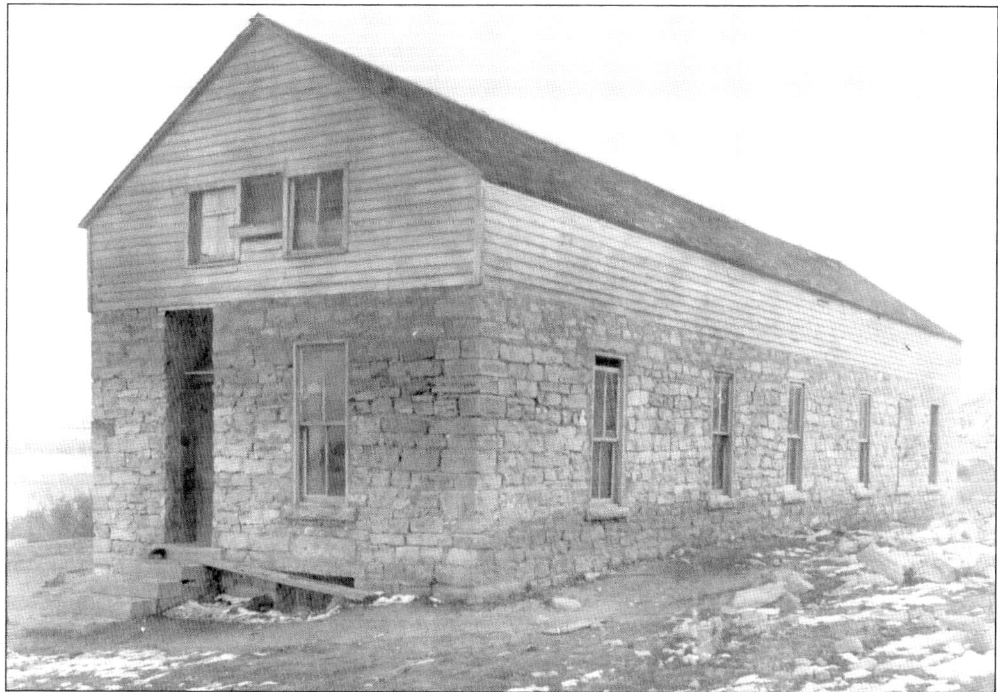

Acequia School. This undated photograph is thought to show Acequia's two-room school built of white limestone in 1911 near the banks of Plum Creek. After the great flood of 1965, the school was torn down to make room for Chatfield Lake and Dam, and a new school was built. (Littleton Museum.)

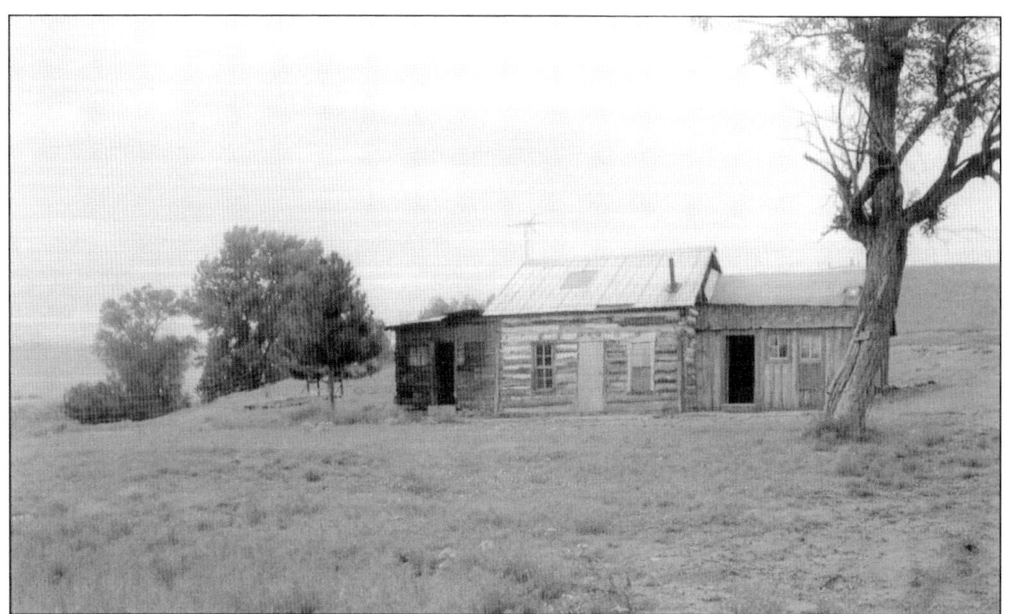

AMOS MIKSCH HOMESTEAD. This is a more modern photograph of Pennsylvanian Amos Miksch's homestead. Miksch built his homestead cabin (the center of the cabin) in the late 1860s and began farming the surrounding land. In 1873, Miksch sold the cabin to Frederick Neumeyer, who farmed there for 10 years. Neumeyer sold it to Austrian immigrants Franz "Frank" and Judith Helmer for $800. (Flo Tonelli.)

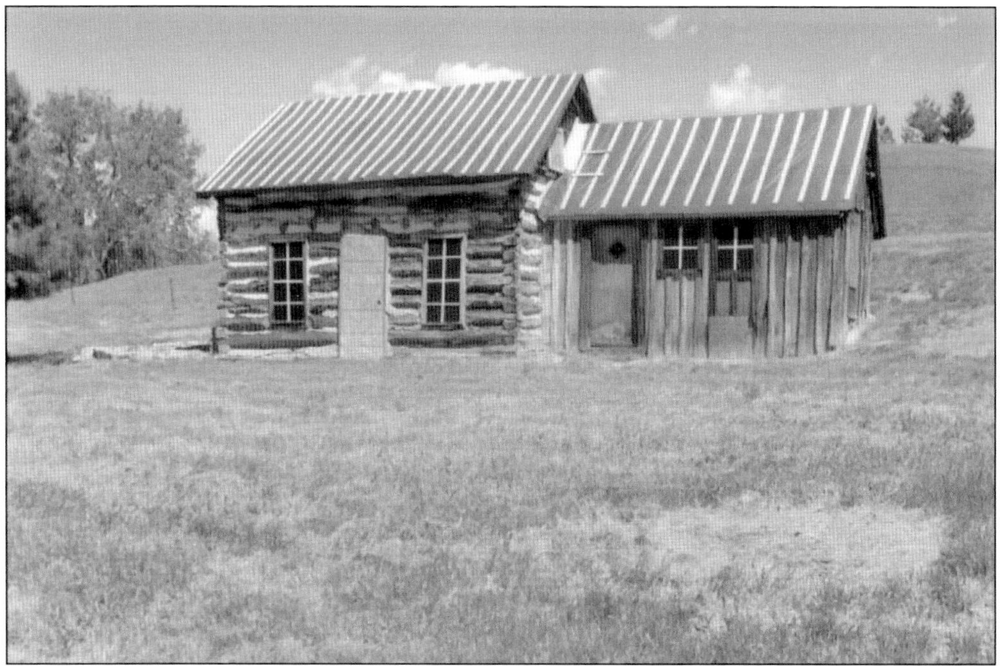

MIKSCH-NEUMEYER-JOHN HELMER HOMESTEAD. The Miksch-Neumeyer-Helmer cabin was owned for more than 100 years by members of the John Helmer family (until 1995) and remained occupied until 2005. Two additions were built during different periods. The one on the west side of the main cabin was removed because it threatened the structure of the original cabin. (Flo Tonelli.)

Two

"Made by Nature Alone"

There are some people who are so moved by nature that they value it for itself alone. Most early explorers left few written accounts of being in Roxborough. It seems many skipped the area altogether as they traveled through the wilderness on the way to somewhere else. The deed between Henry S. Persse (pronounced "purse") and Edward M. Griffith in 1889 was the first legal reference to the land as Roxborough Park. It is uncertain which man suggested the name Roxborough Park in the deed, but subsequent information indicates it was named by Persse after an ancestral estate in Galway, Ireland.

During the middle of the 19th century, most explorers—usually men—came west looking for gold or opportunity. Many were poor; others were entrepreneurs with an education and some family money who simply wanted to see what they could accomplish. It seems Persse was that kind of man. He fell in love with Roxborough and was lucky enough to stumble on a local landowner. Griffith thought it was not worth paying taxes for land filled with rocks. Persse purchased Griffith's land—and, eventually, other homesteads—from the seller's partners until Persse owned most of the land that present-day taxpayers now own in Roxborough State Park.

Persse was an entrepreneur. He had a family and owned a home in Denver. He wrote poems about Roxborough and took pictures of his time there and placed both on postcards. He built a stone house where he entertained visitors, added guest cabins, and invited Denver's A-list to spend time with him in Roxborough. He celebrated Roxborough, and visitors celebrated him. Persse had a dream; he brought partners in to help him make it a reality. He would build a grand resort. But despite a Denver newspaper's glowing description written in large, bold print, it never happened due to a lack of water and a shortfall of money. Both would plague other dreamers who came after him.

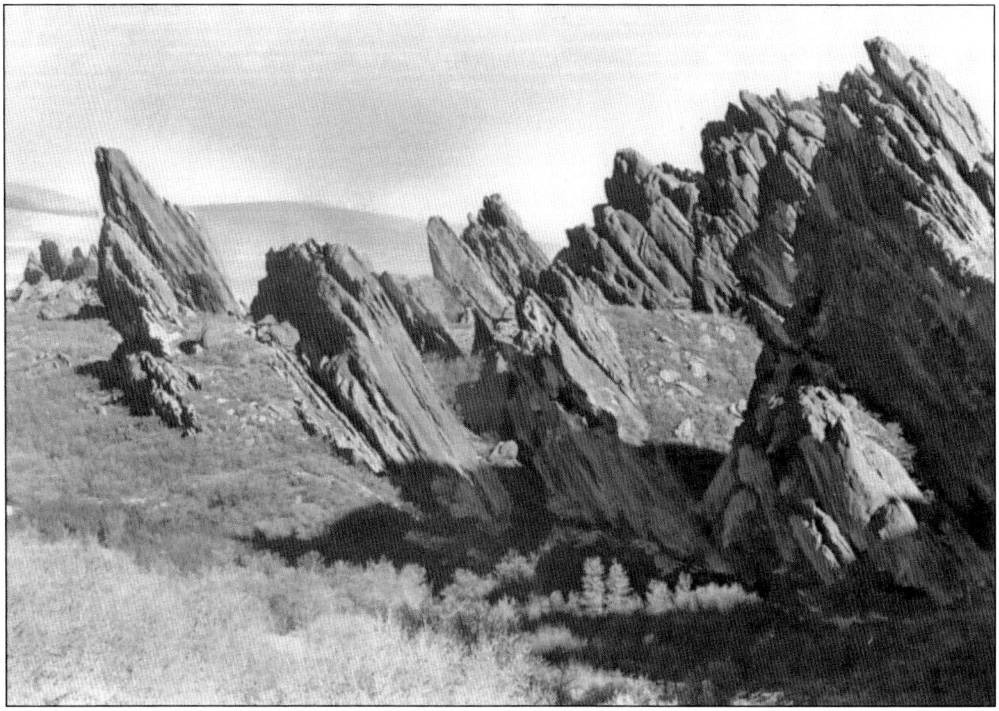

Edward M. Griffith and Henry Stratford Persse. Griffith sold his land to Persse in 1889, claiming that "a bunch of rocks in Colorado were not worth the cost of taxes." Persse saw Roxborough as serene, beautiful, and full of potential. He continued to purchase additional land until he eventually owned 160 acres, making him one of the people who held the most land in Roxborough. (Roxborough State Park.)

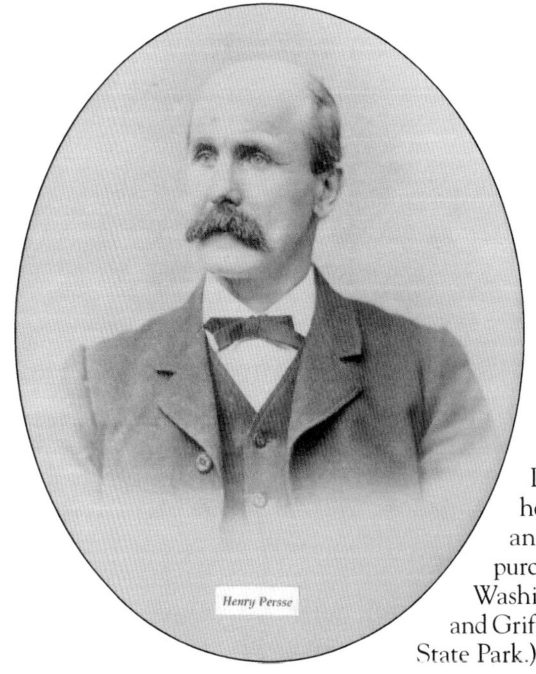

Pioneer Henry S. Persse. Persse, one of the best-known pioneers in Roxborough, was born in New York. He brought his family to Denver in the early 1890s. An entrepreneur, he was a wool dealer and real estate promoter and owned a partial interest in a brewery. He purchased land in what was then known as George Washington Park from the Gray, Carpenter, Everett, and Griffith partnership in the late 1890s. (Roxborough State Park.)

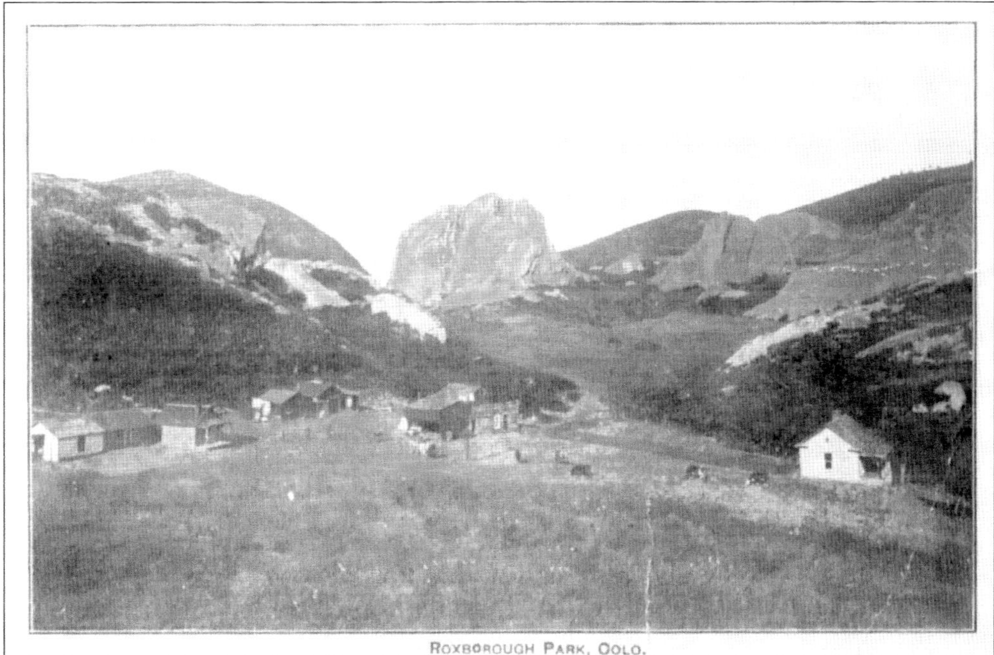

George Washington Park. The property within the soaring 68-million-year-old red rocks was called George Washington Park because of the large rock found in the Fountain Formation that resembled a reclining George Washington. Because of confusion with Denver's Washington Park, the park's name was changed around 1900 to Roxborough. (Ed and Nancy Bathke Collection.)

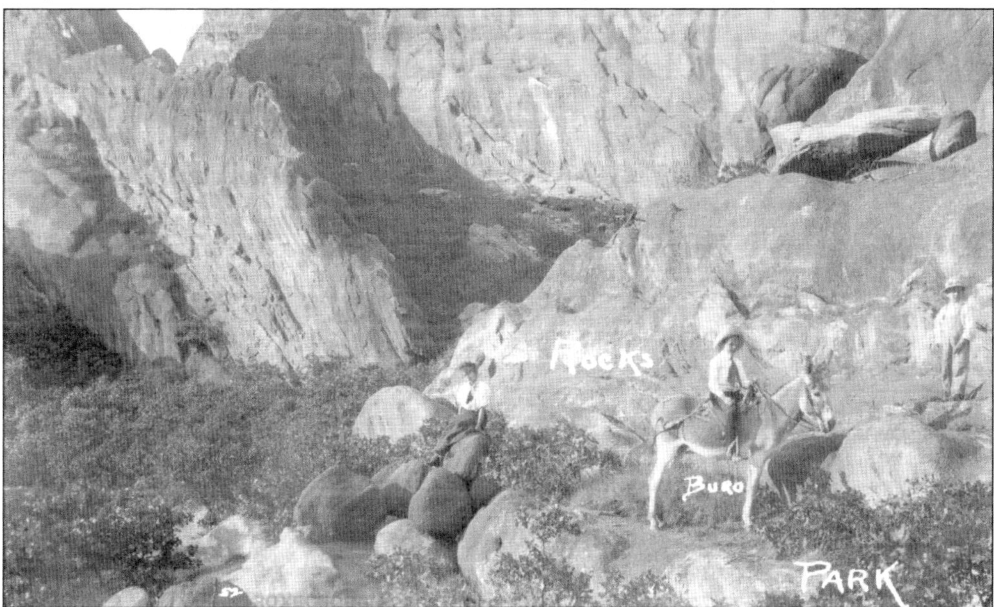

Who Put Roxborough on the Map? Some say it was Edward M. Griffith, one of the first settlers who arrived in the area in the 1860s, who first named the area Roxborough after a place "near his home in England." However, oral history credits Henry S. Persse with naming Roxborough after his English family's estate in Galway, Ireland. This photograph featuring unidentified children and a burro provides a humorous version of the name. (Douglas County Research Center Library.)

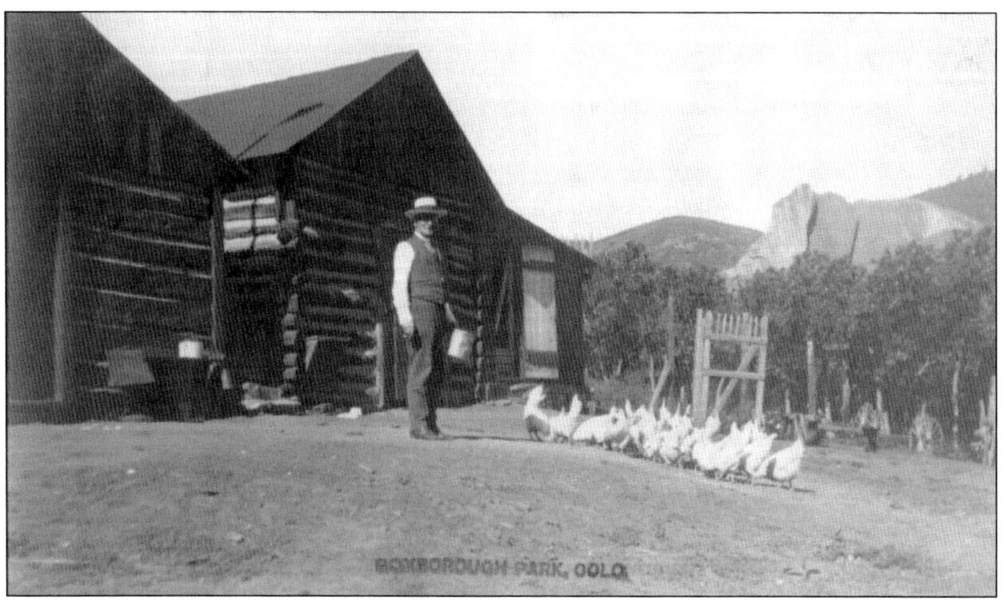

Henry Persse Feeding Chickens at His Roxborough Home. Although Persse continued to make his home in Denver, he built a small, two-room log structure near a spring in Roxborough. A second, smaller log structure was added and inscribed by Persse in 1901. To promote Roxborough, he pictured various local scenes on postcards. This one shows him feeding his chickens. (Ed and Nancy Bathke Collection.)

Post Card.

THIS SIDE FOR ADDRESS ONLY.

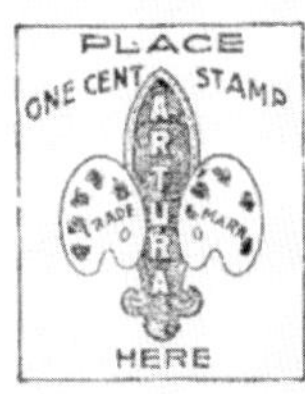

Roxborough Park.

There's a place between the foot hills
And the level, sea-like plain,
Where the peaks loom high behind you
And in front waves golden grain;
'Taint quite high enough for many,
Nor quite low enough for some;
But it's here I've built my cabin,
Far from strife-filled cities hum.

Here the range, behind is golden
With the glowing light of day;
And the prairie's like a painting,
Where the last warm sunbeams lay;
And along the dimpled stretches--
Humble hints of grander heights--
Falls a magic veil of purple
From those fading, dying lights.

Seem's if some folks can't be suited
'Cept upon the highest peak;
And still others, on the lowlands,
Must their fame and fortune seek;
But right here's the happy medium
And it's here contentment dwells,
When the afternoon is dying
'Mongst the Persse's sandstone dells.

An Ode to Henry Persse's Roxborough. This verse is attributed to Persse, who often wrote poems about his beloved Roxborough Park and placed them on postcards. In this ode, he writes: "Taint quite high enough for many, Nor quite low enough for some; But it's here I've built my cabin, Far from strife-filled cities hum." (Douglas County History Research Center.)

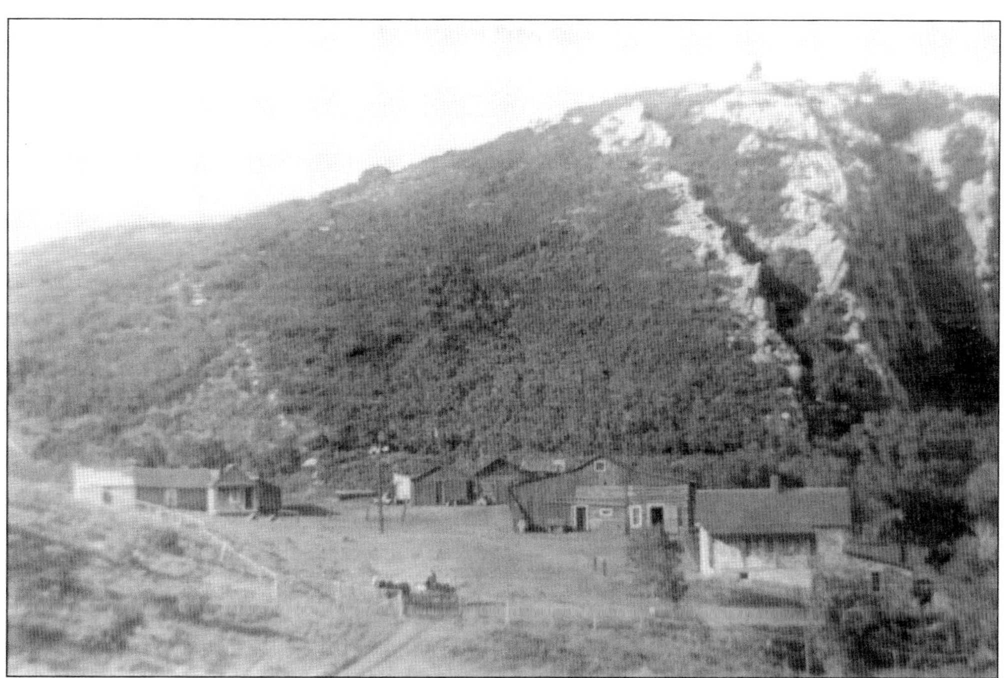

Henry Persse's Resort. Persse believed Roxborough could be a resort area and invited Denver's finest citizens to visit. He continued to expand his holdings and built the guesthouses pictured here. (Roxborough State Park.)

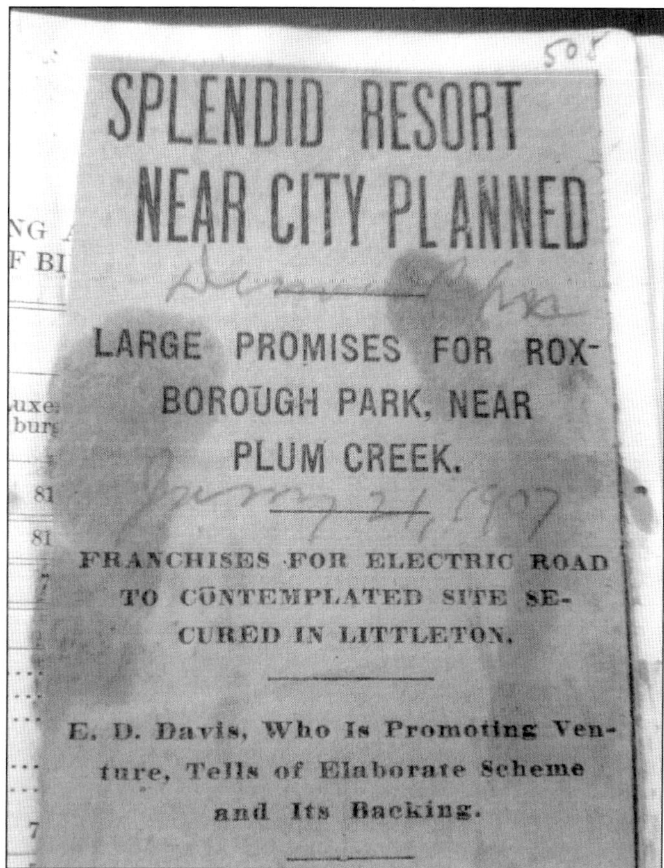

SPLENDID RESORT NEAR CITY PLANNED

LARGE PROMISES FOR ROXBOROUGH PARK, NEAR PLUM CREEK.

FRANCHISES FOR ELECTRIC ROAD TO CONTEMPLATED SITE SECURED IN LITTLETON.

E. D. Davis, Who Is Promoting Venture, Tells of Elaborate Scheme and Its Backing.

Henry Persse's "Splendid" Resort. A January 1907 headline announced: "Splendid Resort Near City Planned. Large Promises for Roxborough Park, Near Plum Creek Park." Plans called for an "electric road" consisting of 20 miles of double track running south from Englewood into the foothills. The electric railway would transport Denver citizens "to an all the year round resort for the patronage of the best class of people in the country." (History Colorado.)

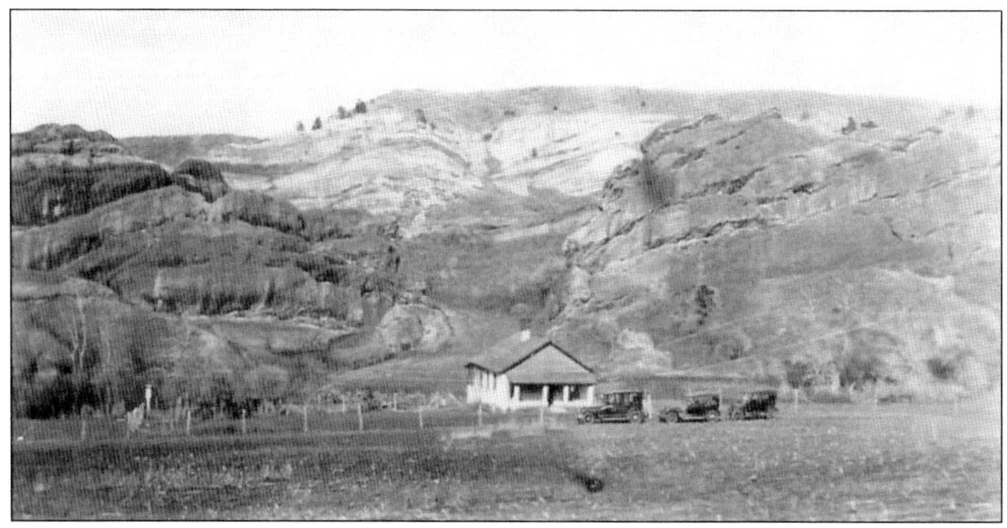

Henry Persse and Partners' Grandiose Plans. A 200-room hotel would be built of white silica brick. A unique sanitation system was promised: "The sewage would pass through a series of tanks filled with quicklime and come out eventually in the shape of a colorless and odorless fluid that makes excellent fertilizer." Amenities would be placed "in surroundings of Roxborough Park a natural beauty spot located in the hills near Plum Creek." (Ed and Nancy Bathke Collection.)

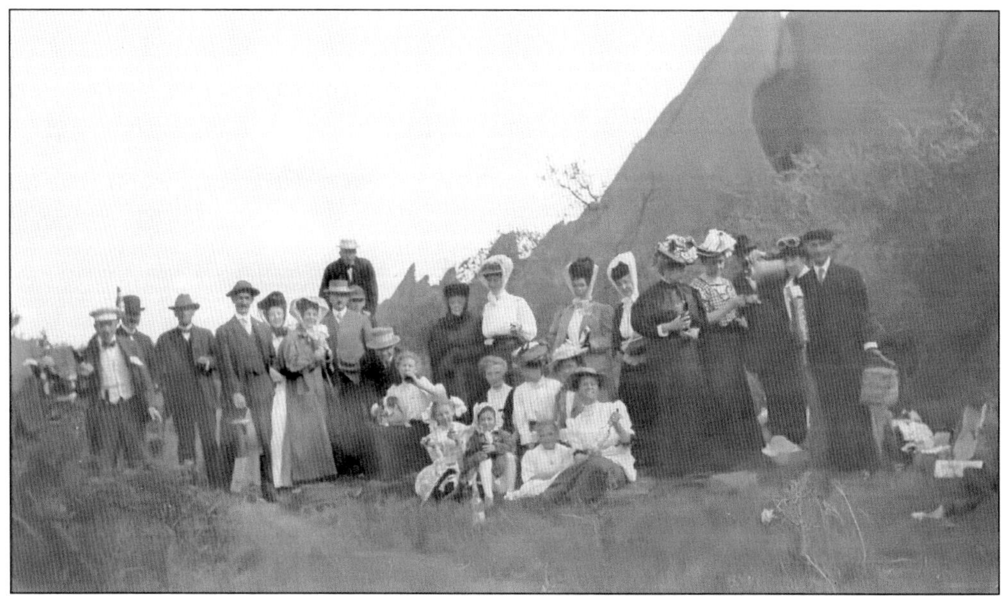

Celebrations. This undated photograph shows an unidentified group celebrating in Roxborough. Many famous people visited Roxborough Park between 1905 and 1913, and several wrote about its beauty in Persse's guestbook. One person wrote: "Seven autos. Thirty people. A lovely place." Another wrote, "A park made by Nature's Hands Alone." (Douglas County History Research Center, Roxborough State Park Collection.)

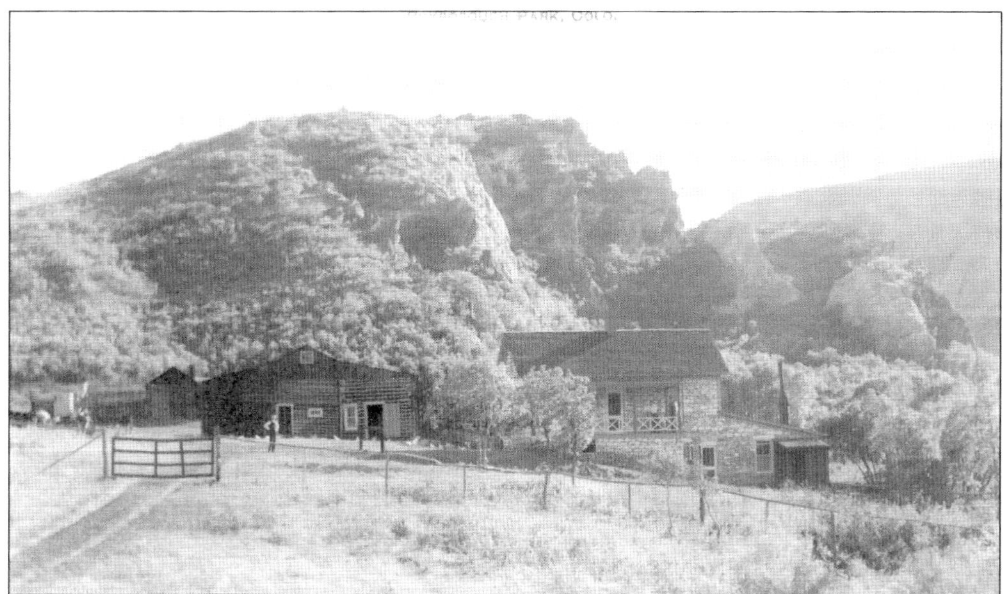

Henry Persse's Stone House. Persse's stone house was constructed in 1903. In an oral interview given years later, rancher Toney Helmer said his father, Anton, helped build the house and noted the mortar was made of red mud and water. The home's base was made from sandstone extracted from the Lyons Formation and remains one of the best examples of the white-hued material. (Douglas County History Center Library.)

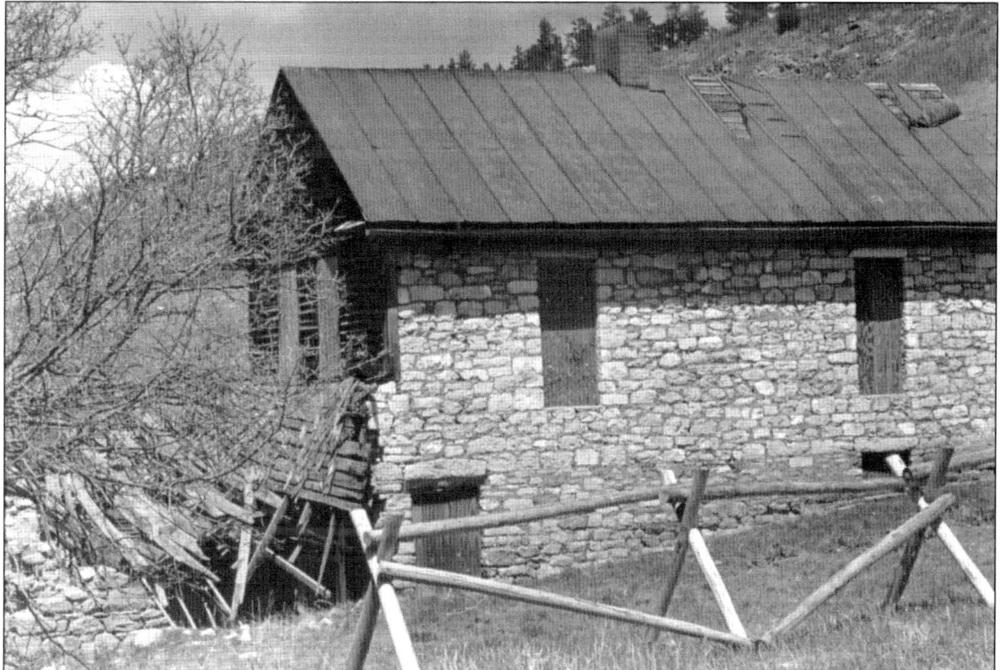

A House in Disrepair. Henry Persse's house was built into a grassy hill and had a single chimney in the center of the shake shingled roof. Through the years, it fell into disrepair, was restored, and is still standing in Roxborough State Park; visitors can walk by as they hike along a nearby trail. State park naturalists often hold open houses at the site. (Ed and Nancy Bathke Collection.)

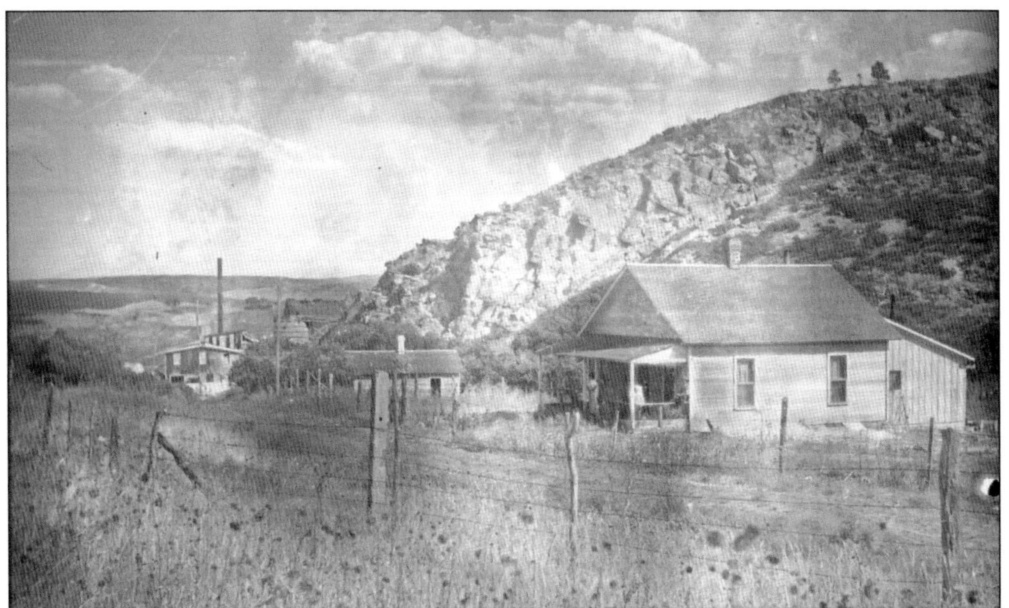

Sale of Roxborough Land. Henry Persse died in 1918 after being struck by a Denver Tramway streetcar. In 1919, Mary Helmer, matriarch of the Helmer family, acquired the property from Persse's Roxborough Land Company, which included the Silica Brick and Clay Company's land and buildings. Although bricks were no longer manufactured in Silica, the Helmer family mined clay and silica until the 1960s. (Douglas County History Research Center, Roxborough State Park Collection.)

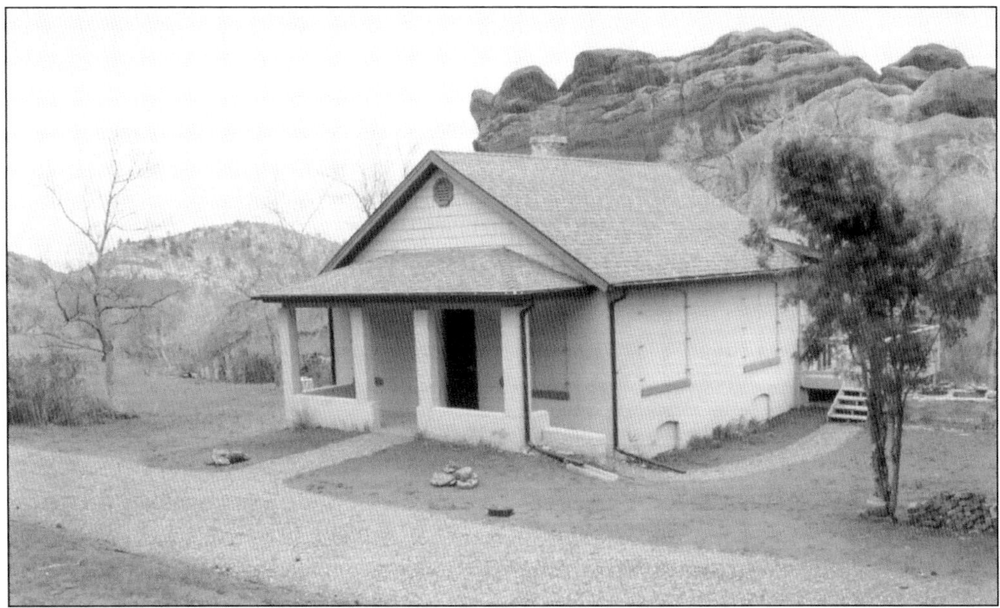

Horace H. Persse Homestead. Horace Persse, Henry's youngest son, lived in Denver but often returned to Roxborough, where he built a small silica-brick home that still stands in Roxborough State Park. David Reed purchased the house from Horace Persse in 1916 and sold it to Eliza Skinner in 1920. The farm was later sold to Grace Church Jones, an artist whose mural can be seen today in Denver's Morey Middle School. (Char Nauman.)

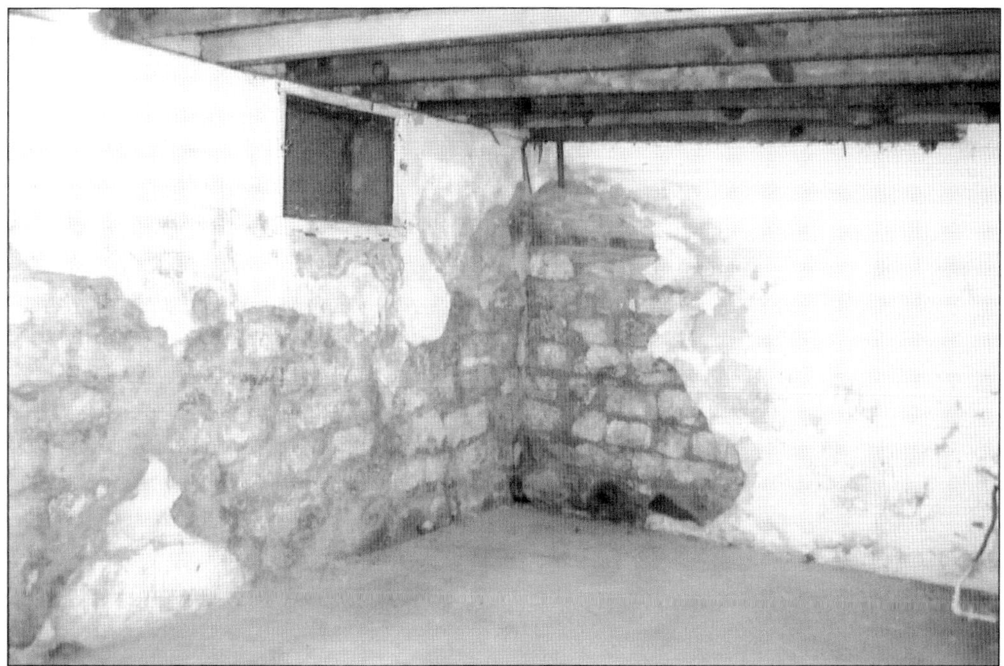

Brick Foundation made from Lyons Formation. Although Horace Persse's home was made of silica brick, its foundation was made of sandstone from the Lyons Formation. The home is still standing in Roxborough State Park. (Char Nauman.)

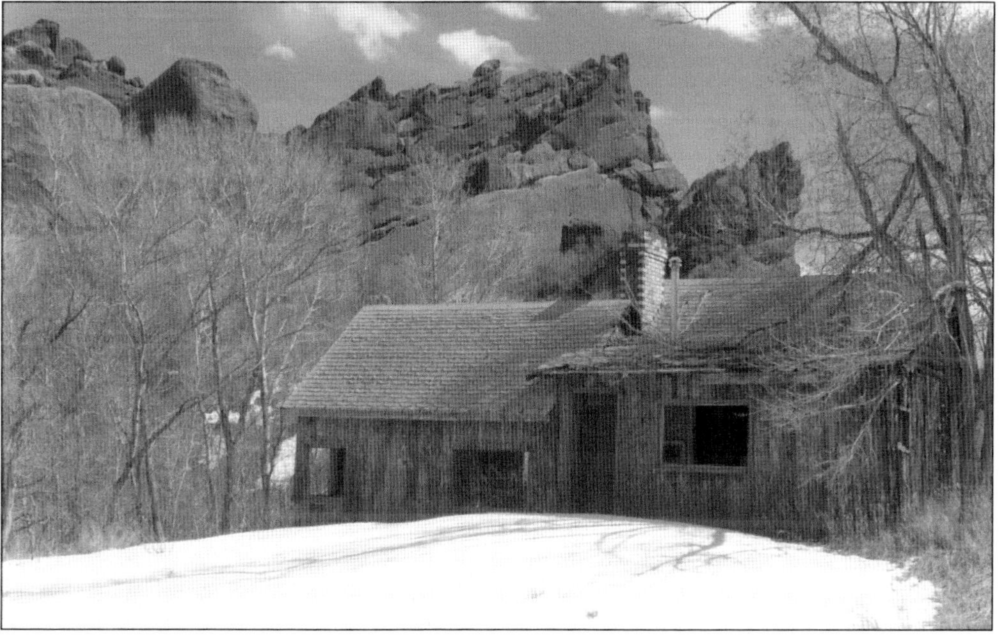

Sundance Ranch. In 1946, W. Bonner and La Cleta Brice purchased the property once owned by Horace Persse. The Brice family owned the ranch for 60 years. They named the property Sundance Ranch and dreamed of developing it into a dude ranch. This photograph shows one of the cabins they built for visitors. In 2002, the family sold parts of the land to the State of Colorado as an addition to Roxborough State Park. (Lance W. Moreland.)

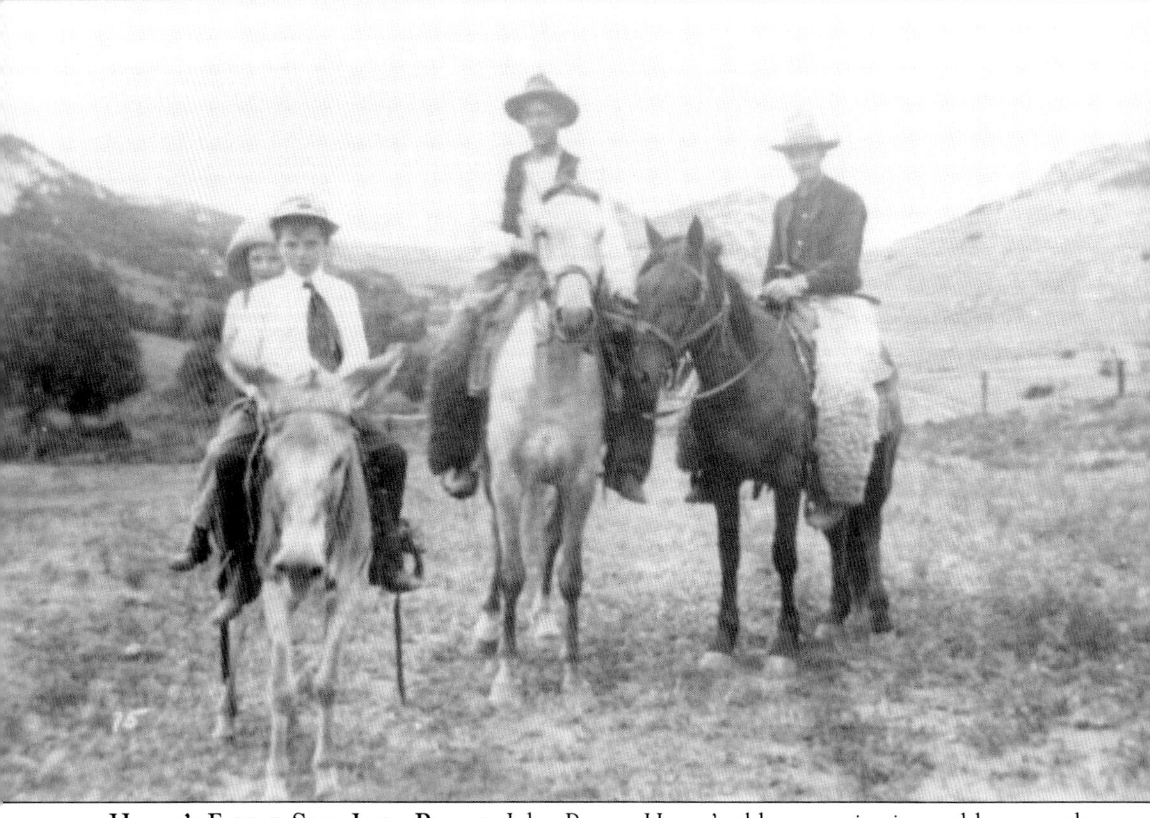

Henry's Eldest Son, John Persse. John Persse, Henry's eldest son, is pictured here on the right. His finely dressed children are on a burro. The man on the white horse is unidentified. John was the last Persse family member to live in Roxborough. He worked for the Denver Police Department, and after his retirement, he resided in his father's stone house until his death in 1937. (Roxborough State Park.)

Three

Water!

Water in the arid west was as valuable as gold, and early pioneers viewed the pure mountain flow of the South Platte River as a golden vein tumbling down from the high peaks of the Rockies. Settlers established homesteads close to the river and nearby creeks, then dug trenches to irrigate their small farms. In 1860, Colorado was not yet a state when the Kansas Territory legislature began construction on the City Ditch in Platte Canyon (Waterton Canyon). By 1867, water was delivered via the City Ditch to towns, farms, and Denver's Capitol Hill.

In 1894, the Denver Union Water Company was formed by a group of prominent business leaders who successfully combined several water departments into one. At the turn of the 20th century, the company began enlarging existing sand filter beds and building a Platte Canyon Reservoir near the mouth of the South Platte River. Given the isolation of Platte Valley at the foot of the mountains, a town was needed to house workers. Scores of men were put to work building the town of Kassler and constructing sand beds and the reservoir.

Within a few years, Kassler became the first slow-sand filter plant west of the Mississippi, capable of releasing 50 million gallons of clean water per day. Platte Canyon Reservoir provided water for the sand beds. Within 10 years, Denver Union Water Company's town of Kassler contained one of the largest sand filter plants in the country.

In 1918, Denver residents voted to create a Board of Water Commissioners and buy Denver Union Water Company's water system, including Kassler. In 1985, Kassler was decommissioned, but many of its original buildings were preserved. Today, thousands of people per year pass by deserted Kassler to hike, bike, fish, and enjoy wildlife in Waterton Canyon. Most are unaware that the little town of Kassler provided clean, clear mountain water to Denver citizens for more than eight decades.

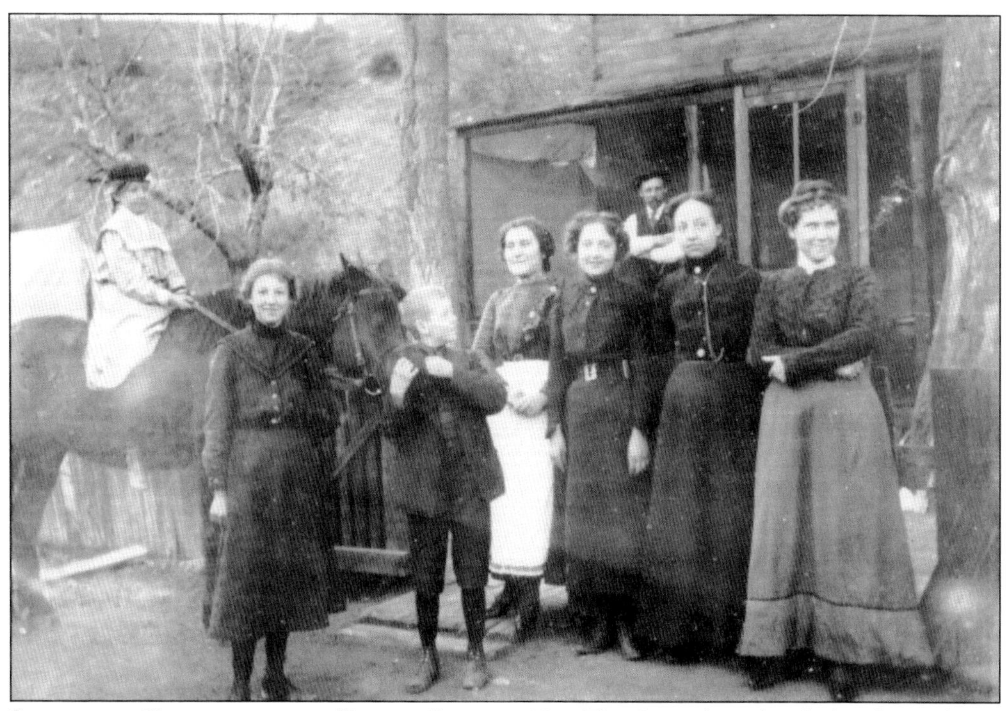

Samuelson Home along the Platte River, 1897. The Samuelson family lived in a frame home close to the railroad tracks along the South Platte River. Mr. ? Samuelson operated the pump that provided water to trains' engines. Pictured here are, from left to right, Thelma Phillips, Merle Phillips Montgomery, Chester Samuelson, Maud Wilson, Elsie Brodthe, ? Samuelson, Clara Brodthe, and Florence Wilson. (Littleton Museum.)

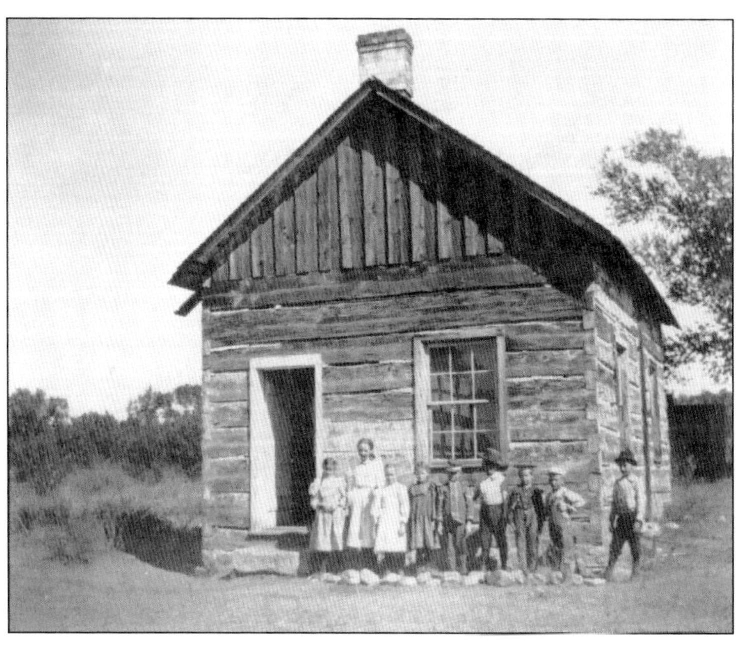

Platte Canyon School, 1897. The Platte Canyon School was the first school located in Waterton Canyon. Pictured here are, from left to right, Merle Phillips Montgomery, Elsie Bradtke, Ruby Wise, Thelma Phillips Dietler, Chester Samuelson, Floyd Phillips, Audrey Bivens, Ralph Wise, and Ralph Bradtke. (Littleton Museum.)

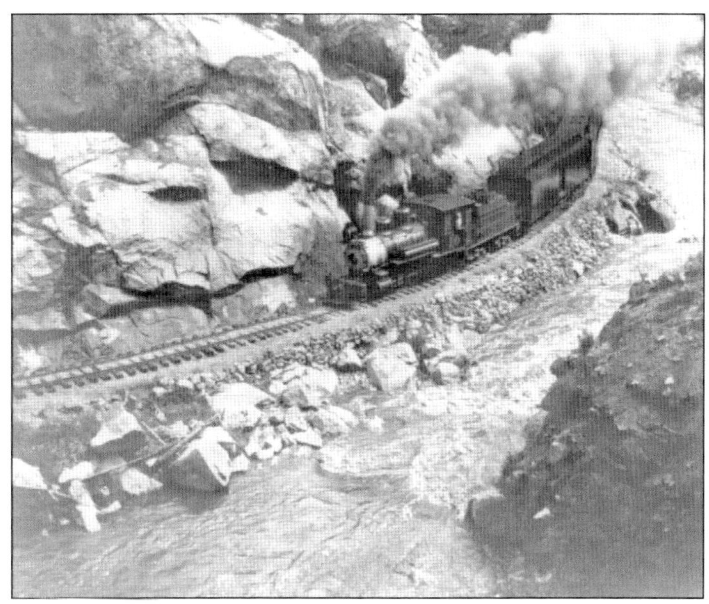

Rounding a Curve in Platte Canyon, 1908. In 1874, the Colorado & Southern Railway was extended from Denver along the South Platte River. Narrow-gauge trains traveled along tight riverbeds from Denver to Leadville, stopping at mountain communities along the way to deliver freight, passengers, and mail. In 1909, a spur was built to two new communities, Silica and Canyon Spur (later called Waterton). (Littleton Museum, photograph by Harkey Browning.)

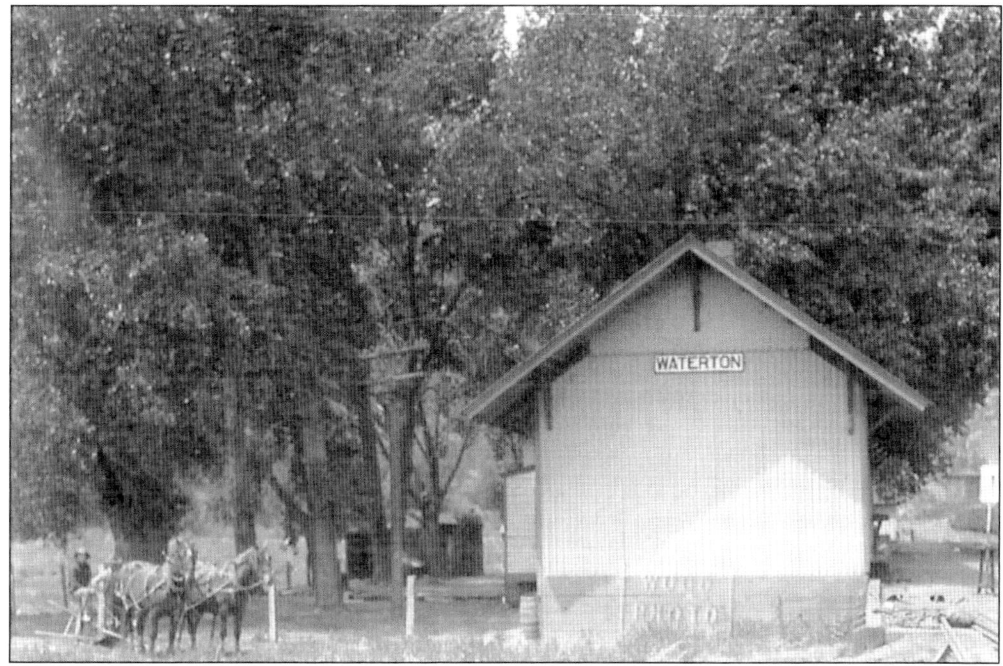

What's in a Name? The names Platte Canyon, Platte Valley, Waterton, Kassler, and Roxborough have been interchangeable for more than a century. Land to the southeast was called Roxborough. The area along the South Platte River was called Platte Canyon. In 1916, the nearby train stop became known as Waterton. Denver Union Water Company called its company town Kassler. (Mary Lou Helmer family.)

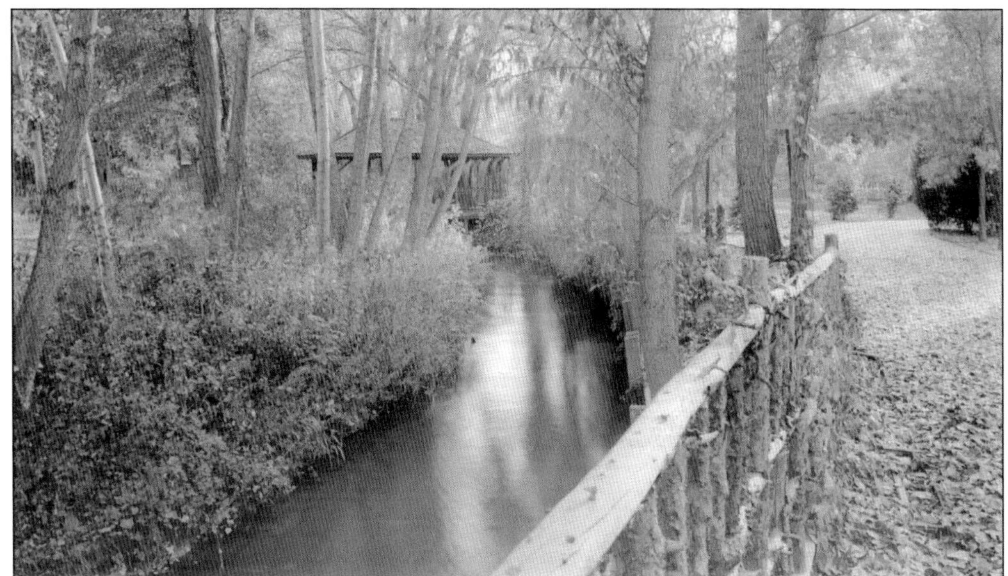

Early Waterways Provided Needed Irrigation. In 1860, the City Ditch became synonymous with spring when the headgates were opened, permitting water from the South Platte River to takes its 37-mile journey to Denver's Capitol Hill. In 1879, construction began on the 84-mile High Line Canal. Water in the canal began a journey across the plains to Denver and transformed the semiarid lands. (Denver Public Library.)

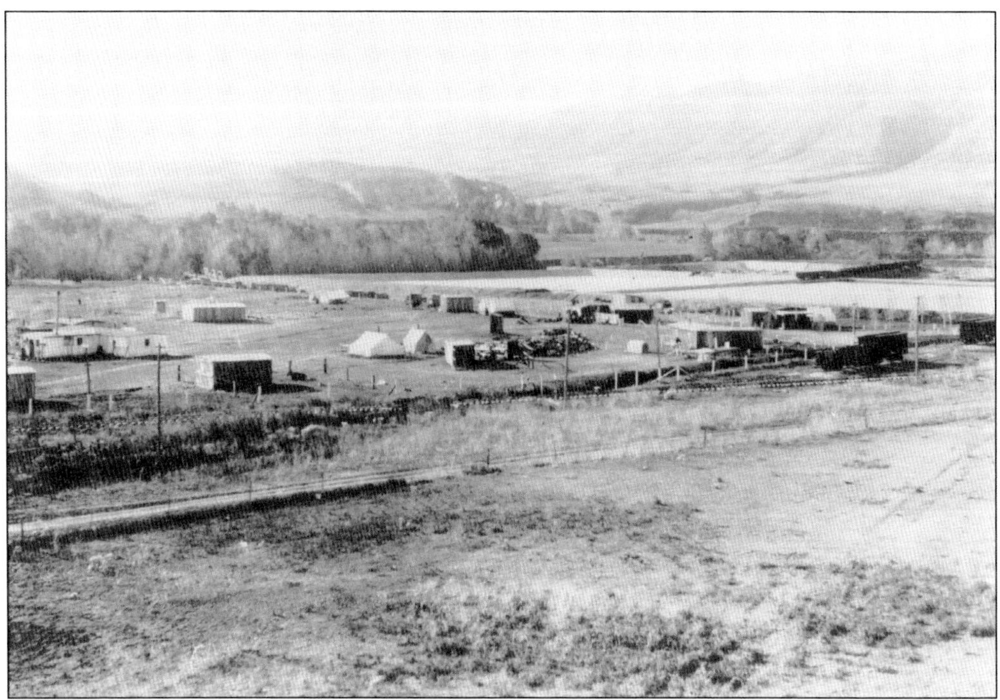

Worker's Camp at Platte Canyon. This photograph provides a close-up view of the Platte Canyon workers' camp in 1901. The camp housed workers until more permanent housing could be provided in Kassler. The large sand beds are to the upper right of the camp. (Littleton Museum.)

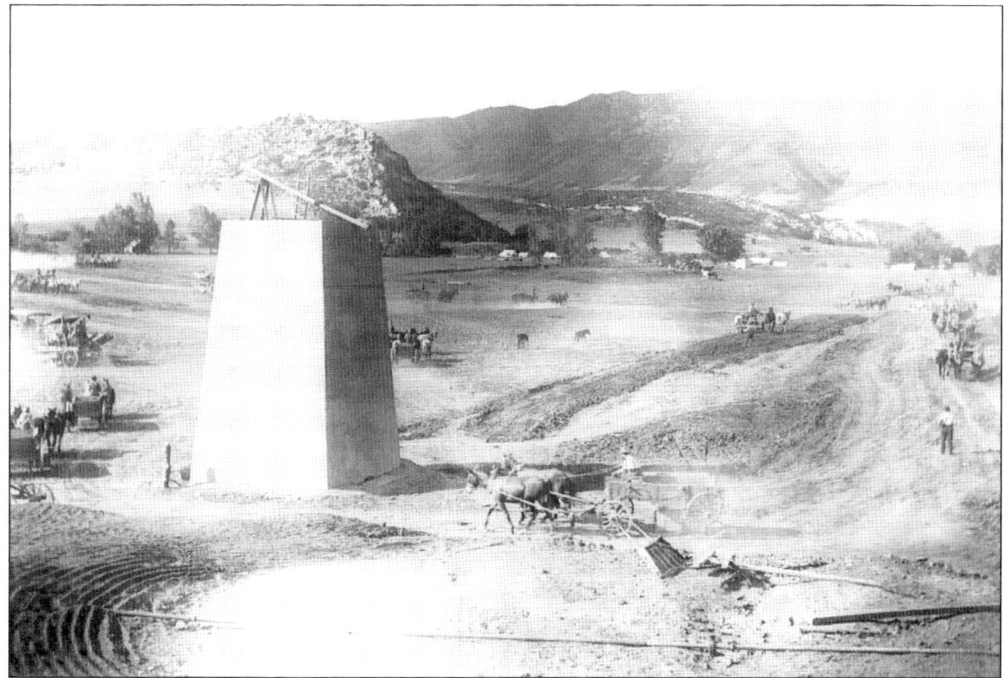

CONSTRUCTION OF THE PLATTE CANYON RESERVOIR. In 1904, the Denver Union Water Company completed the Platte Canyon Reservoir at Kassler, north of present-day Waterton. The large concrete structure in the center contained the valve house. Two valves let water in, and one valve regulated water that went to the sand beds. (Douglas County History Research Center.)

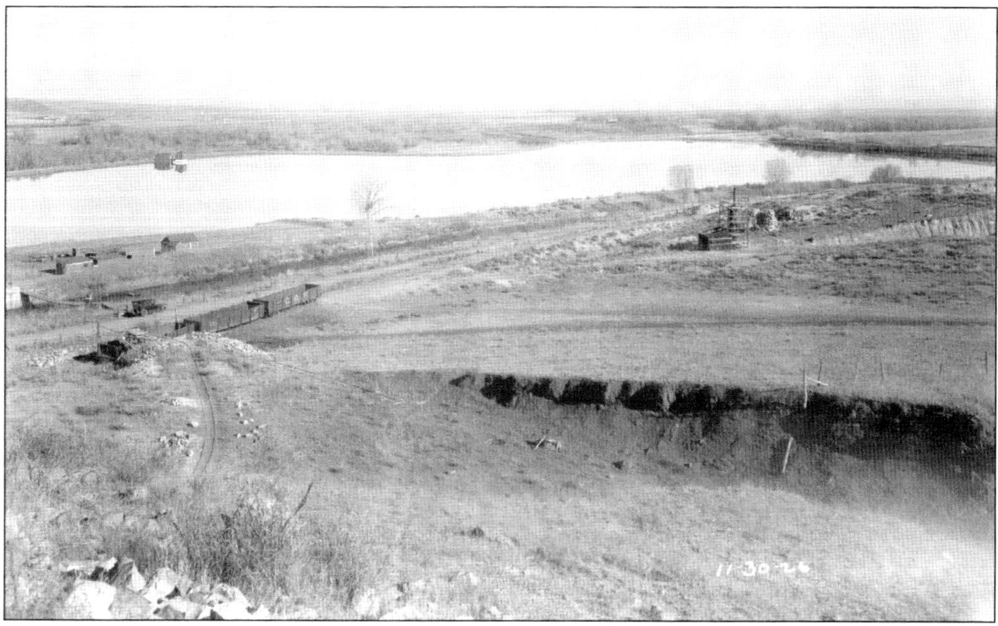

PLATTE CANYON RESERVOIR, 1906. Initially, water came from the South Platte River. Later, after the Platte Canyon Reservoir was completed, water for filtering sand at Kassler came from the reservoir, bypassed the sedimentation basins, and went directly into the 10.5-acre filter beds. When water reached the bottom, it was drained off through perforated clay pipes. (Denver Water.)

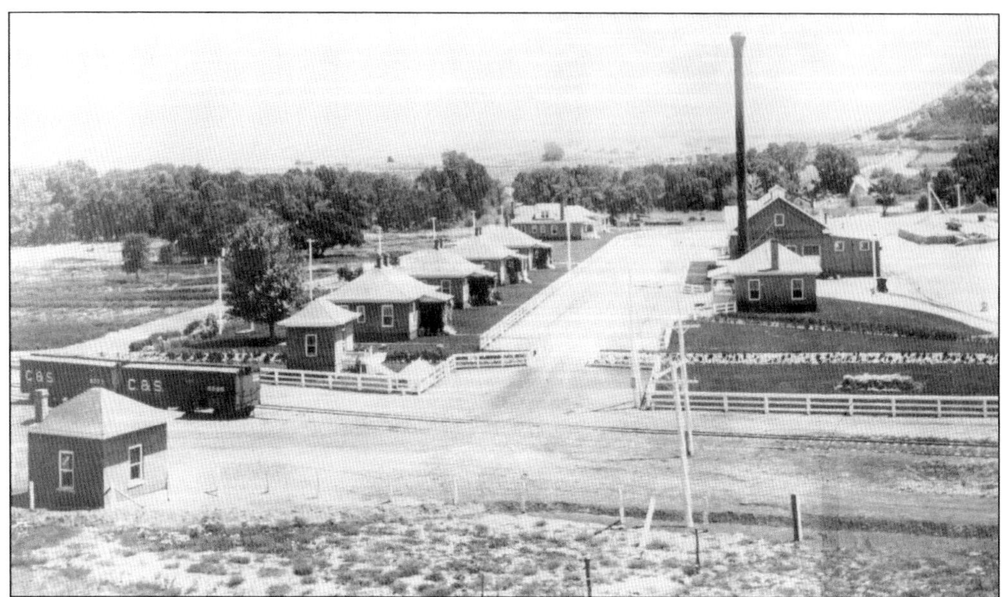

Kassler, c. 1918. Given the isolation at the foot of the mountains, the company town of Kassler was essential to the construction and maintenance of the Platte Canyon Reservoir. This photograph was taken looking southwest. Kassler's four brick buildings (on the left) were built for supervisors. The large building on the left at the end of the road served as bachelors' quarters. Framed houses for workers were smaller and had fewer amenities than the supervisors' homes. (Douglas County History Research Center.)

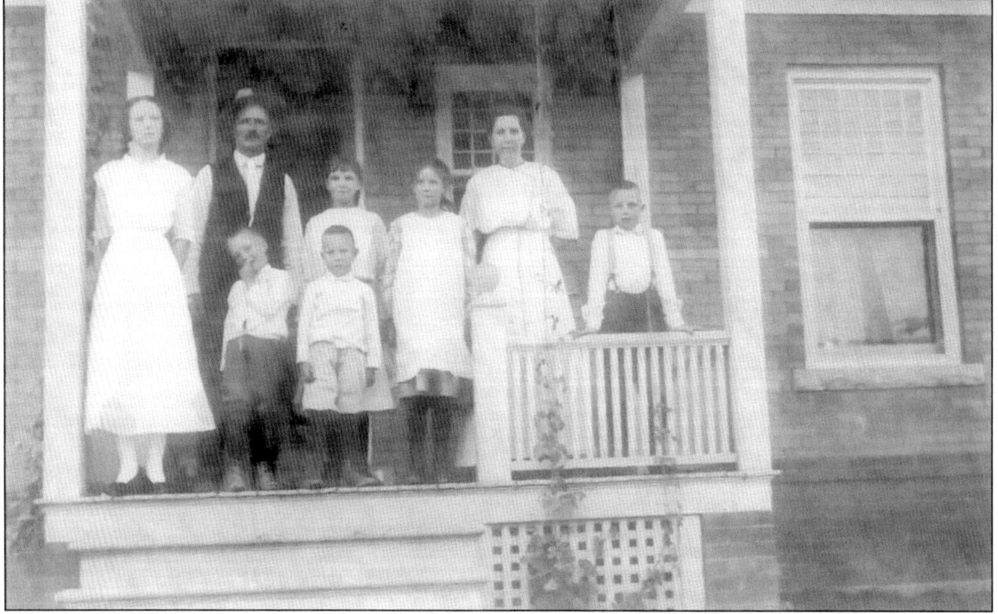

Zebulon Vance Swan. Zebulon Swan is credited with saving lives when, in 1890, water began flowing over an earthen dam up the canyon and "Zeb" rode a horse down the gorge to warn those below. Since his homestead was needed when Cheesman Dam was built, Swan was provided a larger home for his wife and seven children adjacent to the Platte Canyon Reservoir at Kassler. (Bob Swan.)

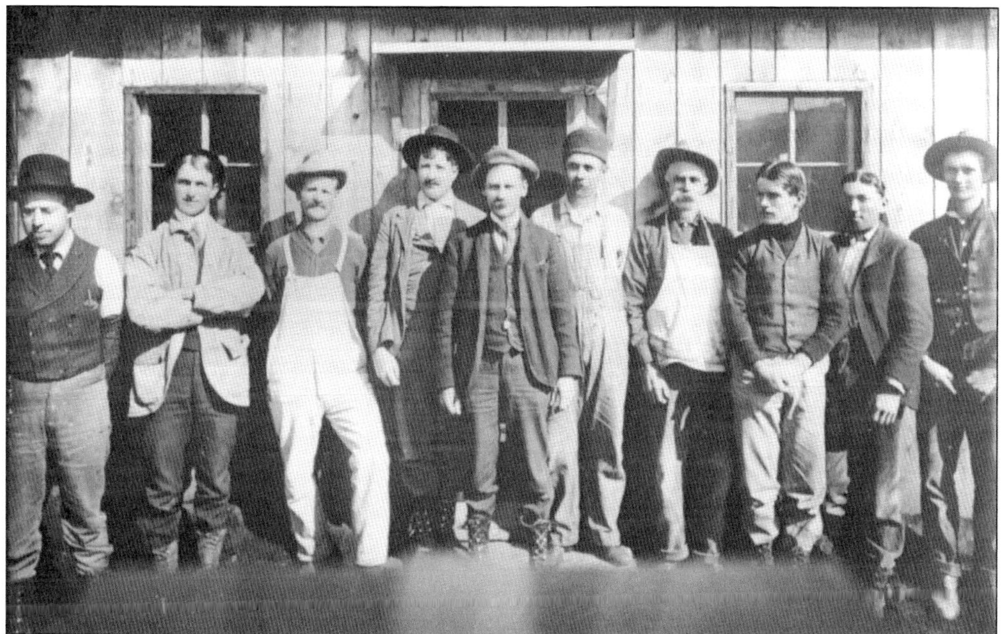

Kassler Work Gang, c. 1904. Zebulon Vance Swan is the second man from the left in this photograph; the others are unidentified. Swan became foreman of the plant. His son David became the superintendent in 1962 and lived with his family in the supervisor's house, which is still referred to as the Swan House. (Douglas County History Research Center.)

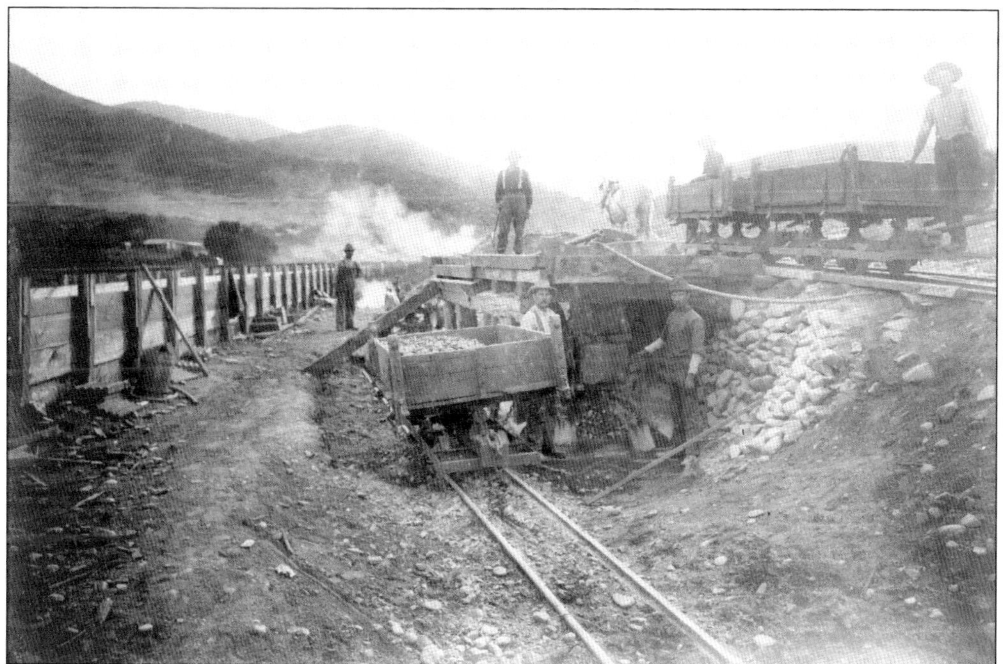

Filter Bed Rock Crushers, 1905. Rock was crushed into different sizes, hauled to and from the sand beds on wooden narrow-gauge railcars, and layered atop the perforated pipe. Later, stone taken from the South Platte River was used, and a rock crusher was no longer needed. (Denver Water.)

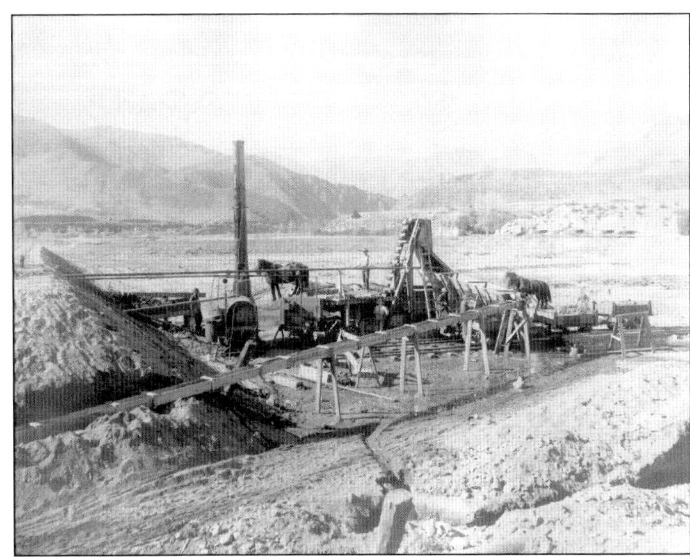

SAND WASHER UNDER CONSTRUCTION, 1901–1905. Four unidentified men work on constructing a sand washer. The sand had to be cleaned before placing it in the filter beds. In the beds, a concrete base was built, followed by perforated tiles, rocks of different sizes, and clean, fine sand. (Denver Water.)

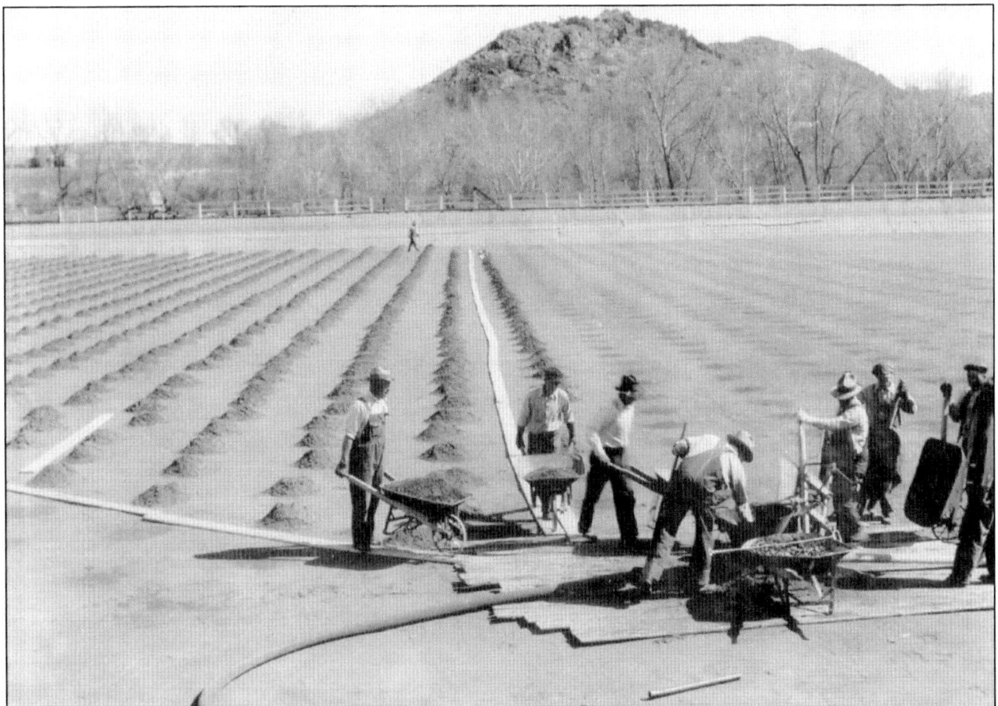

WORK GANGS LAYER THE SAND BEDS. The filtration beds and sedimentation basins were located west of the buildings. Sand beds had to be washed frequently to remove bacteria and remaining debris. The water filtered by the sand was carried off through pipes at the bottom. Men in work gangs used basic tools to skim sediment from the sand beds. All work was done by hand until the 1950s. (Denver Water.)

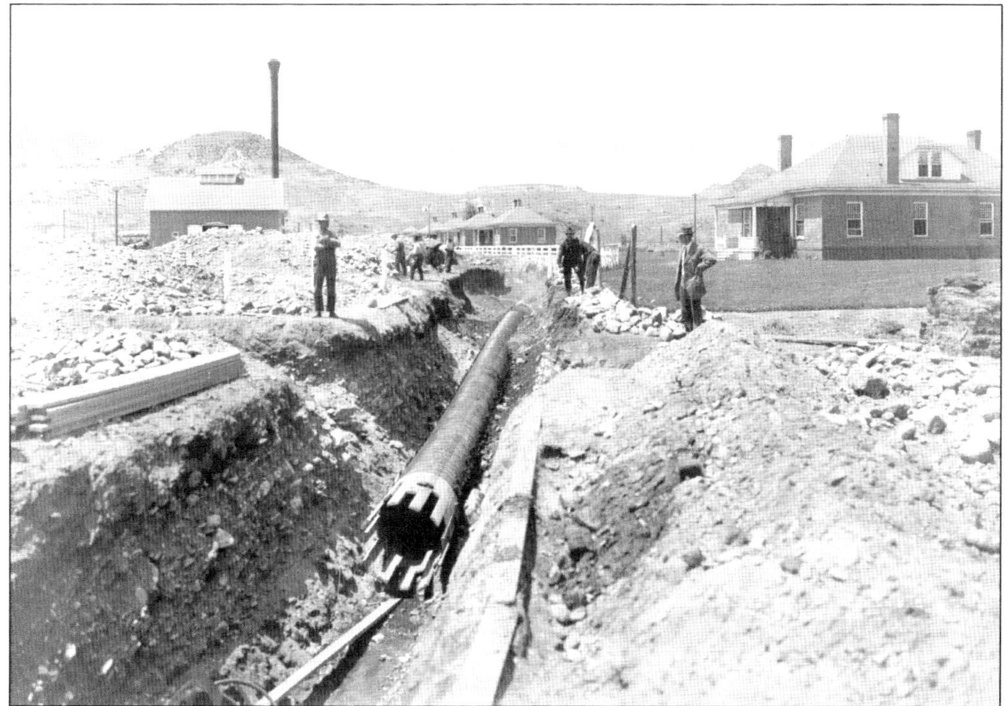

Pipes to Platte Canyon Reservoir, 1912. A 36-inch-diameter conduit was set by the work gang to deliver water back to the Platte Canyon Reservoir. Equipment was maintained in the blacksmith shop (to the left of the trench), where tools were made. (Denver Water.)

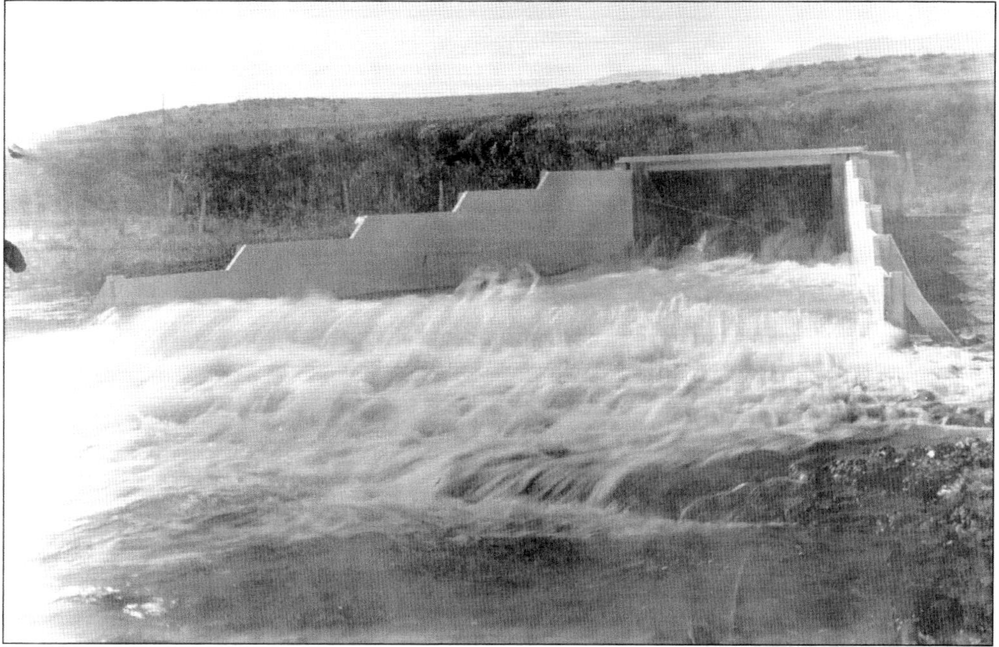

Platte Canyon Reservoir, 1912. Depending on need, 40 million gallons of water rushed out of 36-inch pipes into the Platte Canyon Reservoir each day. Decades later, Kassler was capable of delivering up to 50 million gallons a day. (Denver Water.)

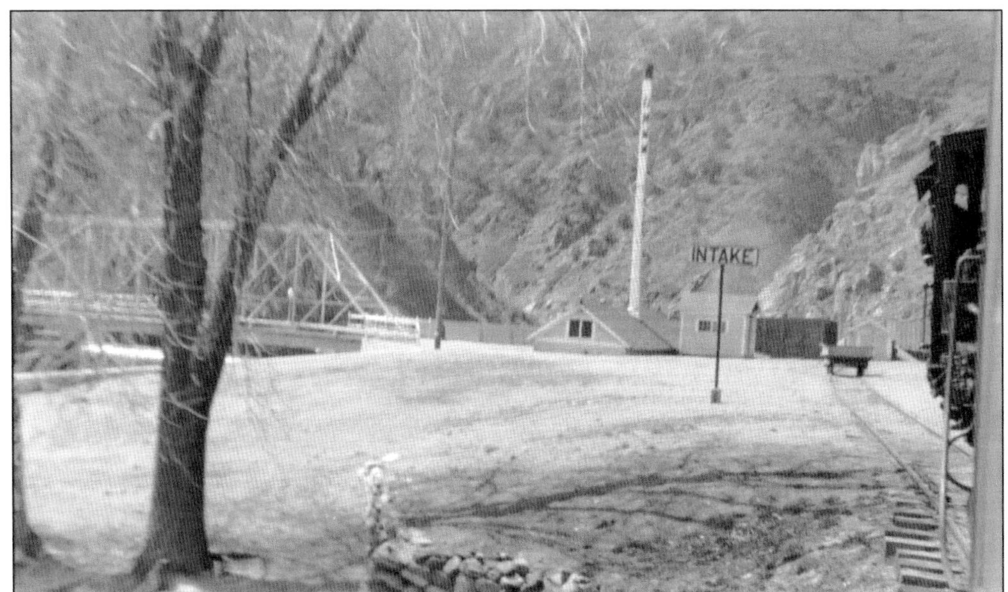

INTAKE AT WATERTON CANYON. This 1937 photograph shows the intake chamber at the upper end of Conduit No. 8, which Denver Union Water Company built in 1912. The site is at milepost 23 (from Denver) on the Colorado & Southern Railway. The dam, intake, boiler, 42-foot stack, and 93-foot lattice girder footbridge were manned around the clock. (Littleton Museum.)

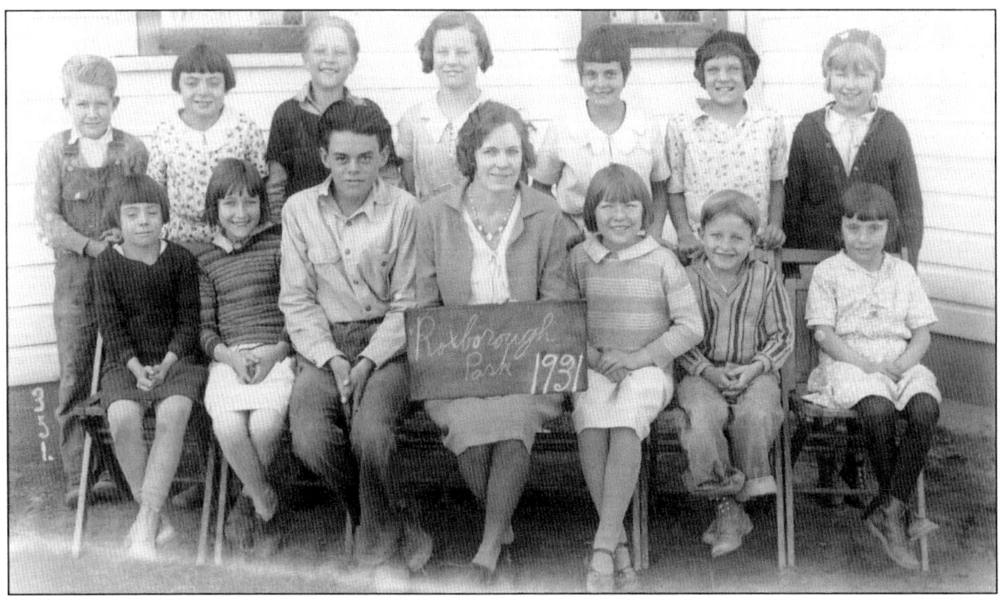

ROXBOROUGH PARK SCHOOL. Teacher Olive Woodward Larsen poses with students in front of Roxborough Park School in 1931. To the right of Larsen is Mary Slocum. Mary's cousin, Margery Slocum, is behind Mary. The other children are unidentified. The school was located where Rampart Range Road ended at Waterton Road. The school's foundation is still standing. (Douglas County History Research Center.)

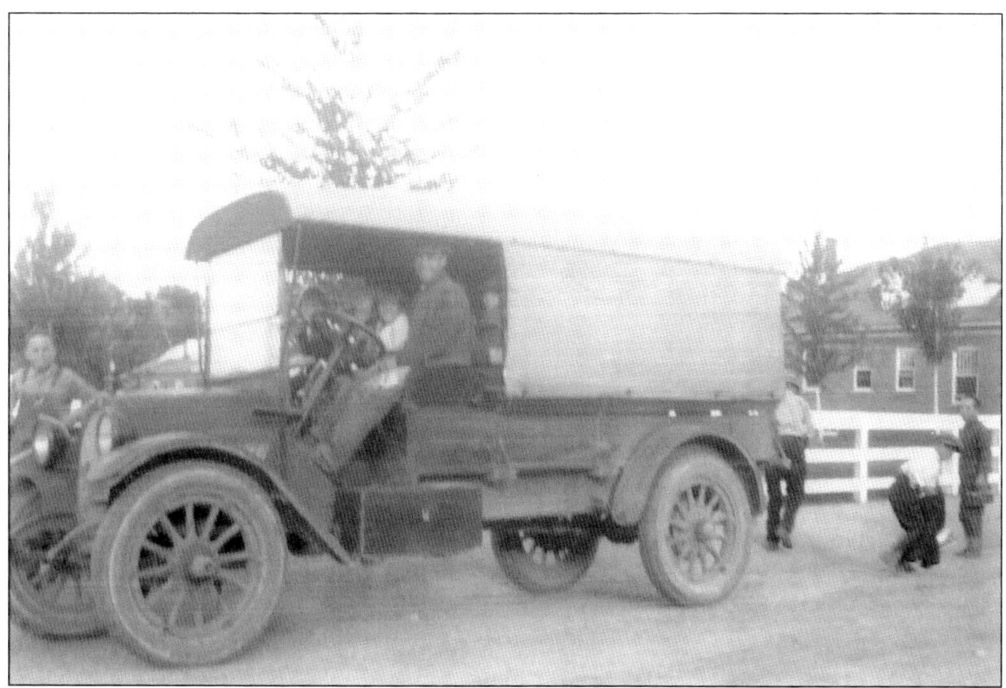

KASSLER SCHOOL BUS. School bus driver Ed Allen smiles as Harry Huster at the front of the bus looks on. Delores Woodward is seated next to Allen. Others in the photograph are unidentified. Children attended local schools. High school students went to Littleton High School until 1956, when they were bussed 17 miles up a dirt road (now four-lane Kipling Parkway) to Bear Creek High School. (Douglas County History Research Center.)

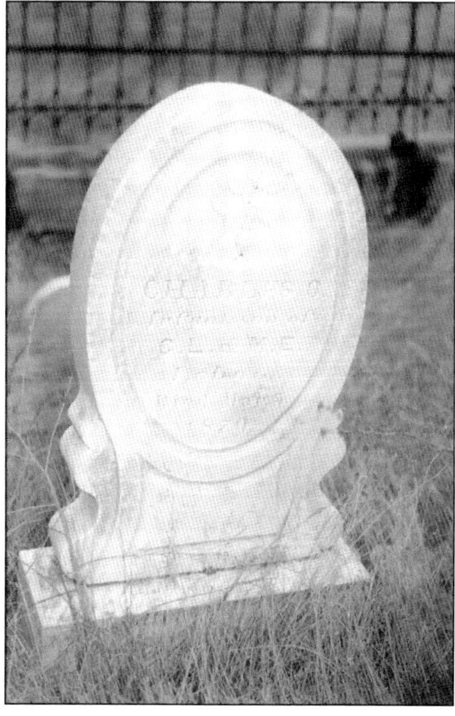

CHARLES OSCAR LEHOW. Brothers Charles and Oscar Lehow purchased a ranch in Platte Canyon in 1866. Charles lived on the ranch with his wife, Mary Elizabeth, and their two children, Charles Oscar and Anna. In 1876, Charles Oscar died at the age of five months. His father and neighboring rancher Benjamin Slocum picked out this burial site on a high bluff overlooking the South Platte River Valley. (Char Nauman.)

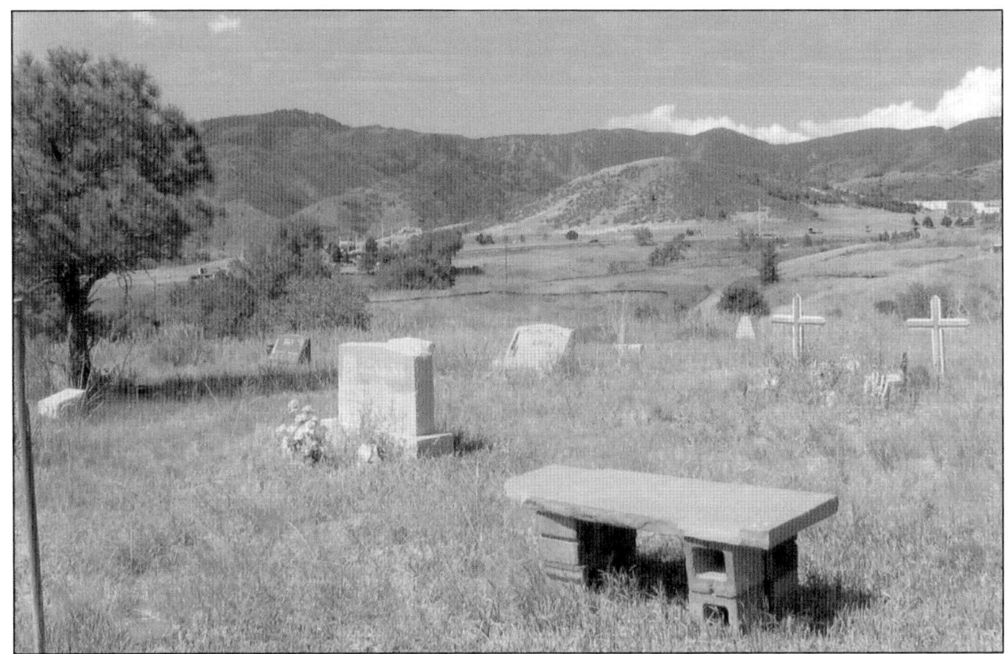

LEHOW CEMETERY. In 1937, Anna "Annie" Lehow deeded the 2.5-acre cemetery to the Lehow Cemetery Association. Workers, spouses, and direct descendants of families who lived and/or worked at the Kassler Filter plant, the old Waterton Railroad Depot, and ranches within a one-mile radius of the cemetery prior to 1954 may be buried at Lehow Cemetery. The rooftops of Lockheed Martin are visible in the photograph. (Char Nauman.)

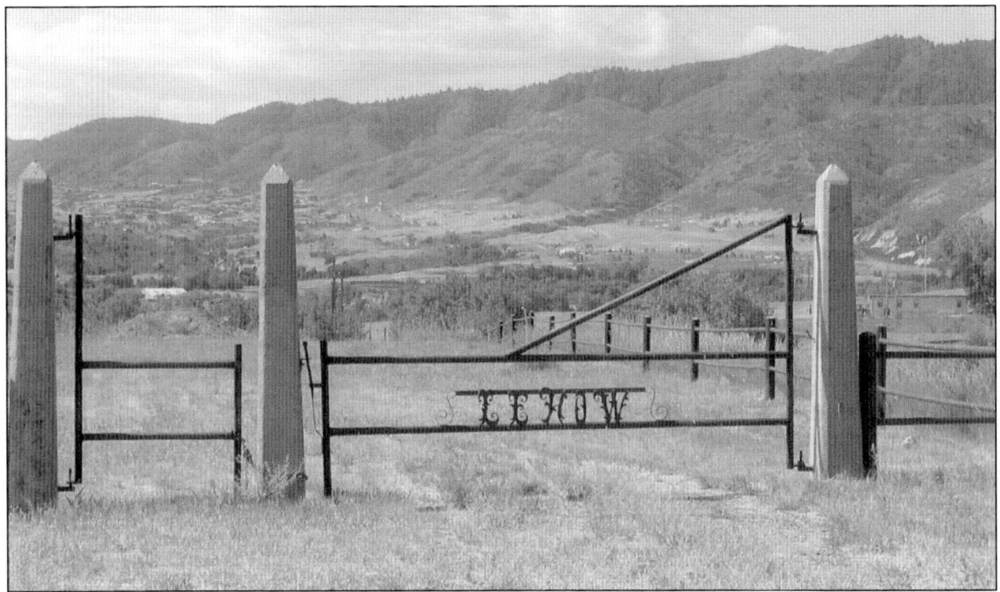

LEHOW CEMETERY SIGN. The 140-year-old cemetery overlooks a vista encompassing part of Roxborough's history: Waterton Canyon, Kassler, Roxborough Park, Roxborough State Park, and Lockheed Martin. A Kassler supervisor, Al Myrick, set the cemetery sign. Rusty Simon, who grew up on a farm just north of Kassler and worked at the Kassler plant for 40 years, set the posts. Roxborough Park homes are visible in the foothills. (Char Nauman.)

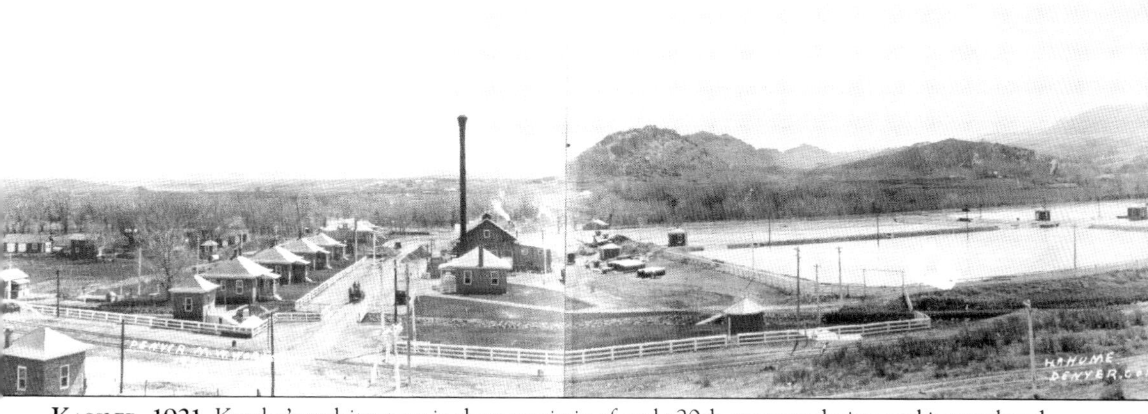

Kassler, 1921. Kassler's architecture is characteristic of early 20th-century design and interrelated to be self-sufficient. Almost everything needed was made for—and by—workers in the blacksmith shop. Twenty machines provided electricity and heat to all the buildings in Kassler. By 1906, the four brick houses to the left of the road were completed for supervisors and their families. In 1915, seventeen frame homes, accommodating 40 to 55 people, were built behind the brick homes. A two-story brick boardinghouse stood at the south end. A small teacher's house is visible near the white fence on the left side of the photograph. Three men ride in a horse-driven buggy. The plant office is on the right; the maintenance shop sits behind the office. The white spaces on the right are filter sand beds. H. Hume took this photograph in 1921. (Douglas County Research Center Library.)

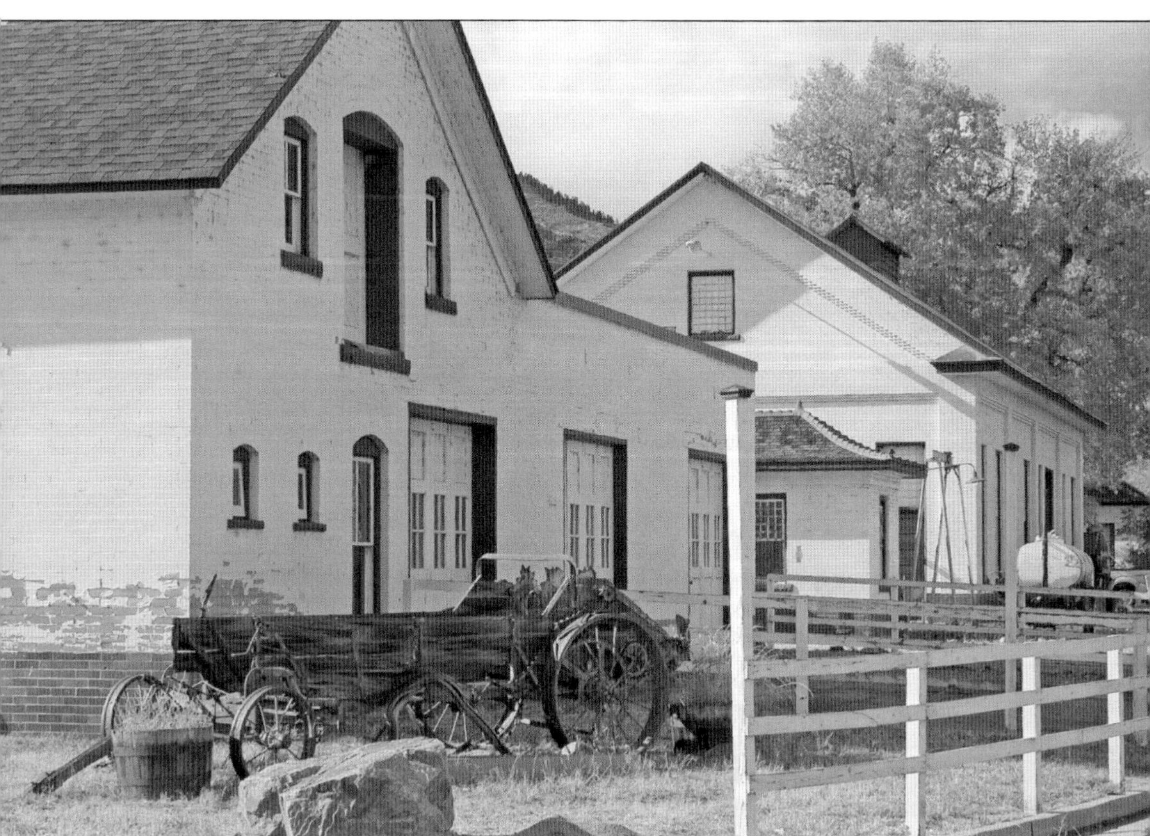

KASSLER, 2015. Kassler's century-old buildings retain much of their original integrity and are in excellent condition. Kassler was officially closed in 1985 but is still maintained by Denver Water. Today, thousands of people pass by Kassler while visiting Waterton Canyon. Most never realize Kassler provided millions of gallons of water per day to Denver for eight decades. (Tom Olkowski.)

Four

The Helmers

The Helmer family's story spans several generations. This chapter is one family's story, but it is also the story of thousands of other families who immigrated to the United States in the late 19th century. They came from simple beginnings with little, other than their youth, determination, and a desire to make a better life for themselves and their children.

Franz and Judith Helmer came to America from Austria in the middle of the 19th century and made what must have been a very difficult journey across the plains to the foot of the Rocky Mountains. Franz, who changed his name to the more Americanized Frank, and Judith had several children. Over a century ago, their eldest son, Anton, and youngest son, John, followed their parents west and homesteaded at the edge of the wilderness to the Platte valley in what is now Roxborough. Anton and John's children stayed and raised their families there, and many of their families' descendants did, too.

Anton Helmer died on his Roxborough ranch at the age of 72 in February 1919. An obituary in the *Littleton Independent* reads: "He was one of the oldest pioneers in this part of the state . . . by conscientious labor and hard work he had accumulated extensive farming interests and was a man that stood high in his community. He was survived by a wife and seven children and a brother (John)."

John and his wife, Nellie Regan, began their life together in 1888 in a small homestead cabin built by Civil War veteran Amos Miksch. Together, John and Nellie worked their farm, raised a family, and contributed to their community. John passed away in January 1944 and was survived by his daughters, June Norman and Polly Campbell, and his son, John "Johnnie."

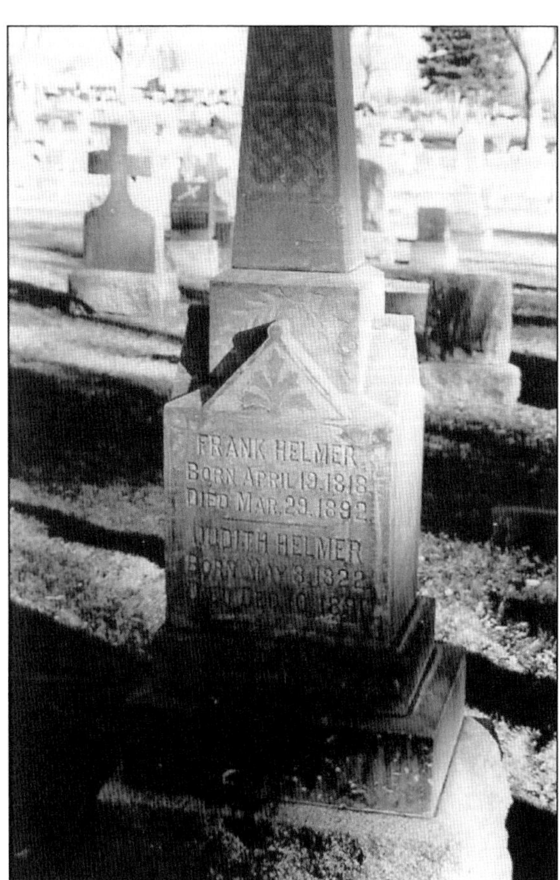

Franz and Judith Helmers' Tombstone. Franz "Frank" Helmer was born in Austria in 1818, married Judith Scholl in 1846, immigrated to the United States in 1858, and traveled to the West under difficult conditions. Over the next several decades, Frank and Judith and their sons, Anton and John, acquired thousands of acres in Platte Canyon Valley. Frank and Judith died in the 1890s. (Mary Lou Helmer family.)

Anton Helmer. Anton—born in 1847 in Innsbruck, Austria—was the eldest child of Frank and Judith Helmer. In 1866, Anton traveled west, where he was reunited with his father and his younger brother, John, who had traveled with his father to what was then the Kansas Territory. Anton and John's mother, Judith, soon followed. The Helmers would go on to become one of Roxborough's oldest pioneer patriarchs. (Mary Lou Helmer family.)

Anton and Mary Jaksch Helmer. At age 36, Anton married 20-year-old Mary Jaksch in Denver in 1863. They homesteaded east of the hogback near today's Roxborough Village. Of their seven children, only Anthony "Toney," George, and Cecelia "Cel" remained in Roxborough. The *Littleton Independent* noted that Mary, "one of the original subscribers to the paper, would . . . in the early days . . . feed Indians biscuits when they came to her door." (Mary Lou Helmer family.)

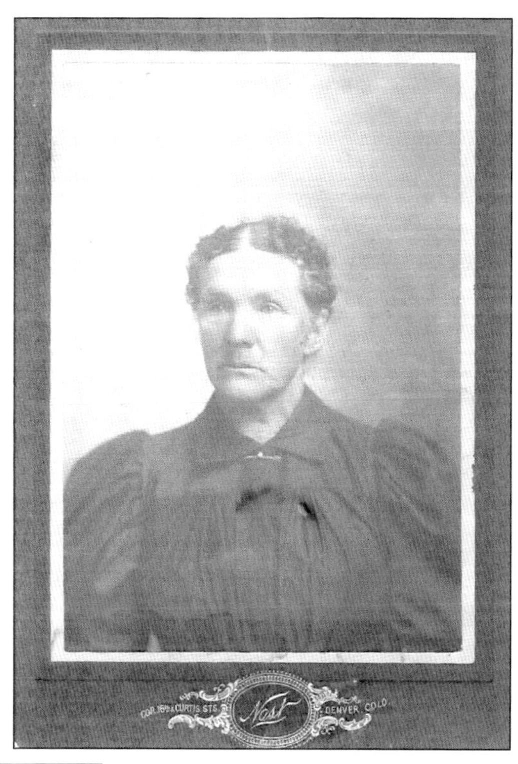

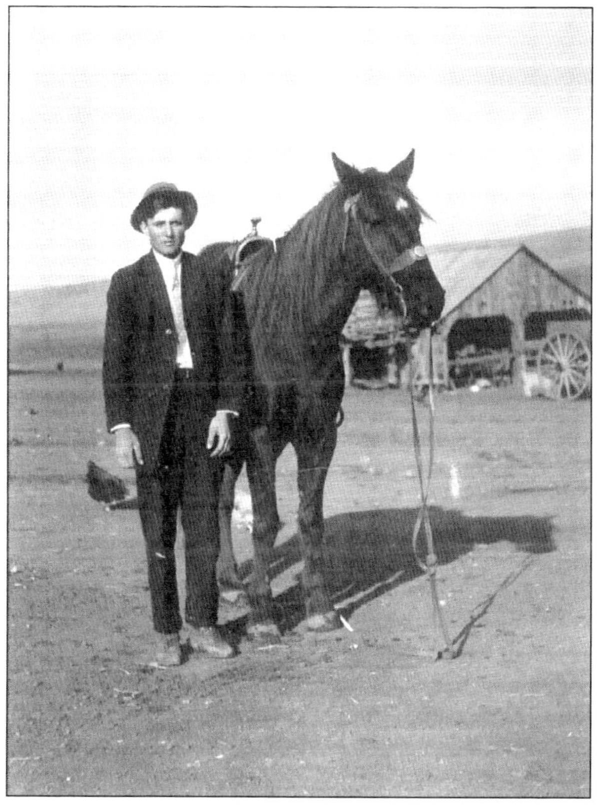

Anthony "Toney" Helmer Marries Helen Skinner. Toney Helmer, son of Anton and Mary Jaksch Helmer, married Helen Skinner on June 29, 1921. Helen's family owned the Horace Persse homestead, where the family raised hogs. According to the *Littleton Independent*, the newlyweds lived in the homestead (later called Sundance Ranch) but soon moved two miles north to the Helmer ranch headquarters. Toney and Helen had three daughters. (Mary Lou Helmer family.)

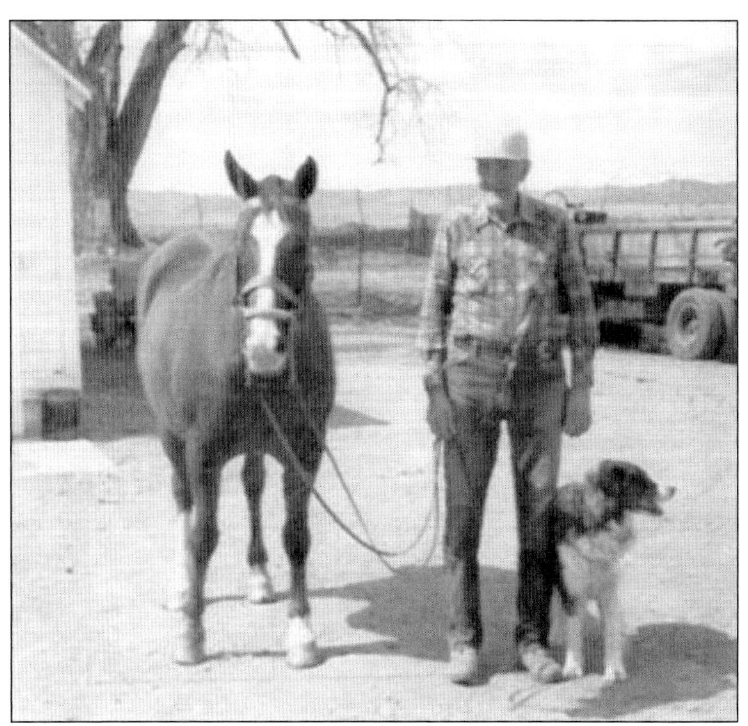

George Helmer. George Helmer was born in 1897 and made his home on the original homestead. George married Hazel Scott in 1919. They were married 46 years and had two daughters, Ramona and Nellie. After Hazel's death in 1965, George married Gladys Waller. George was known for his ability to manage the variety of animals on the Helmer cattle ranch. (Mary Lou Helmer family.)

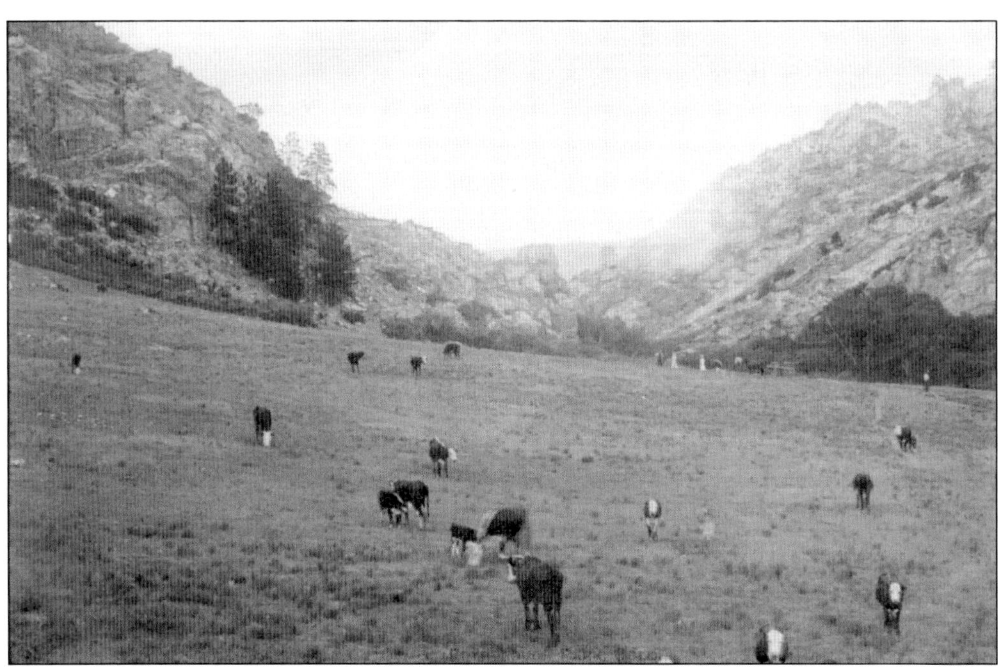

Picturesque Pasture on Helmer Ranch. The Helmer family owned about 200 head of registered Hereford cattle, which roamed freely through the ranch's pristine grasses and among the red sandstone monoliths. The Helmer brothers (George and Toney) were well known as hardworking ranchers. Their livestock was exhibited throughout the West at stock shows and competitions. (Ed and Nancy Bathke Collection.)

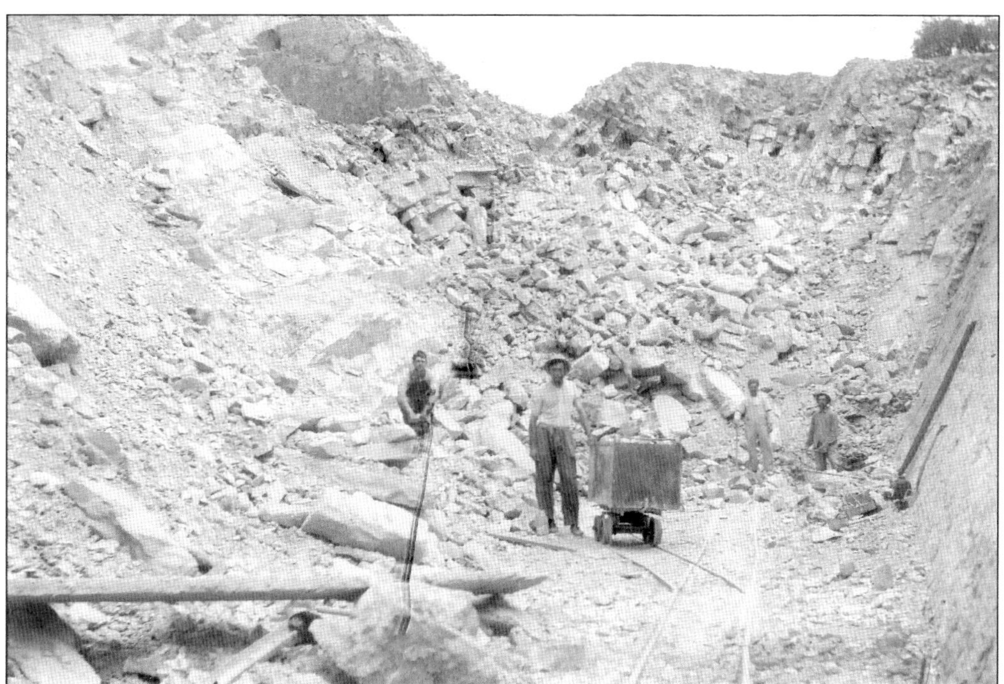

The Helmers' Mining Interests. In 1919, matriarch Mary Helmer purchased the Silica Brick Company's holdings, which her son Toney claimed had gone broke because of poor management. This undated photograph shows unidentified miners working in the Dakota Hogback. Carts carried the stone and clay on tracks where they could be loaded on trains on their way to Denver. (Ed and Nancy Bathke Collection.)

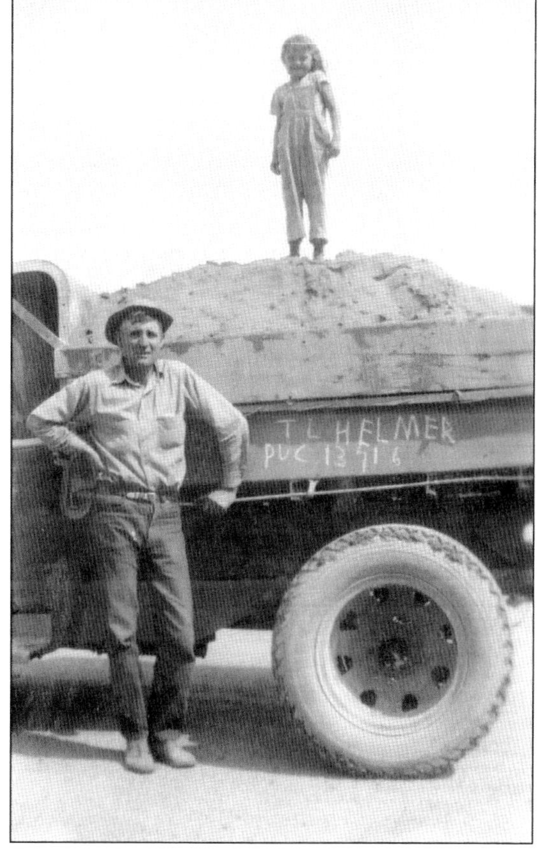

Mary Lou and Toney Helmer. Toney Helmer stands beside a truck he used to haul dirt, sand, and rock from Silica mines to customers' sites. His youngest daughter, Mary Lou (pictured on top of the load), remembers her father making sales to companies all over Colorado. A mid-1950s contract with the federal government provided supplies to build the US Air Force Academy near Colorado Springs. (Douglas County History Research Center.)

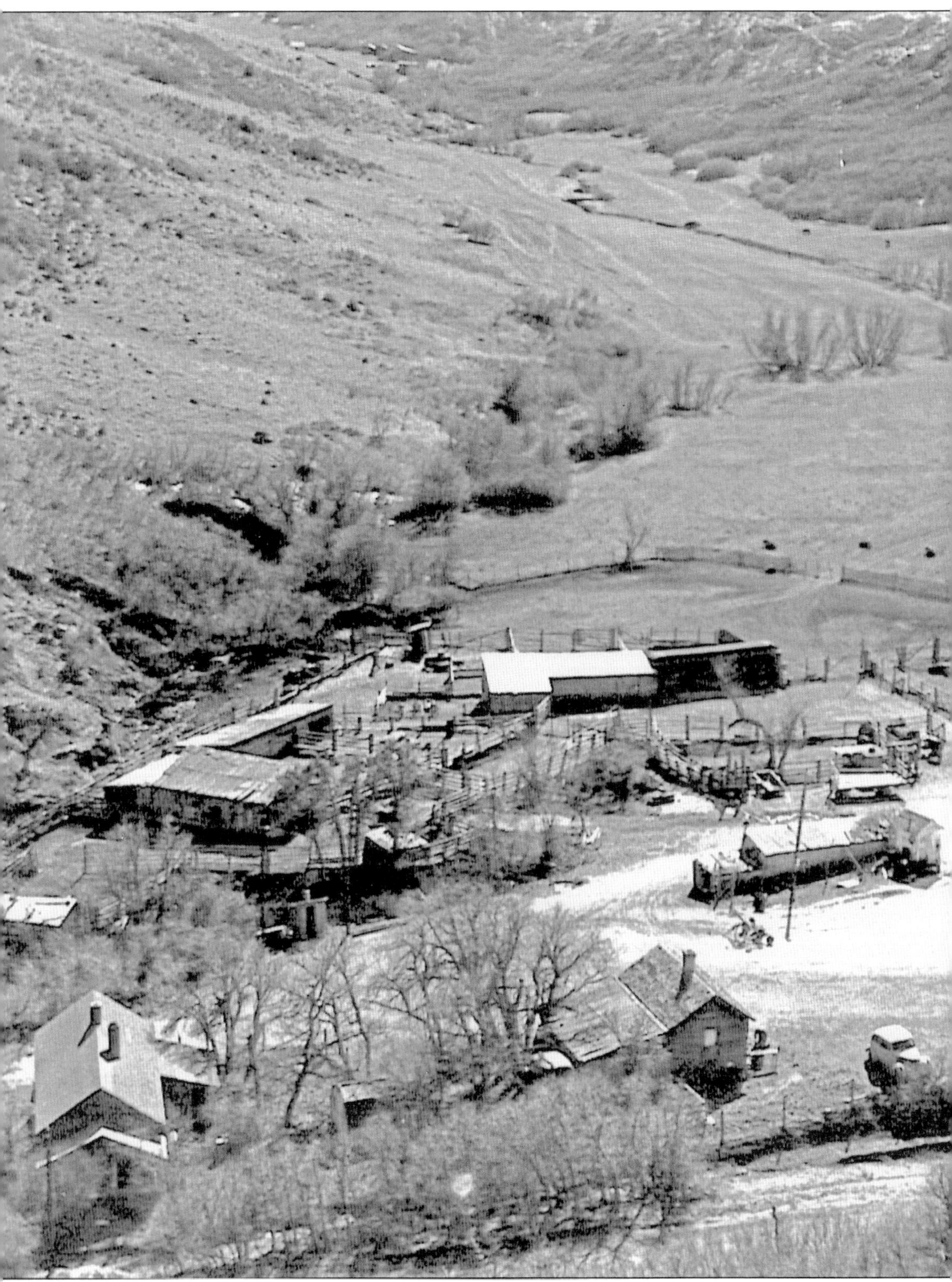

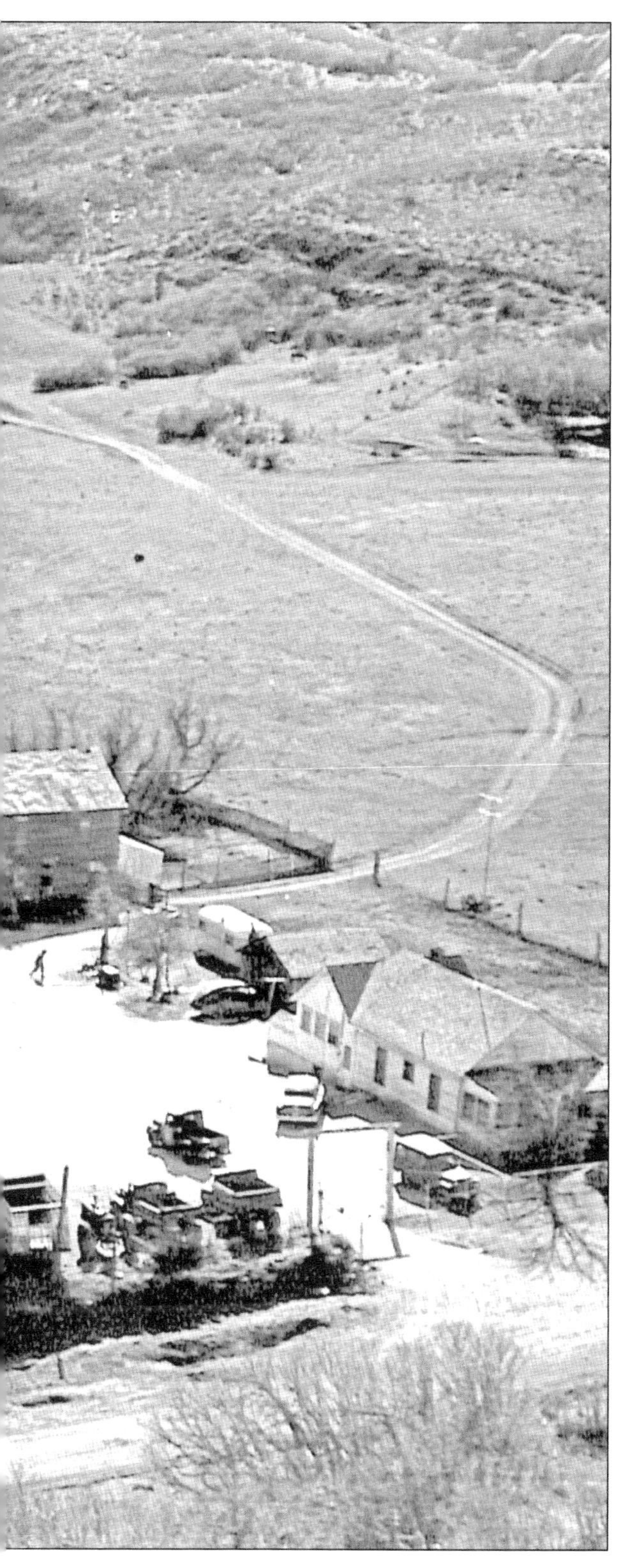

Bird's-Eye View of the Helmer Ranch. This undated photograph was taken from the Dakota Hogback looking down on Toney Helmer's home and the former Silica Brick and Clay Company. Mary Lou Helmer remembers her uncle George handled the cattle, her father, Toney, managed the mining business, and her aunt Cecelia "Cel" and uncle Mel Head (Cel's husband) contributed to ranch operations. Toney's family moved into the old Silica superintendents' dwelling and used other buildings on Silica's land to house Helmer family members and livestock. The Helmers successfully operated the mining business for decades. Mary, Toney, George, and Cel accumulated property, including much of the land held by Henry Persse's original Roxborough Land Company. By 1970, the Helmers owned more than 3,600 acres stretching from Waterton to Sundance Ranch. In 1970, the family sold 3,200 acres to the Woodmoor Corporation for the development of a private residential area (called Roxborough Park), another large residential community (Roxborough Village), and portions of what is presently Roxborough State Park. (Mary Lou Helmer family.)

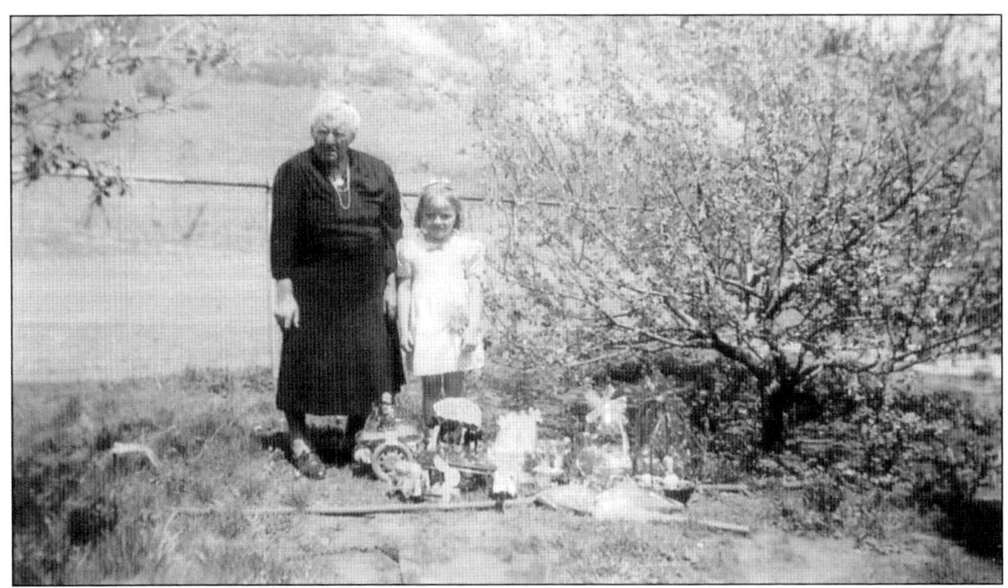

Mary Jaksch Helmer. Mary Lou Helmer is pictured with her paternal grandmother, Mary. The Helmer children grew up on the family ranch with an extended family of aunts, uncles, cousins, and their grandmother. Mary Lou remained on the ranch after her marriage to Jimmy Shields and the birth of their three children. She remembers telling her children to remain on the front porch while she ensured there were no rattlesnakes in the yard. (Mary Lou Helmer family.)

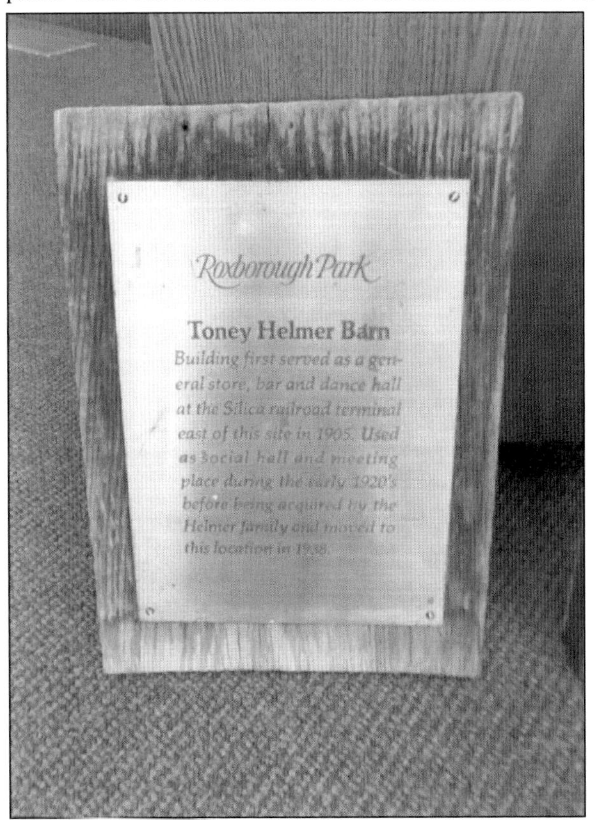

Plaque Commemorating Silica-Helmer Historical Barn. When the Woodmoor Corporation purchased the Helmer ranch in 1970, the company destroyed most of the structures on the property, including the barn, built in 1905, that had been the Silica railroad terminal, general store, bar, and dance hall. The Helmers used it as a social hall and meeting place during the 1920s. Mary Lou Helmer remembers the family was saddened when the historic barn was demolished. (Mary Lou Helmer family.)

CATTLE SALE CATALOG, 1970. This photograph shows the front page from a catalog circulated among cattlemen to announce the sale of the Helmers' award-winning cattle. It contained photographs and descriptions of the Helmer ranch's last registered Herefords. (Mary Lou Helmer family.)

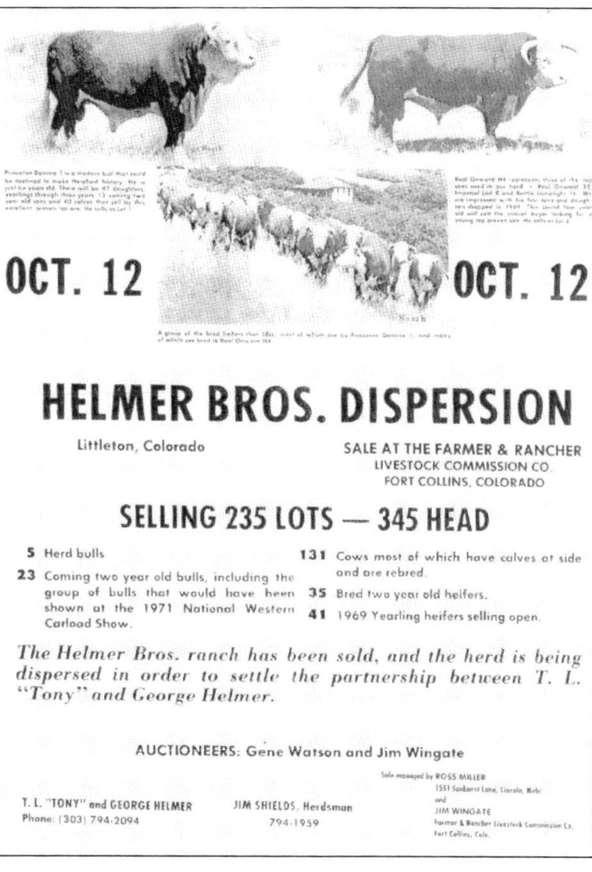

OCT. 12 OCT. 12

HELMER BROS. DISPERSION

Littleton, Colorado

SALE AT THE FARMER & RANCHER
LIVESTOCK COMMISSION CO.
FORT COLLINS, COLORADO

SELLING 235 LOTS — 345 HEAD

5 Herd bulls

23 Coming two year old bulls, including the group of bulls that would have been shown at the 1971 National Western Carload Show.

131 Cows most of which have calves at side and are rebred.

35 Bred two year old heifers.

41 1969 Yearling heifers selling open.

The Helmer Bros. ranch has been sold, and the herd is being dispersed in order to settle the partnership between T. L. "Tony" and George Helmer.

AUCTIONEERS: Gene Watson and Jim Wingate

T. L. "TONY" and GEORGE HELMER
Phone: (303) 794-2094

JIM SHIELDS, Herdsman
794-1959

Sale managed by ROSS MILLER
1551 Sunburst Lane, Lincoln, Nebr.
and
JIM WINGATE
Farmer & Rancher Livestock Commission Co.
Fort Collins, Colo.

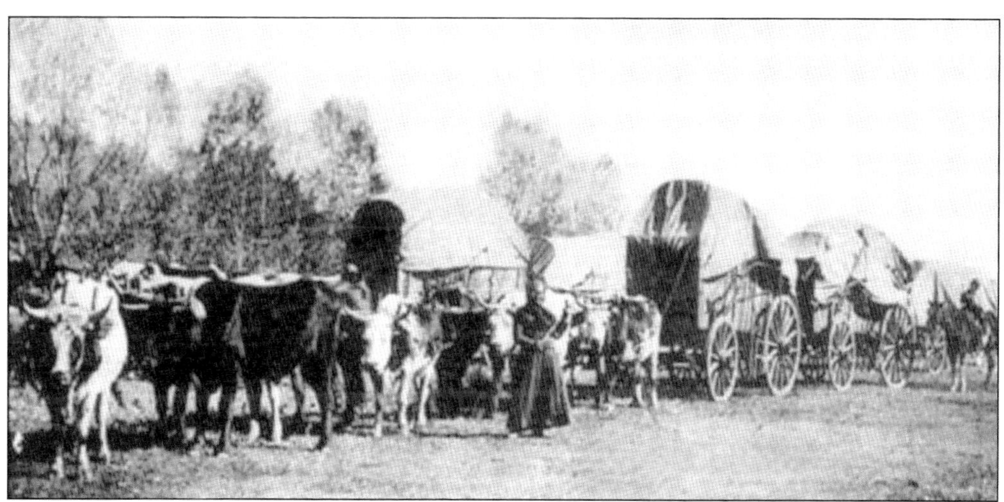

PIONEER JOHN HELMER. Born in Austria in 1858, John Helmer was the youngest son of Franz and Judith Helmer. As a boy, he walked across the prairie with his father to the Kansas Territory, and at age 18, he hauled freight by wagon over plains and mountain routes. By some accounts, when the weather was cold, he had to keep moving so the potatoes he was transporting would not freeze.

To all whom it may concern:

Know ye, That A. C. Miksch a Private of Captain S. M. Logan's Company (B.) First Cavalry Regiment of Colorado VOLUNTEERS, who was enrolled on the 30th day of July one thousand eight hundred and sixty one to serve ___ years or during the war, is hereby Discharged from the service of the United States this Seventh day of January 1864, at Camp Collins by reason of his Enlistment as a veteran Volunteer under provisions G.O. 191 War Dept. 1863. (No objection to his being re-enlisted is known to exist.*)

Said A. C. Miksch was born in in the State of Pennsylvania is twenty three years of age, five feet ten inches high, Light complexion, Hazel eyes, Light hair, and by occupation when enrolled, a Farmer

Given at Camp Collins this Seventh day of January 1864.

Jno. C. Anderson Capt. 1 Cav. of Colorado
Ast. Comsy. of Musters
Commanding the Reg't.
Dist Colorado

*This sentence will be erased should there be anything in the conduct or physical condition of the soldier rendering him unfit for the Army.

S. M. Hawkins 1st Lieut 1st Cav. of Col
Comd'g Co. "B"

I hereby certify that the above is a true copy of a certificate of discharge exhibited to me by Amos C. Miksch this 11th day of August 1873.

Louis Dugal
Register

AMOS MIKSCH. Born in 1838 in Pennsylvania, pioneer Amos Miksch came to Colorado as a young man and worked as a miner in Central City. This 1864 document shows Miksch's discharge and reenlistment as a "veteran volunteer" in the First Calvary Regiment of the Colorado Volunteers. In 1864, Miksch witnessed the Sand Creek Massacre and later testified about the atrocities committed there. (Douglas County History Research Center.)

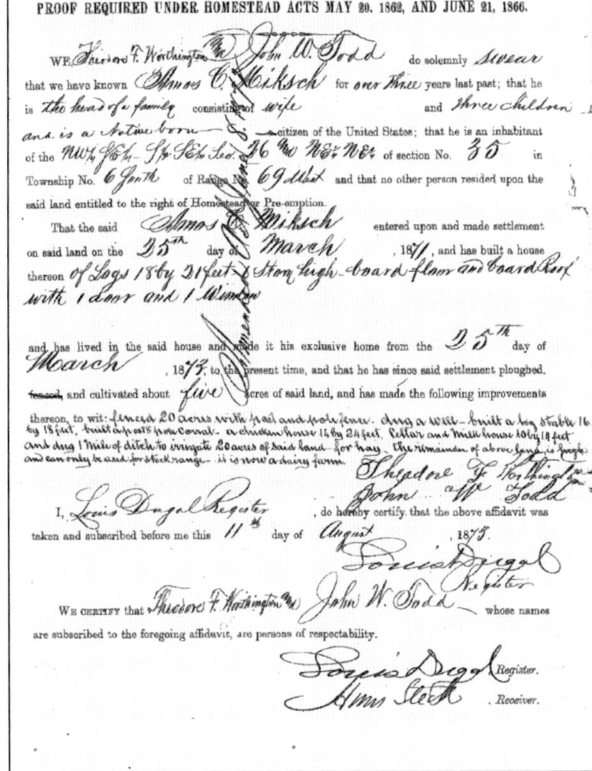

PROOF REQUIRED UNDER HOMESTEAD ACTS MAY 20, 1862, AND JUNE 21, 1866.

WE, Theodore F. Worthington and John W. Todd do solemnly swear that we have known Amos C. Miksch for over three years last past; that he is the head of a family consisting of wife and three children and is a native born citizen of the United States; that he is an inhabitant of the NW¼ of SE¼ - S½ of SE¼ Sec. 26 and NE¼ NE¼ of section No. 35 in Township No. 6 South of Range No. 69 West and that no other person resided upon the said land entitled to the right of Homestead or Pre-emption.

That the said Amos C. Miksch entered upon and made settlement on said land on the 25th day of March, 1871, and has built a house thereon of Logs 18 by 21 feet 1 Story high - board floor and board Roof with 1 Door and 1 Window

and has lived in the said house and made it his exclusive home from the 25th day of March, 1873, to the present time, and that he has since said settlement ploughed, ~~fenced~~, and cultivated about five acres of said land, and has made the following improvements thereon, to wit: fenced 20 acres with post and pole fence - dug a well - built a log stable 16 by 18 feet, built a post and pole Corral - a chicken house 14 by 24 feet, Cellar and Milk house 10 by 14 feet and dug 1 Mile of ditch to irrigate 20 acres of said land for hay. The remainder of above land is arid and can only be used for stock range. It is now a dairy farm.

Theodore F. Worthington
John W. Todd

I, Louis Dugal Register, do hereby certify that the above affidavit was taken and subscribed before me this 11th day of August, 1873.

Louis Dugal
Register

WE CERTIFY that Theodore F. Worthington and John W. Todd whose names are subscribed to the foregoing affidavit, are persons of respectability.

Louis Dugal, Register.
Amos Steck, Receiver.

AMOS MIKSCH'S HOMESTEAD PATENT. Miksch filed this affidavit in 1873 affirming he improved the land, built a house of logs with one door and one window, and made it his exclusive home. He cultivated five acres, fenced 20 acres, dug a well, built a 14-by-24-foot chicken house and a 10-by-14-foot cellar and milk house, and dug a one-mile ditch to irrigate "the arid land." It was this cabin and land that John Helmer purchased in 1888. (Douglas County History Research Center.)

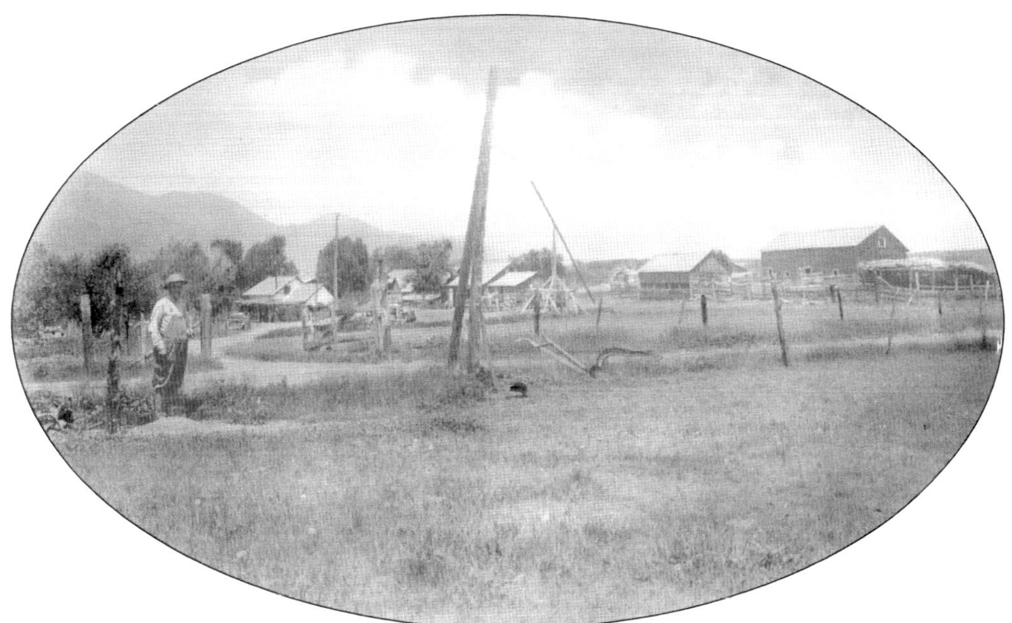

John Helmer and Nellie Regan. John Helmer married Irish-born Nellie Regan and purchased the cabin and land from his parents. The 1900 US Census shows John, Nellie, and two daughters, Pauline and Julia, living in Platte District. John and Nellie had a son, John William, who died prior to the census. Frank Regan and John William "Johnnie" were born within the next two years. In this 1910 photograph, John Helmer stands in front of his farm. (Douglas County History Research Center.)

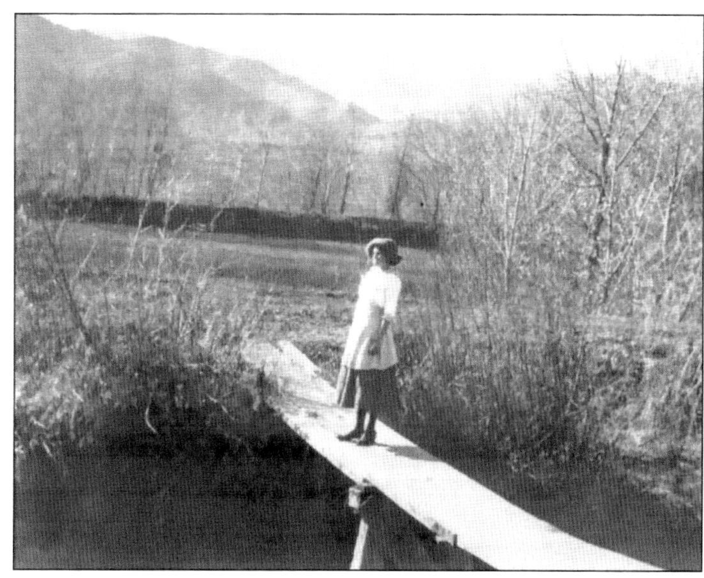

John Helmer's Family Life. Julia Helmer remembered her family raised cattle, sold milk, and irrigated crops by utilizing the nearby High Line Canal. The John Helmer family's life was typical of families in the Platte community. Their social and political activities appeared in newspapers, often under the news of Acequia. Pauline Helmer is pictured on a board stretched across the High Line Canal. (Bobbie Elder Collection.)

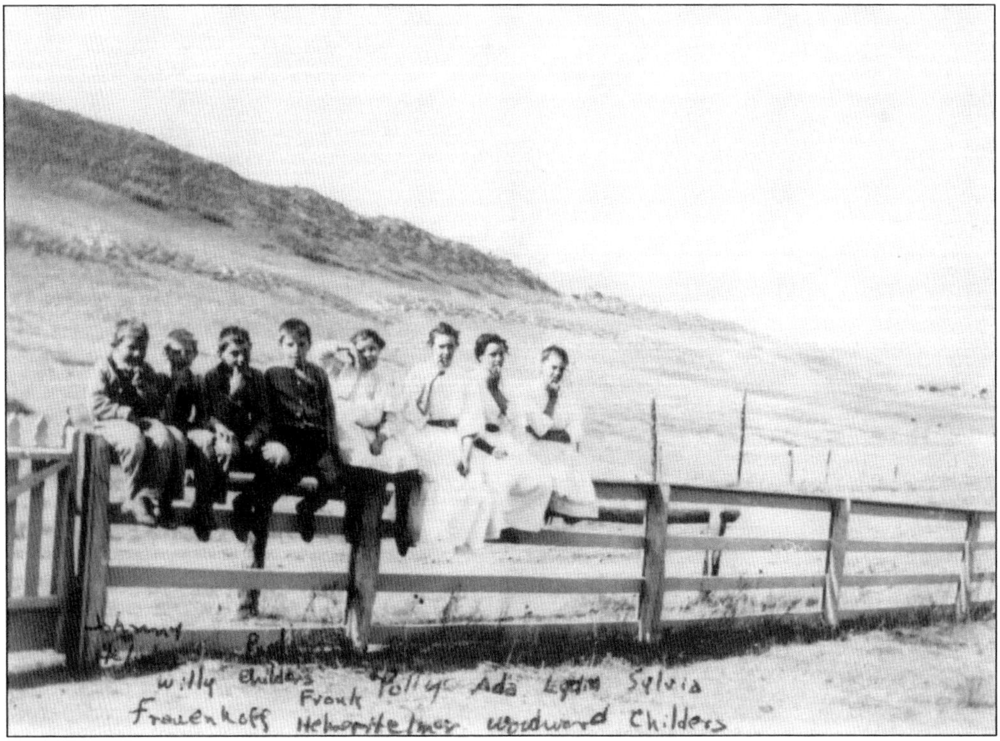

CHILDREN ON THE FENCE. In a small farming and ranching community, children played with their siblings, cousins, and friends. Pictured in this undated photograph are, from left to right, Johnnie Helmer, Willie Frauenhoff, Paul Childers, Frank Helmer, Polly Helmer, Ada Woodward, Lydia Woodward, and Sylvia Childers. (Douglas County History Research Center Library, Norman Collection.)

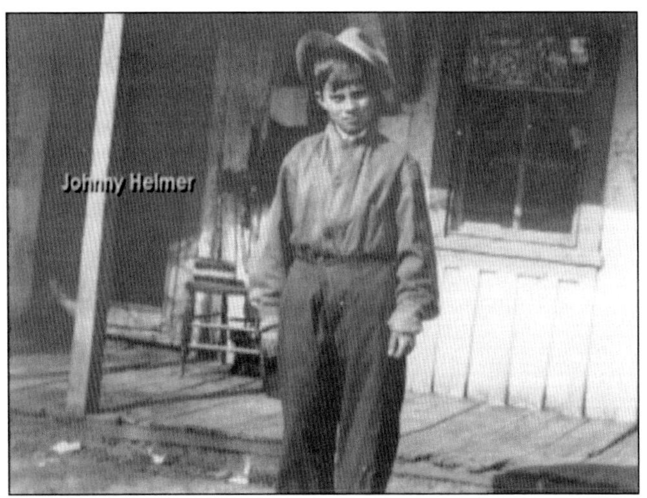

JOHNNIE HELMER ON THE PORCH. Little Johnnie Helmer is pictured on the porch of his family's cabin. Much later, after the death of his mother, Nellie, in 1938, Johnnie lived with his 88-year-old father, John, in the Miksch-Helmer cabin. In the early 1940s, financial troubles and the elder John Helmer's poor health required that the family rent the cabin and sell some of the property to pay back taxes. (Douglas County History Research Center Library, Norman Collection.)

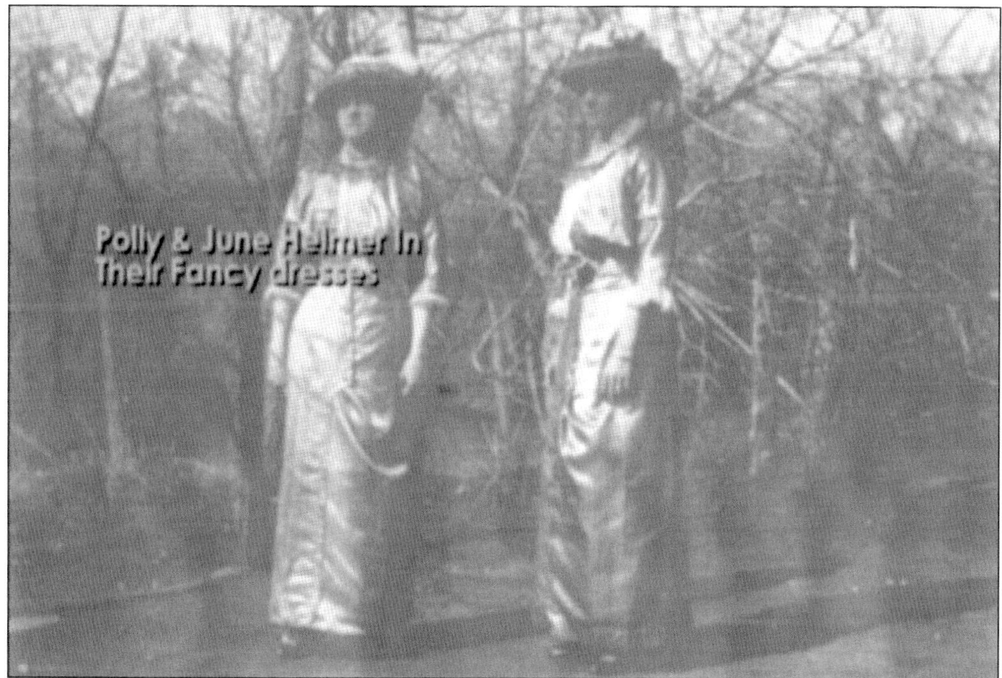

John Helmer's Daughters on Their Wedding Day. This photograph is thought to show the wedding day of Pauline "Polly" and Julia "June" Helmer. The sisters' double wedding on April 14, 1914, made the front page of the *Douglas County Record Journal*. Polly married Walter Campbell, and June married William Norman. (Douglas County History Research Center Library, Norman Collection.)

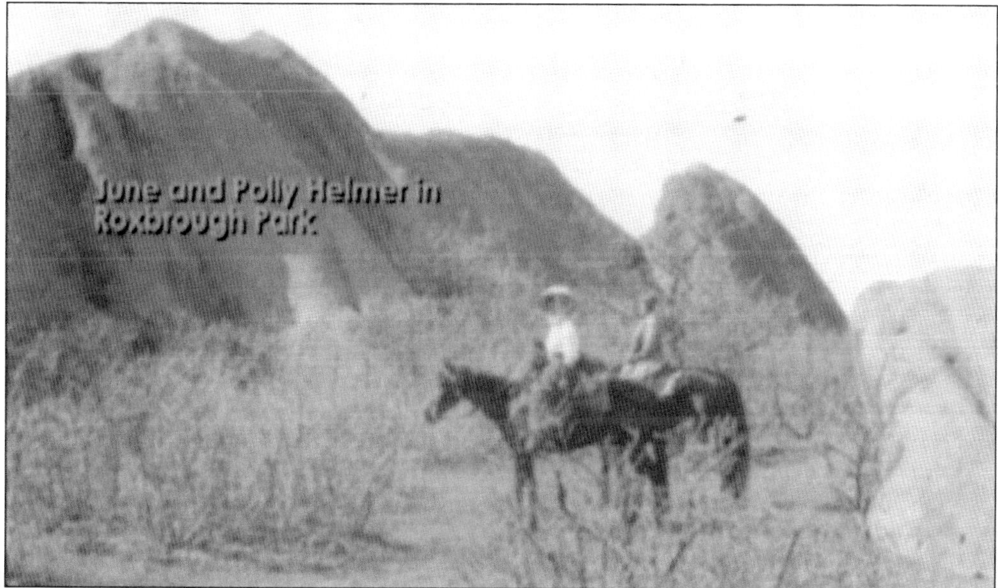

June and Polly Helmer Riding Horses. June and Polly remained in Roxborough and were able to continue their close relationship. In this undated photograph, they are riding horses along the red rocks of Roxborough. (Douglas County History Research Center Library, Norman Collection.)

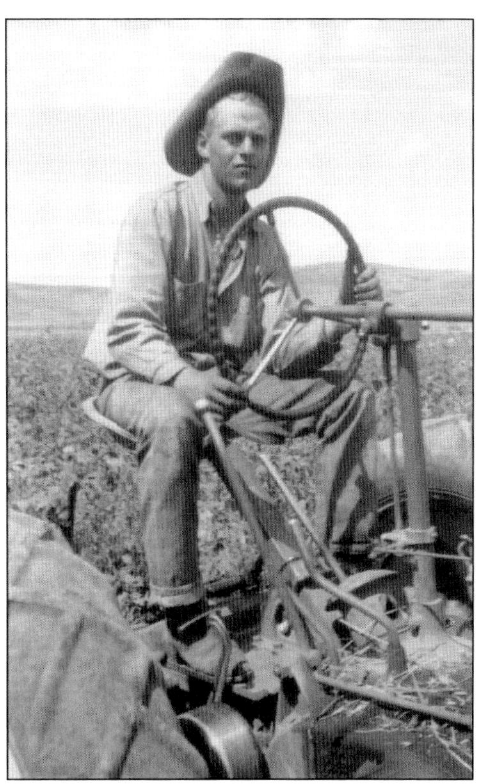

YOUNG FRANK NORMAN ON A TRACTOR. After Julia (June) Helmer married William R. Norman they remained in Roxborough and raised three children: Harold, Kathryn, and Frank born in 1927. The children attended Roxborough Park School with their Helmer cousins and friend Rusty Simon. In 1968, Frank became a school bus driver in Roxborough. He drove younger children to Plum Creek School and older students to Castle Rock's Douglas County High School. (Douglas County History Research Center Library, Norman Collection.)

JOHN "JOHNNIE" HELMER. In 1948, Johnnie Helmer married Margaret Hildebrand. They lived in the Hildebrand ranch house until the 1970s, when the Army Corps of Engineers acquired part of the ranch for the construction of Chatfield Dam. After both Johnnie and Margaret died in the 1990s, Margaret's daughter, Florence Stockwell, inherited the house. Her son, John Stockwell Jr., sold the 1871 cabin in 2005. This certificate was obtained from Art Cornell's report on the Hildebrand ranch. (Art Cornell.)

BOOK 24, PAGE 160
FILED FOR RECORD MAY 28, 1948 at 8:50 A. M.
EARL K. DOWNING REC.

CERTIFICATE OF MARRIAGE

I Rev. F. D. McCallin
a Catholic Priest residing at Littleton
in the County of Arapahoe in the State of Colorado do certify that in accordance with the authority on me conferred by the above License, I did, on this 23rd
day of May in the year A.D. 1948 at Littleton
in the County of Arapahoe in the State of Colorado solemnize the Rites of Matrimony
between John W Helmer of Littleton
in the County of Arapahoe in the State of Colo
and Dorothy Hildebrand of Littleton
in the County of Arapahoe in the State of Colo
in the presence of Robert Campbell and Dorothy Huggins
Witness my hand and seal at the County aforesaid this 23rd day of
May A.D. 1948.

SIGNED IN PRESENCE OF

Robert P Campbell Rev. F. D. McCallin SEAL
Dorothy Huggins Littleton

Five

Mining Roxborough's Hogback

A rush of people moved west in 1849 to find gold. Colorado saw its share of miners, but most moved higher into the mountains, where rich mother lodes were found. Others panned along the South Platte River and small creeks in and near Roxborough. Some gold was found on the northwest side of Carpenter Peak, but it was not enough to start a stampede to Roxborough.

The Dakota Hogback, a long, sharp ridge at the eastern fringe of the Rocky Mountains, is clearly visible in Roxborough as the first line of ridges along the western edge of the Great Plains. Much of the hogback is scarred from a century of mining—not for gold but for the interesting and useful rock found in the Dakota Hogback. Over millions of years, sediments from the shallow sea that once covered the area were compressed into a soft rock. Oyster and clamshells, sand, and mud dissolved and formed layers of sandstone, shale, limestone, and clay, which are materials needed for constructing items ranging from homes to roadways.

Mining became very important in Roxborough's early days, offering jobs at which a man could earn a decent wage to live simply; unlike deep underground mining, this was not dangerous. For ranchers like the Helmer brothers Toney and George and sister Cel and her husband, Mel Head, the hogback that ran through their property provided an additional source of income. For Denver companies like Robinson Brick, General Shale, and others, the clay in the hogback was a source that could be used to make bricks to construct homes and commercial buildings.

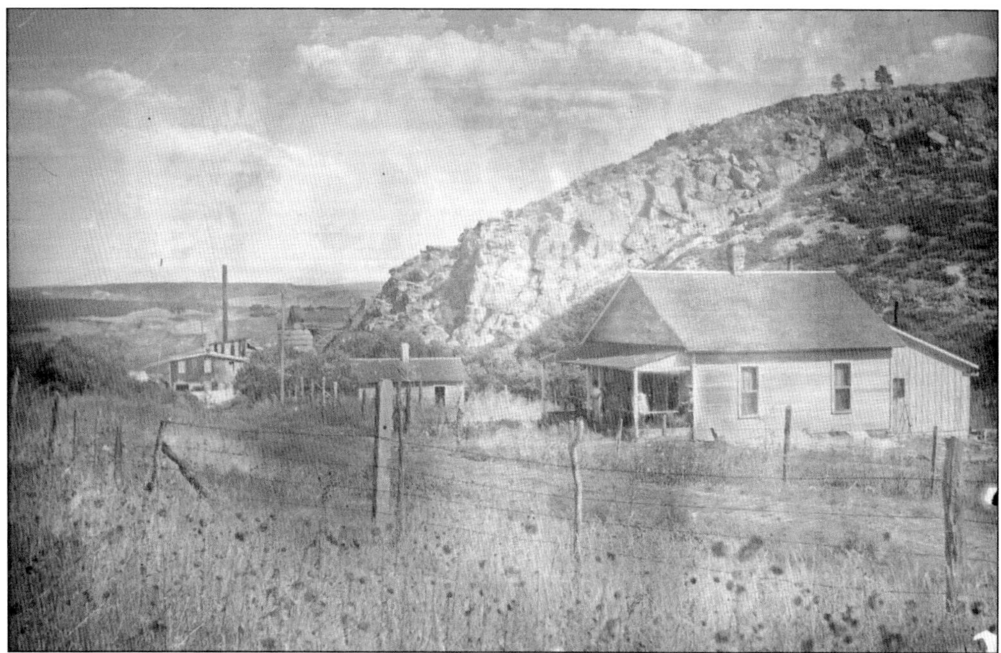

Roxborough Land Company. In 1889, Henry S. Persse purchased property that included what would one day become the small industrial town of Silica. In 1904, Persse's Roxborough Land Company granted a land and mineral lease to the Silicated Brick and Clay Company, which soon constructed manufacturing buildings and installed telephone and telegraph lines. This photograph shows miners' homes in Silica. (Roxborough State Park.)

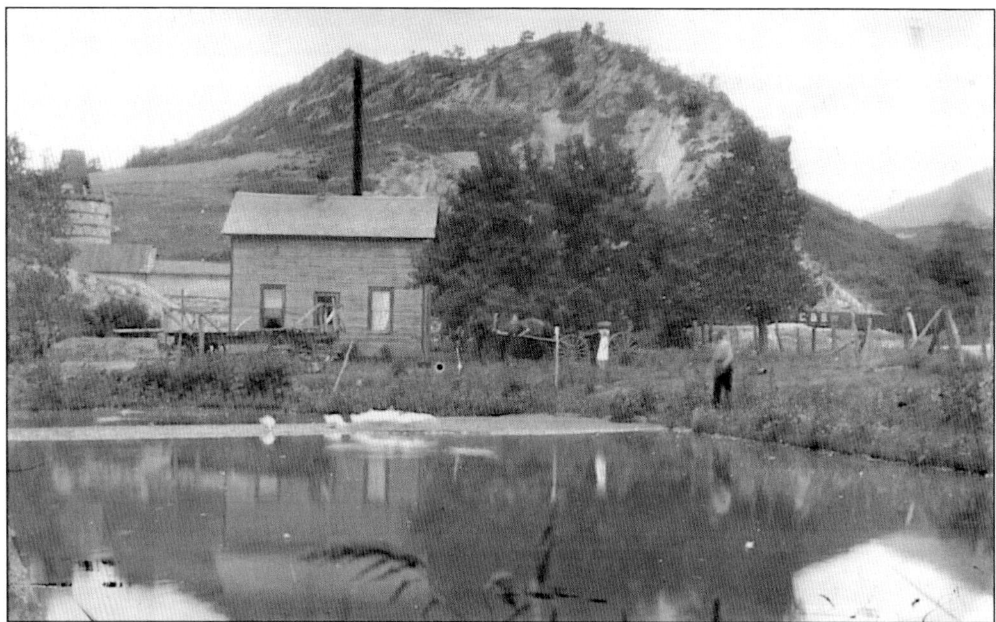

Silicated Brick and Clay Company. Because of the remoteness of the operations, the company developed a small settlement called Silica to support workers who made bricks with sand excavated from a nearby hogback that contained feldspar deposits mixed with calcium silicates—excellent elements for making distinctive white silica bricks. (Douglas County History Research Center.)

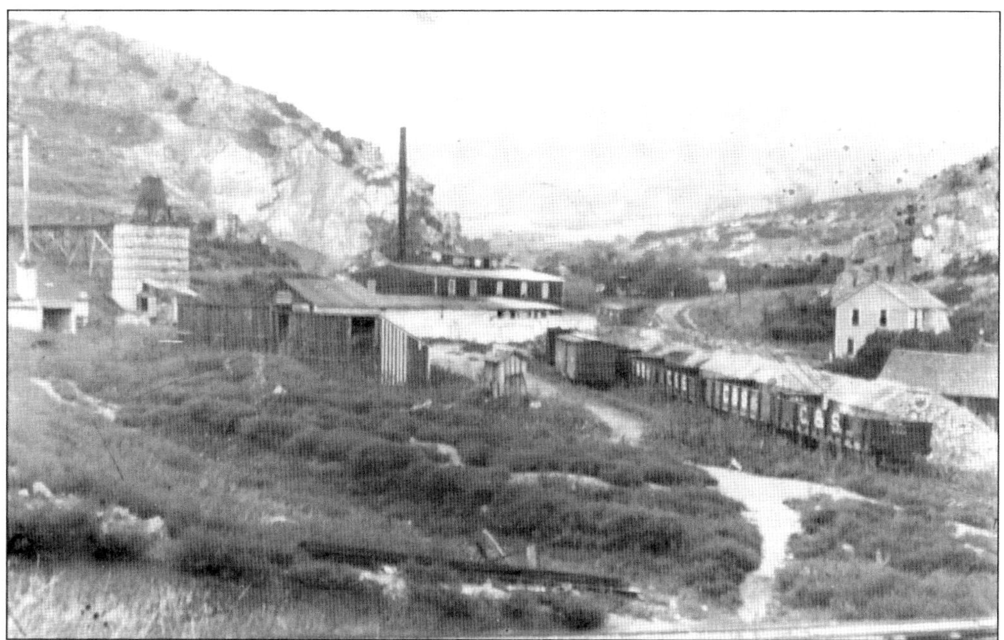

Colorado & Southern Railway Spur to Silica. In 1876, the Colorado & Southern (C&S) Railway reached Platte Canyon. In 1909, the C&S Railway built a four-mile railroad spur to the Silica Brick Company. The spur maintained operations for mining companies along the hogback until 1941. Oral history maintains the tracks were pulled up in 1941 to assist with the World War II effort. (Douglas County History Research Center.)

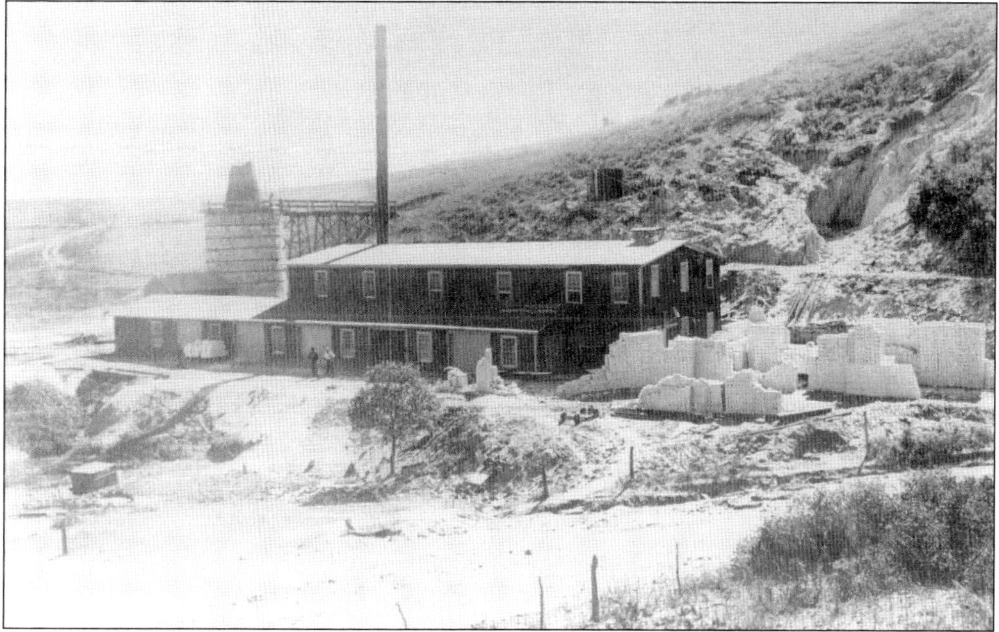

Silicated Brick Company's Failure. Some said supervisor George Hedges created the distinctive white silica bricks using a secret formula he crafted. Supposedly, after Hedges died in 1919, his formula and the company died with him. Cattleman Anton Helmer said the brick company closed because of poor management. (Ed and Nancy Bathke Collection.)

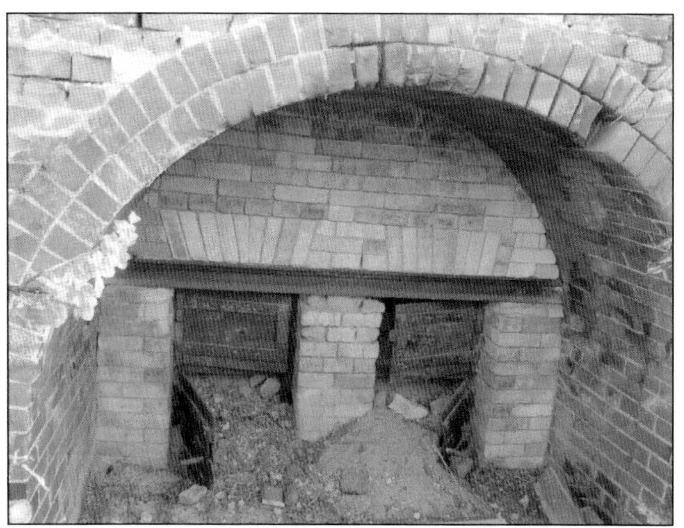

Kiln Opening. In the *Archaeological Assessment of the Roxborough Kiln*, Kimberly D. Dugan states: "The distinctive bricks . . . were made from a mixture of ground lime rock and silica sand, quarried from the nearby hills directly to the south and west of the kiln. The bricks were placed on small cars and pushed into a steel boiler where they were steamed under high pressure overnight." (Douglas County History Research Center.)

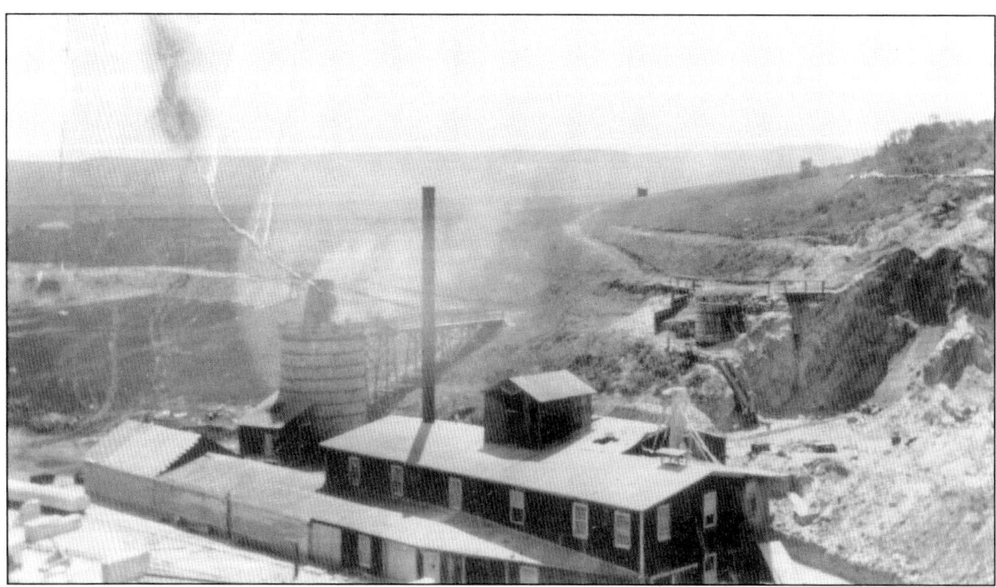

Helmer Family and the Brick Company. After Henry S. Persse's death in 1918, the Helmer family's matriarch, Mary Helmer, purchased property from Persse's Roxborough Land Company that included the brick and clay company. Bricks were no longer manufactured, but clay, sand, and rocks were mined and sold until 1970, when mining interests—along with thousands of acres of the Helmers' cattle ranch—were sold to the Woodmoor Corporation. (Douglas County History Research Center.)

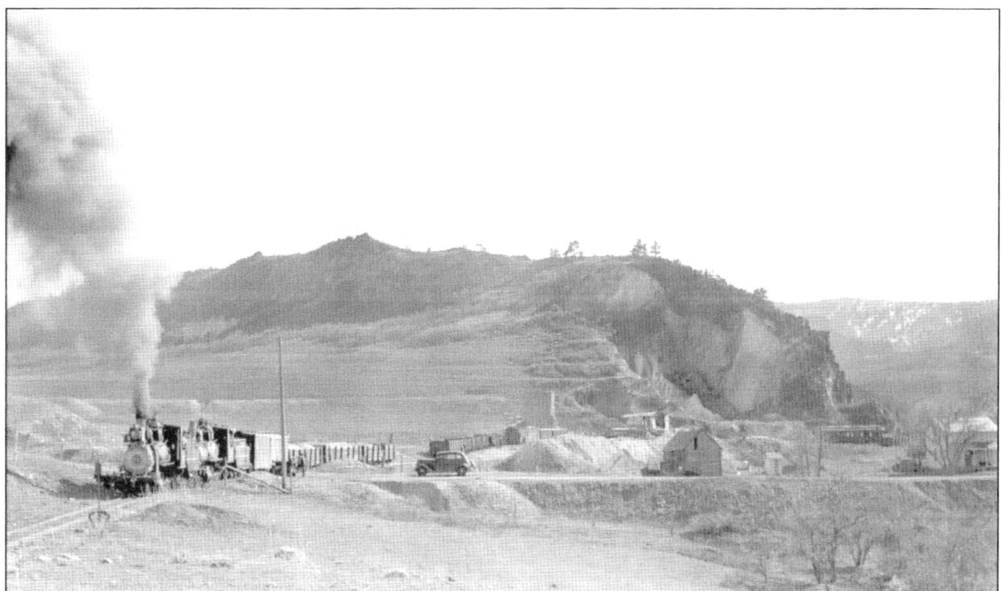

The Last Train from Silica. The town of Silica appeared on Douglas County maps until 1937. The last train departed from Silica around 1941. According to Toney Helmer's daughter, Mary Lou Helmer, the Helmer family made the superintendent's office their home and lived there until they sold the property in 1970. The Helmers used other buildings to house family members and workers or for business purposes. (Greg Liptak Collection.)

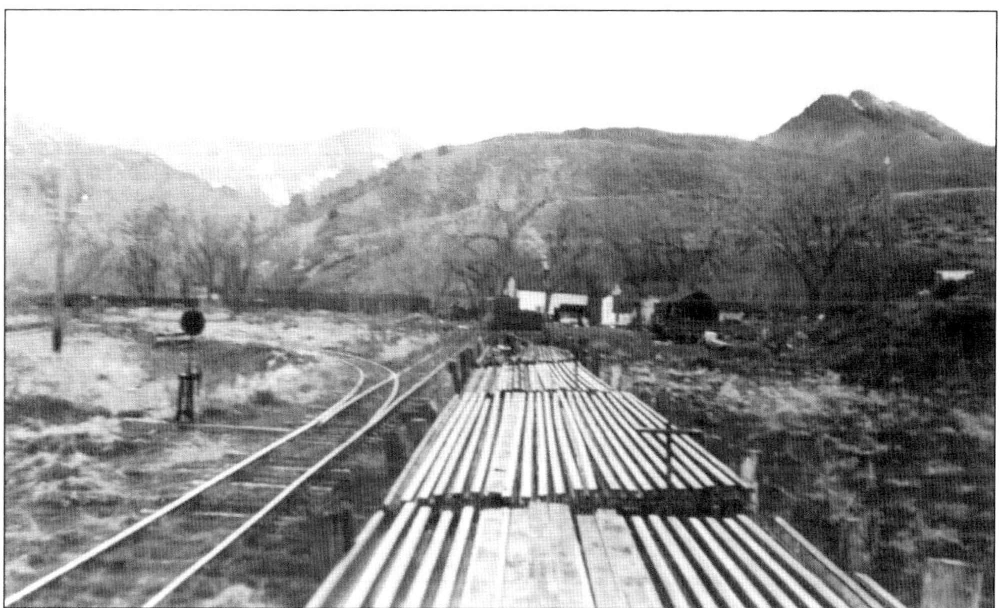

Removing Silica's Railroad Tracks. The Colorado & Southern railroad spur continued to serve Silica—and other mines throughout the area—until the early 1940s. According to oral history, the tracks were dismantled for the war effort in 1941. The Helmer family continued to mine clay and silica until the late 1960s, transporting the materials by truck. (Littleton Museum.)

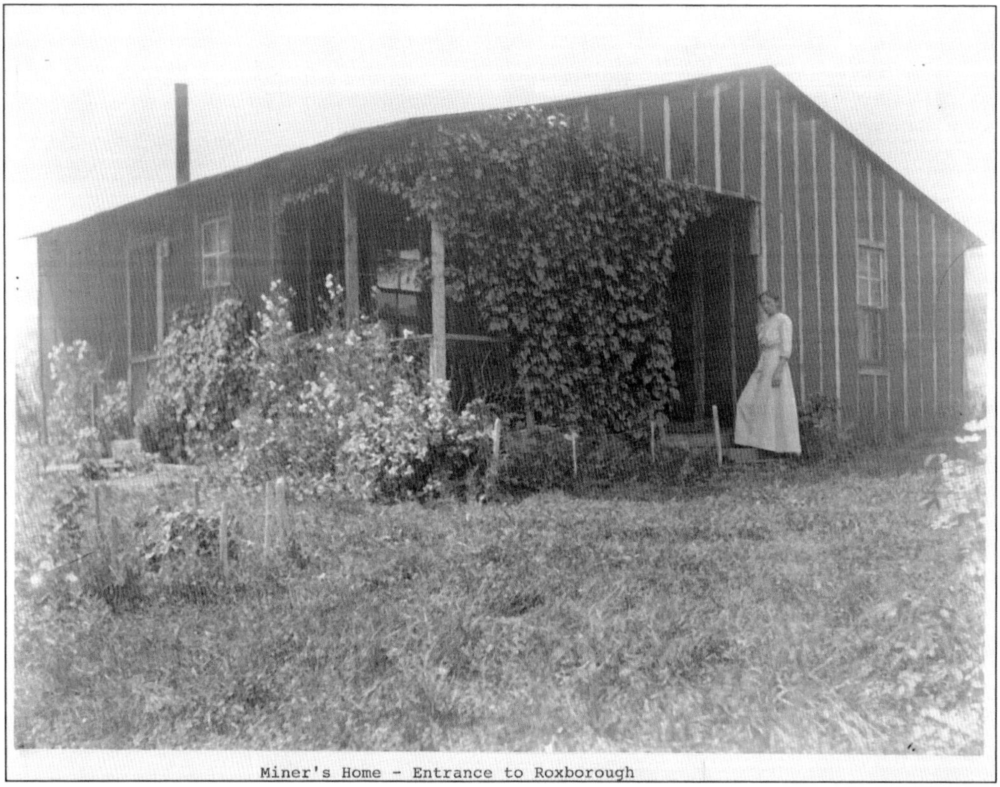

Miner's Home - Entrance to Roxborough

SILICA MINER'S HOME. An unidentified woman is standing outside a miner's home in Roxborough. It is likely that her husband did not have to go far because he worked nearby in Silica. In the early 1900s, clay, feldspar, lime, and other materials were mined from the nearby hogbacks (long, sharply crested ridges found along the east side of Roxborough's foothills.) Silica workers made bricks used for building homes and other structures that were shipped by rail to Denver. (Roxborough State Park.)

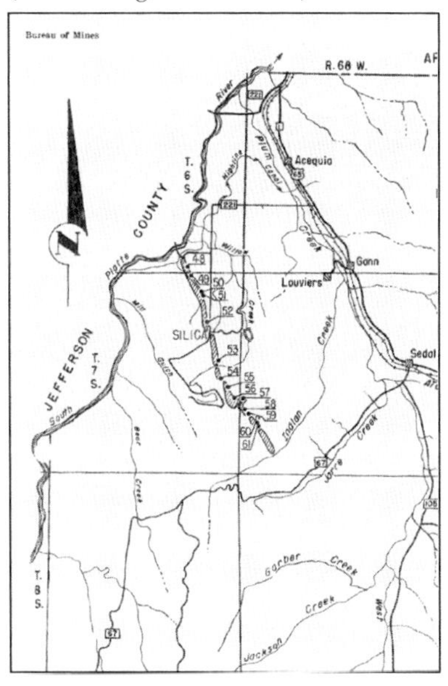

ROXBOROUGH'S CLAY MINES. This map shows the location of mines operating along the Dakota Hogback in Roxborough during the 1950s. No. 48 was a mine acquired by Robinson Brick and Tile Company of Denver in 1949. By 1955, it was the largest clay mine in the area. Some of the mines are active today along the western border of the Roxborough Village West residential community. The mines are active or inactive depending on building needs. (US Bureau of Mines.)

THE HILLSIDE MINE. Hillside Mine No. 49 was leased by W.H. Hedley from Slocum Brothers and operated from 1953 to 1954. It was entered through 15 feet of sandstone that formed a hanging wall on the clay bed and the crest of the hogback. The portal and drifts were made large enough to accommodate a truck. Two men operated the Hillside Mine and produced an average of 15 tons of clay, sandstone, feldspar, or rocks per day. (US Bureau of Mines.)

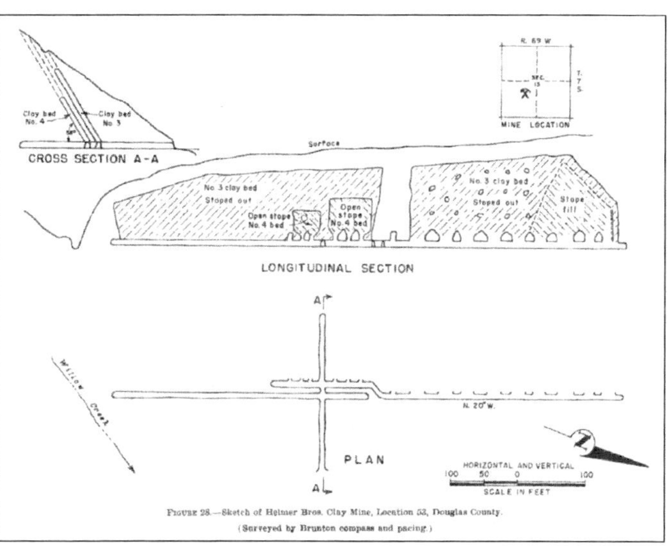

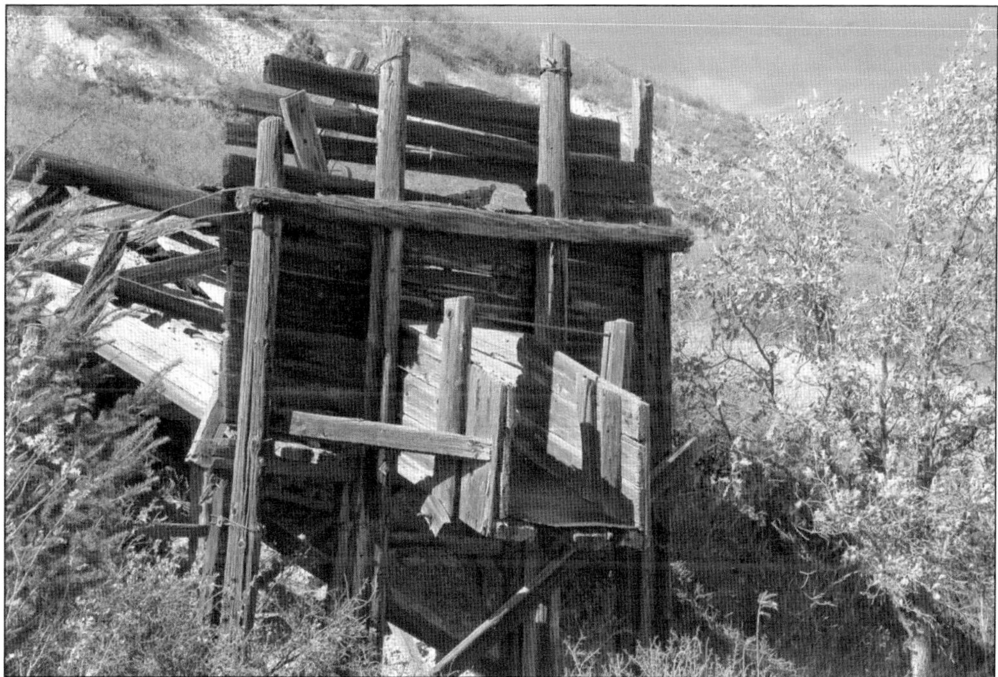

THE HELMER BROTHERS MINE, LOCATION NO. 53. The Helmer family operated the area's only underground mine, which was located one mile south of Silica. Opened in 1930, it was leased intermittently until 1954. The four men employed there mined clay, sandy shale, and sandstone, producing about 25 tons per day. Parts of the adit's wooden structure are still visible in Roxborough State Park. (Tom Olkowski.)

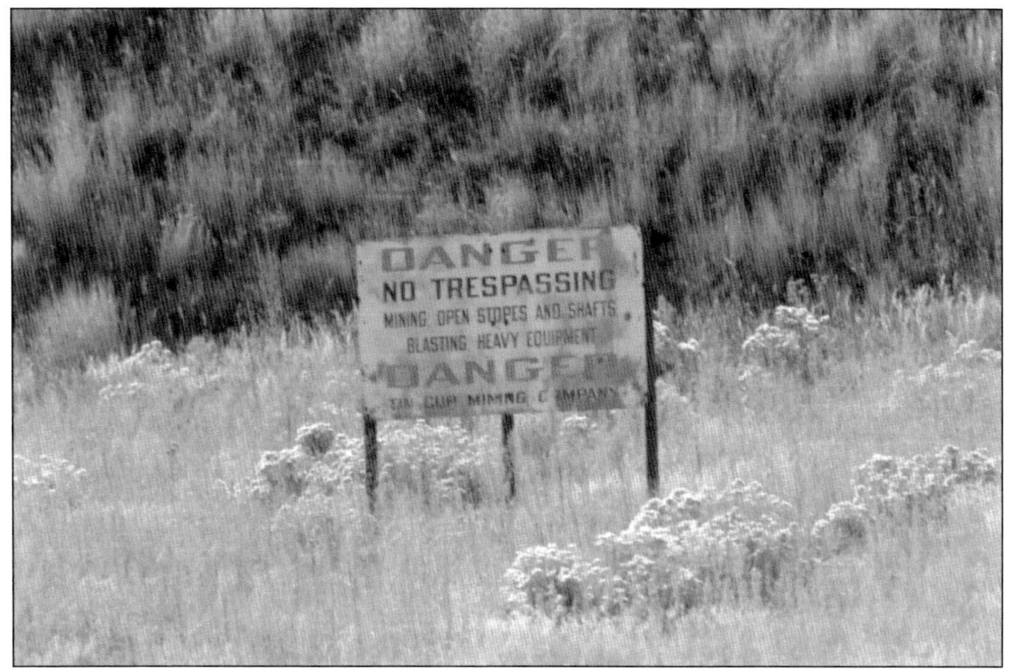

ROBINSON BRICK COMPANY'S TIN CUP MINES, 1943–1990. In 1943, the Robinson Brick Company signed an agreement with the Slocums to lease property along the hogback. In 1960, Robinson Brick signed a lease that made the term of the lease perpetual so long as clay was produced and there was no cessation of mining operations for a period of six months. (Tom Olkowski.)

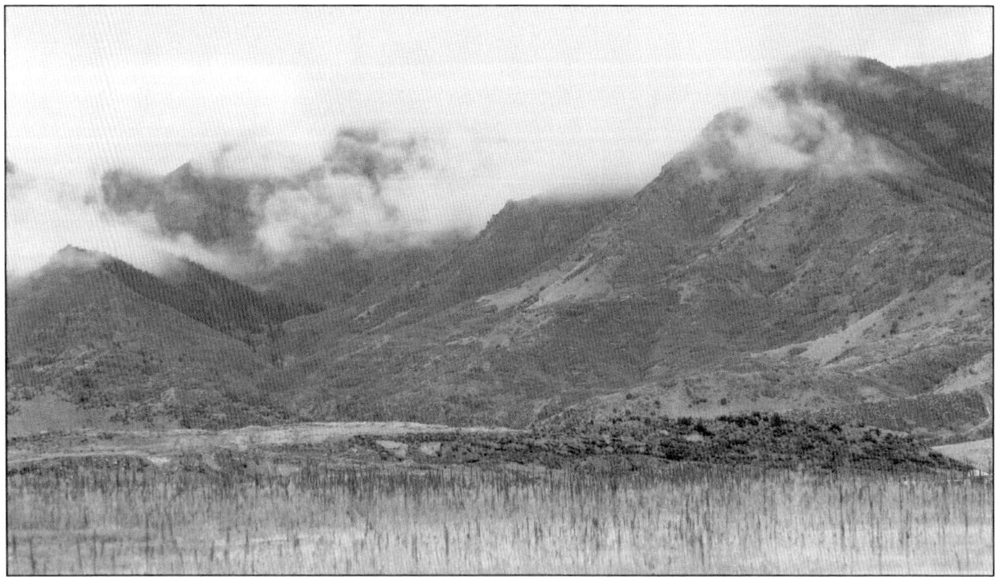

ROXBOROUGH VILLAGE AND MINING COMPANIES. From 1968 to 1992, the Tin Cup Mining Company, a subsidiary of Robinson Brick Company, purchased 180 acres of lease property along Dakota Hogback. An agreement between Tin Cup Mining Company and Roxborough/Village Joint Venture allowed the construction of the county road across a portion of the property. In this photograph, the mining scar on the hogback can be seen running behind Roxborough Village West. (Tom Olkowski.)

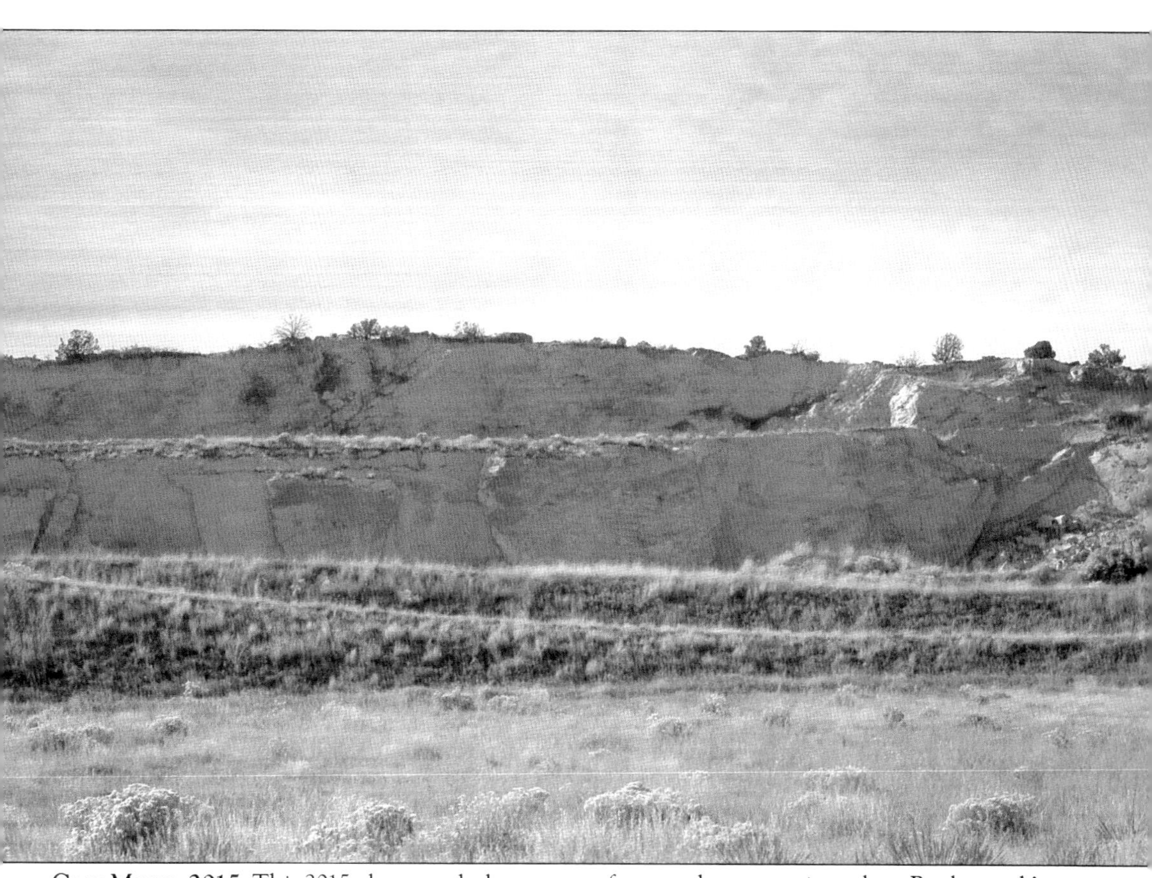

Clay Mines, 2015. This 2015 photograph shows scars of past and present mines along Roxborough's Dakota Hogback. Not pictured is Roxborough Village West, the residential community to the east of the hogback, where this picture was taken. (Tom Olkowski.)

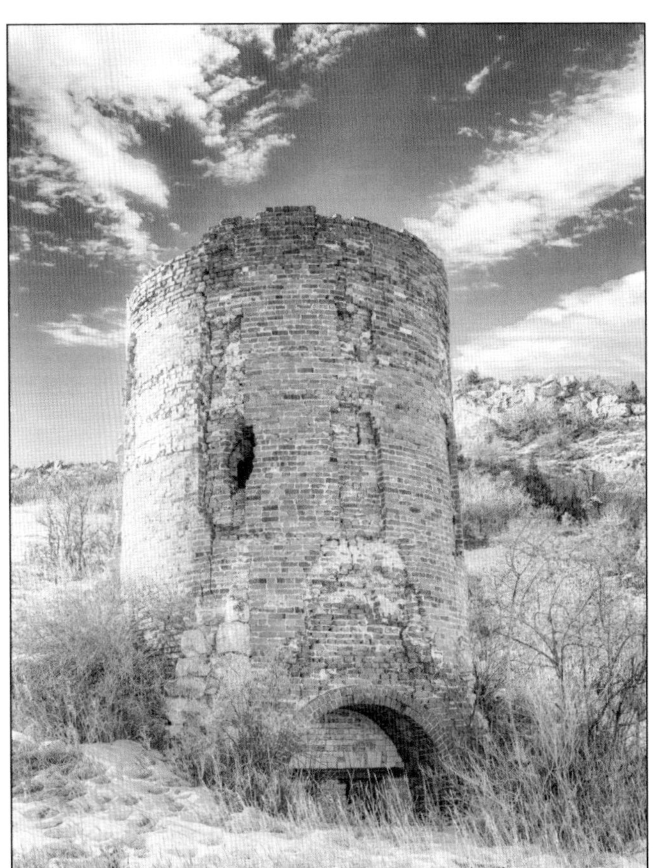

The Roxborough Lime Kiln. With the exception of the lime kiln, most of Silica's structures were removed after the sale of the Helmer Ranch in 1970. Because of Silica's significant role in the industrial development and growth of Douglas County, the Roxborough Kiln site was designated a Douglas County Landmark in 2007. (Bert Paredes.)

Silica, A Ghost Town. The town of Silica gradually disappeared over several decades. Only the deteriorating lime kiln stands as a reminder of the people, industrial buildings, and small town that provided white bricks, sand, and clay for more than 50 years. Each day, hundreds of cars pass by what was once Silica, replaced by the West Metro Fire Station and a road to Roxborough State Park. (Tom Olkowski.)

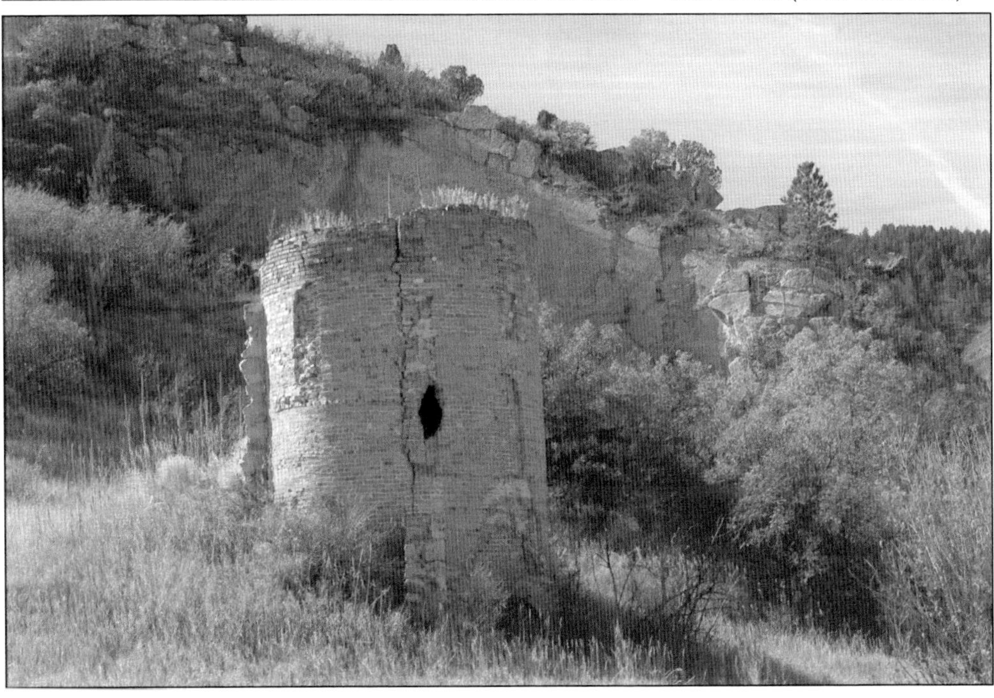

Six

Tourists, Farmers, Ranchers, and Space Cowboys

During the late 19th century, Roxborough remained an isolated, sparsely populated rural community. Farmers, ranchers, miners, and others often found life to be difficult in the area at the foot of the Rocky Mountains. The spectacular beauty of their Roxborough surroundings was overlooked in the daily struggles to make a living for themselves and their families. Although miles of open land separated the locals, strong bonds were forged among them often out of necessity.

Entrepreneur Henry Persse's home was in Denver, but he enjoyed spending time in his beloved Roxborough. He built a small resort among Roxborough's red sandstones and dreamed of creating a spectacular natural getaway for those who could afford it. Throughout the years, others had similar dreams of creating amazing resorts that would bring people to Roxborough. As word spread about Roxborough's beauty, city folks and tourists visited the area by horseback, carriage, and automobile in greater numbers.

However, it was not Roxborough's natural beauty or dreams of building a magnificent resort that drew Glenn L. Martin Airplane Company executives to the northwest Roxborough area in the mid-1950s—it was the area's isolation. The company had been awarded a contract by the US Air Force to build an intercontinental ballistic missile. Secrecy was imperative, and noisy rocket engines needed to be tested. When the company announced plans to build a defense plant on thousands of acres purchased from local ranchers in the foothills northwest of Roxborough and located 15 miles southwest of the small town of Littleton, a new era began.

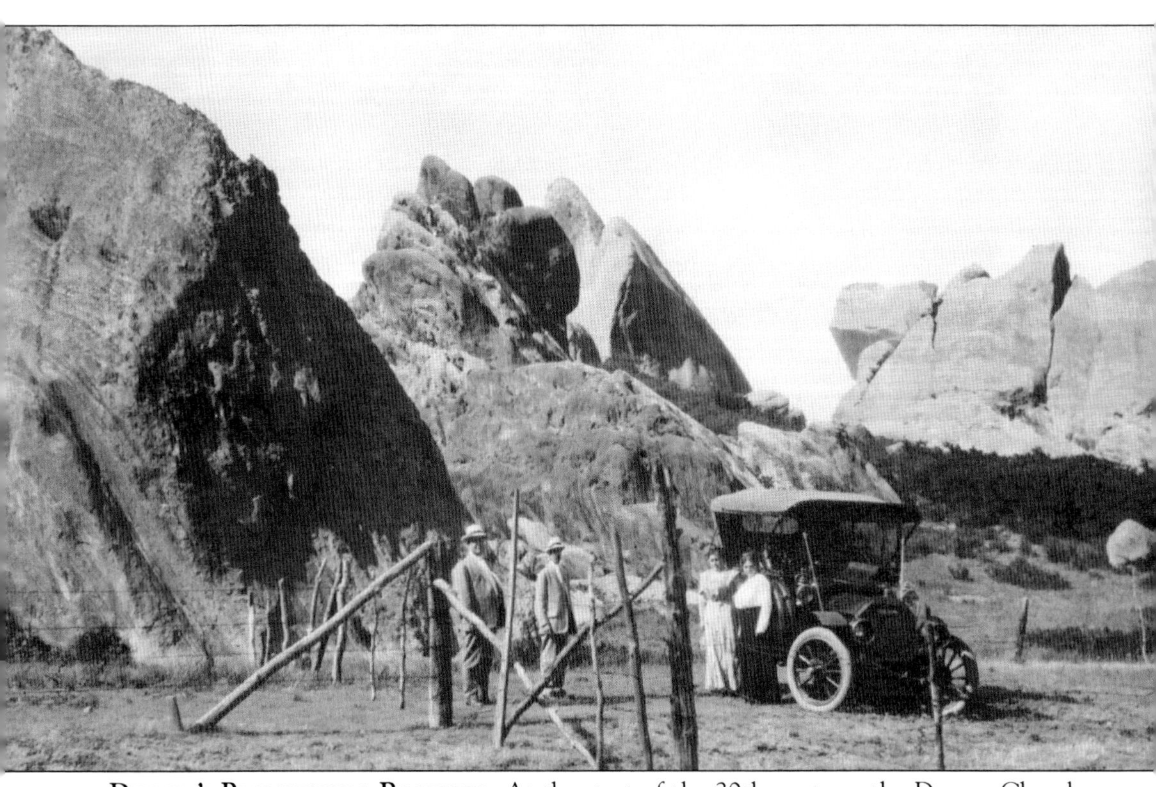

DENVER'S PROMOTIONAL BOOKLETS. At the start of the 20th century, the Denver Chamber of Commerce published several booklets to assist motorists and horse-and-buggy tourists in discovering "the scenic gateway to these playgrounds of the nation." In this undated photograph, two unidentified couples visit Roxborough. (Littleton Museum.)

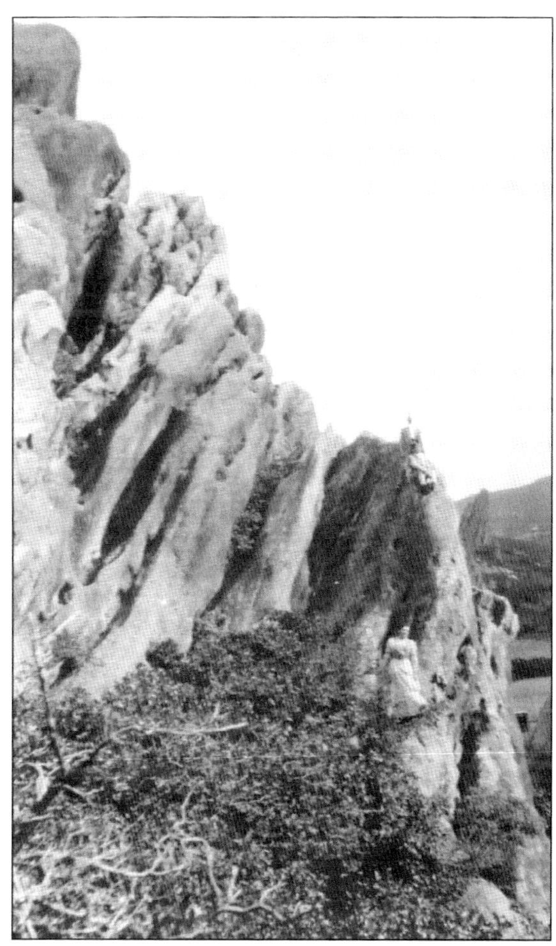

Denver to Roxborough Park and Return. The pamphlet *Denver to Roxborough Park and Return's Route No. 12* promises a scenic roadway where motorists would find scores of beautiful picnic places, a farming area that "will do the city motorist's heart good," and an uninterrupted view of Colorado's mountains. These unidentified visitors climbed the red rocks for pictures. Often, visitors would have to be assisted with getting down off the rocks. (History Colorado.)

An Automobile Day Trip out of Denver. In 1913, Colorado began licensing automobiles. Many folks joined other automobilists to visit places previously difficult to reach. According to one promotional travel booklet, Roxborough's natural beauty was only an hour away. Directions informed motorists that Waterton could be reached through Littleton across the South Platte River, then south on Platte Canyon Road to Chatfield Station, continuing south following the Colorado & Southern Railway tracks. (Douglas County History and Research Center.)

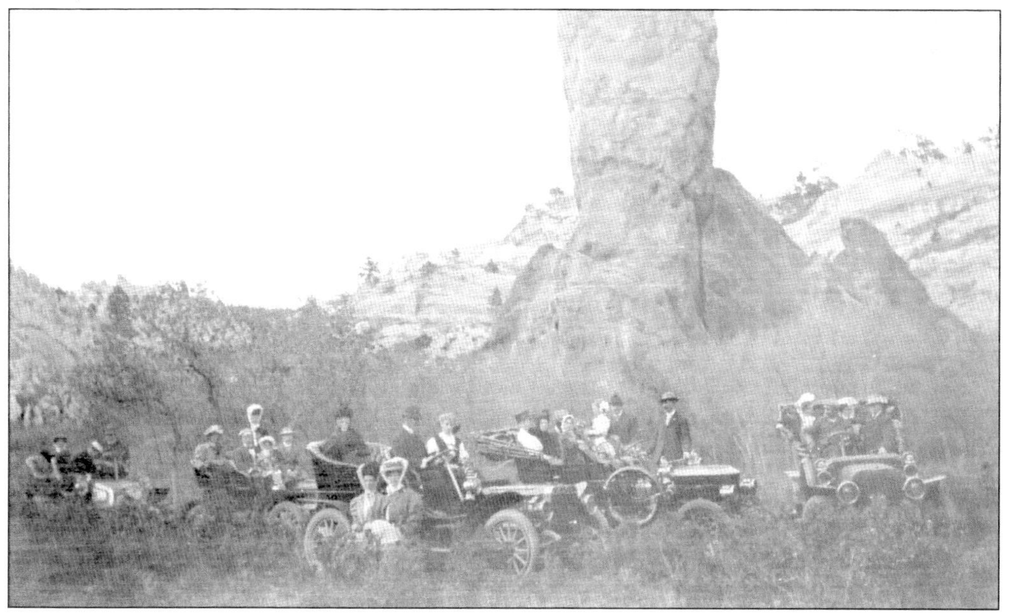

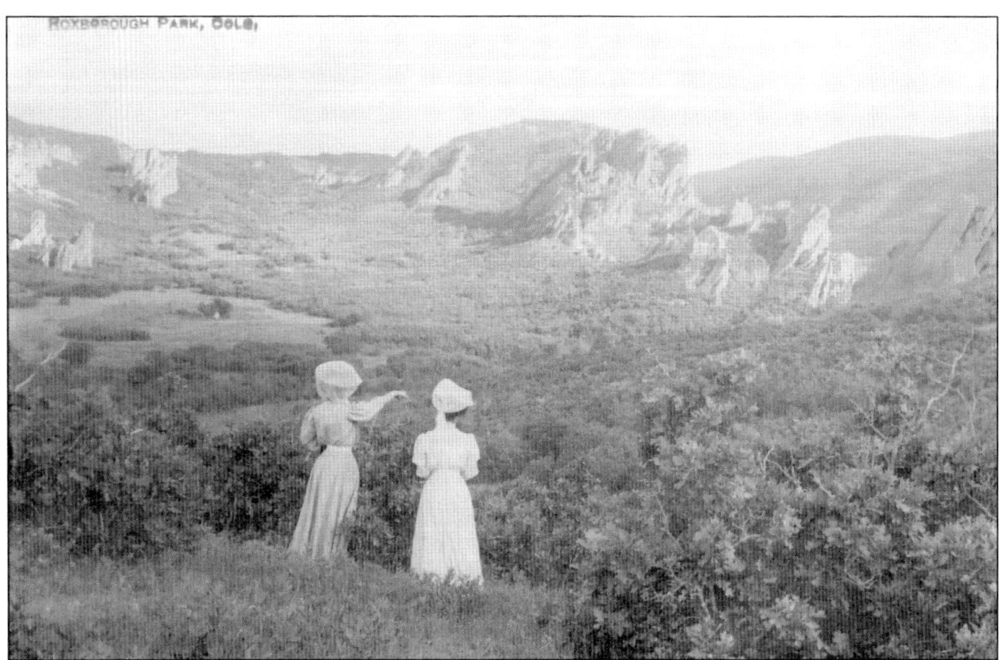

"The Entrance is at the Stone House and Cottages." This popular postcard shows two well-dressed women looking over a valley in Roxborough. One entrance took motorists through Henry Persse's stone house and cottage entrance; the other went through the Helmer Ranch. (Ed and Nancy Bathke Collection.)

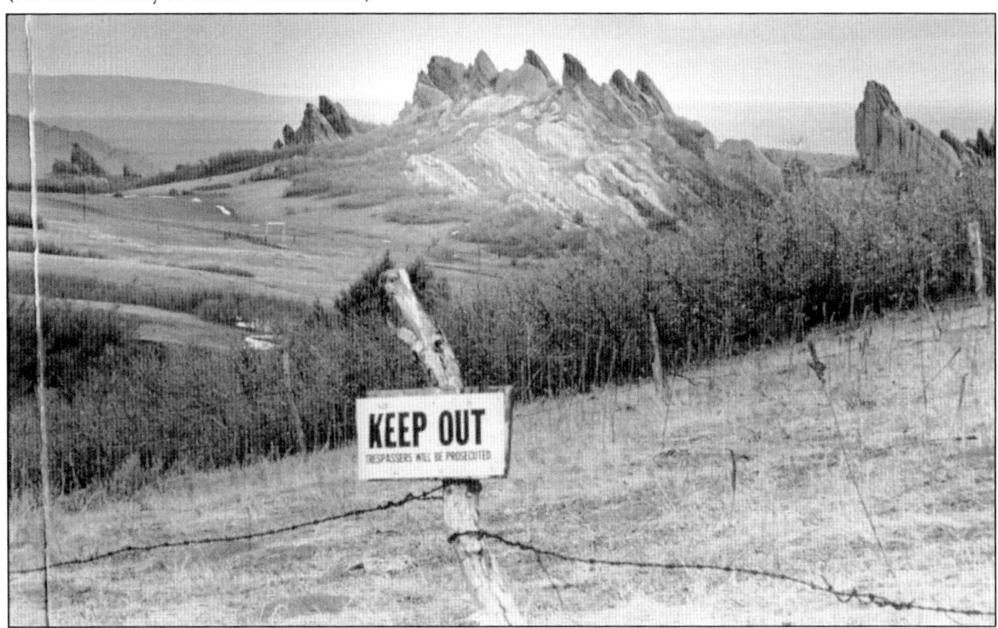

Rancher's Warning. A driving guide mentioned the road inside the park was bad in places due to mud holes. The Helmers discouraged travelers from entering their family ranch. Family members remember that matriarch Mary Helmer would water a ditch to make it difficult for cars to get through. If a driver got stuck, the Helmers charged 25¢ to 50¢ for pushing the automobile out of a rut. (Ed and Nancy Bathke Collection.)

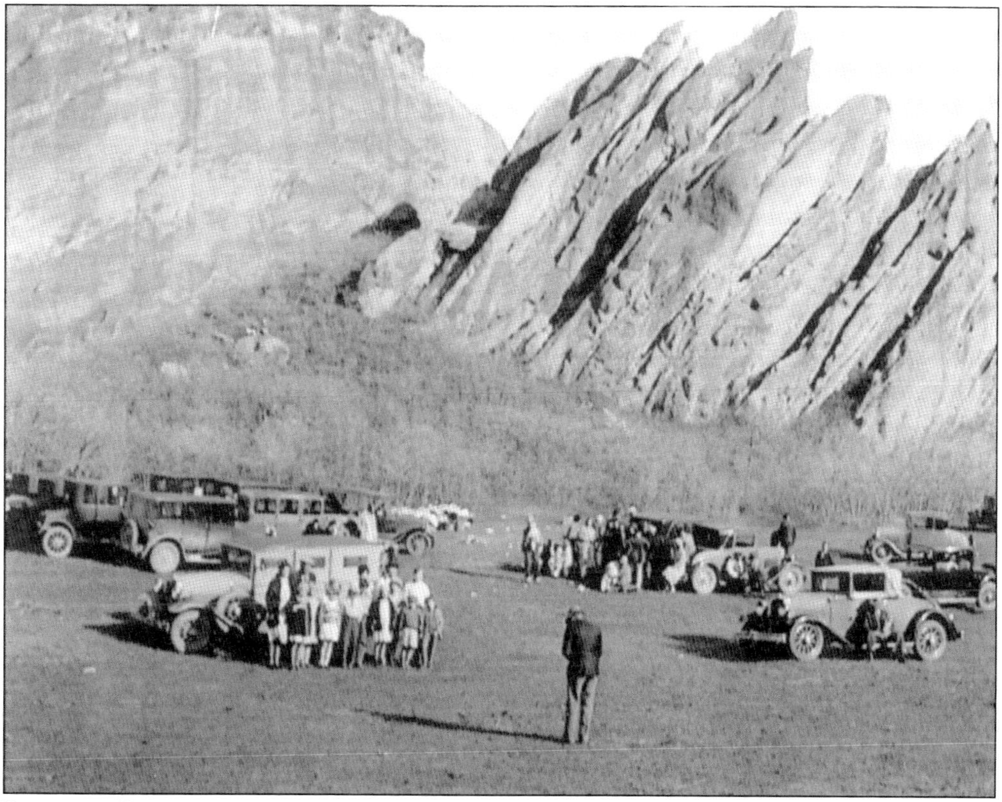

PICNICS IN ROXBOROUGH PARK. Picnics among Roxborough's beautiful 68 million-year-old rocks were not restricted to tourists. In this 1932 photograph, Roxborough Park School students hold a picnic in the valley. Kassler's David E. Swan is pictured sitting on the running board of his 1929 Nash. James Mitchell is taking the picture of the children. Everyone else in the photograph is unidentified. (Bob Swan.)

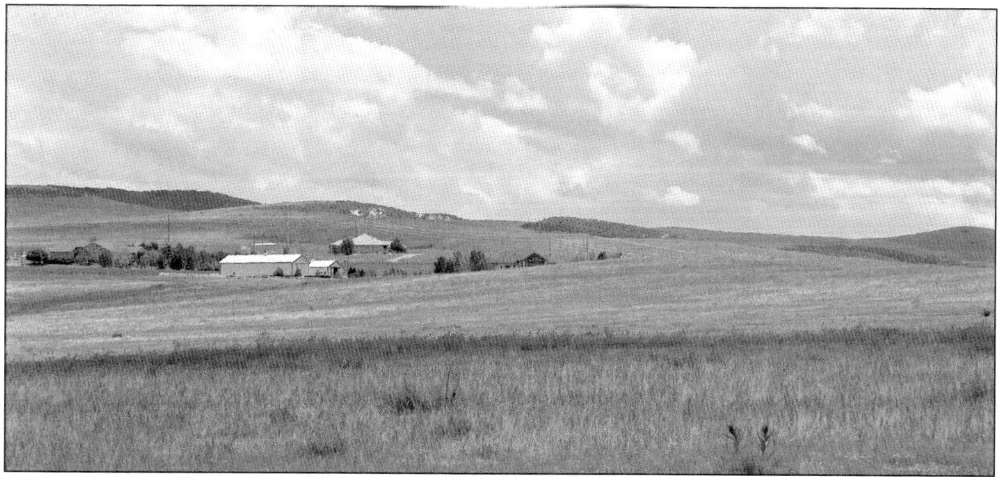

PRAIRIE FARMS AND RANCHLANDS. The vast high prairie grasslands to the north and east of Platte Canyon provided a perfect environment for cattle ranches. Farmers needed access to irrigation, so their homesteads were located closer to the Platte River, High Line Canal, or Plum Creek. Pictured is the ranch house near Platte Canyon Reservoir and Kassler. (Tom Olkowski.)

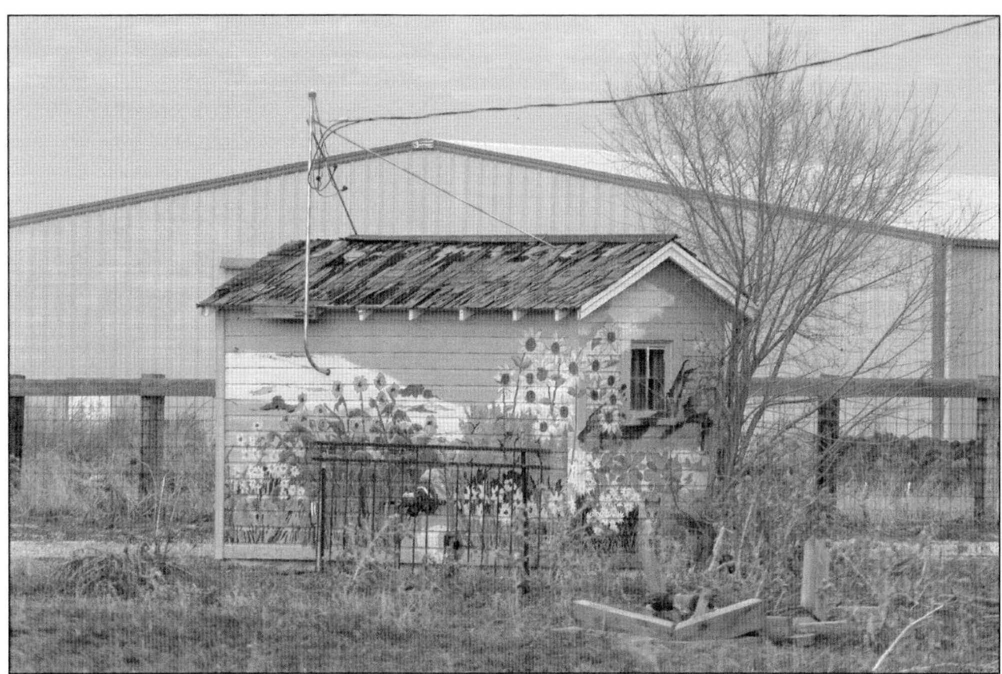

Dairy Farms. In the late 1800s, small creameries developed along the Platte River and Plum Creek valleys. Dairy farmers delivered milk to the nearest creamery, where butter and other dairy products were made and then shipped to Littleton and beyond. This photograph was taken of a small building on what was once the Jones Dairy Farm. Granddaughter Jackie Allis operated it as a small cattle ranch for decades. (Tom Olkowski.)

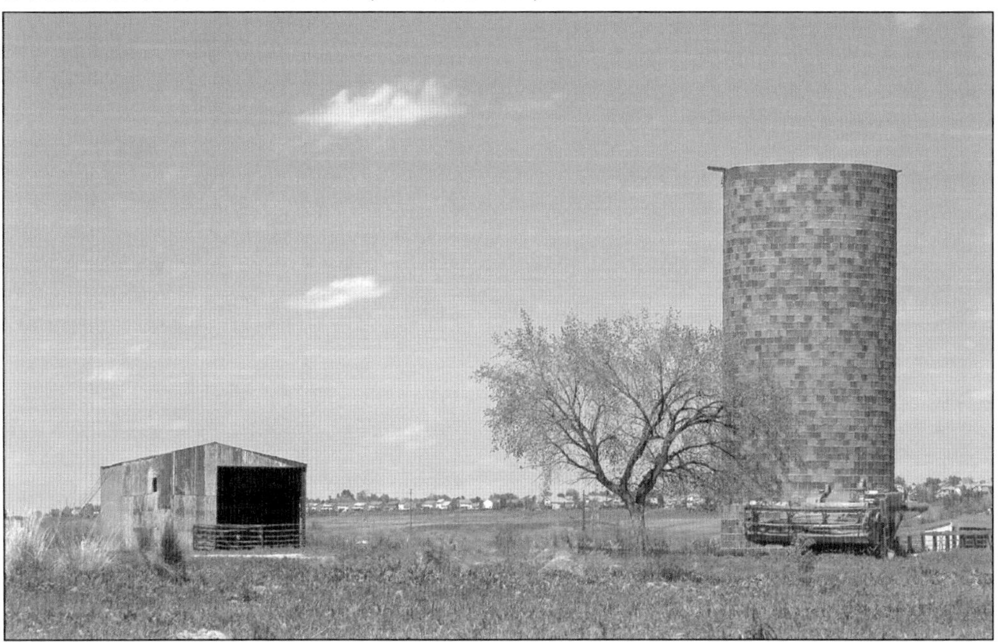

Brick Silo. Pictured is one of the few brick silos left in Roxborough. The silo is currently located on what was once the Allis ranch on Titan Road. The property is now owned by Sterling Ranch Development, which plans to build a roundabout nearby. (Tom Olkowski.)

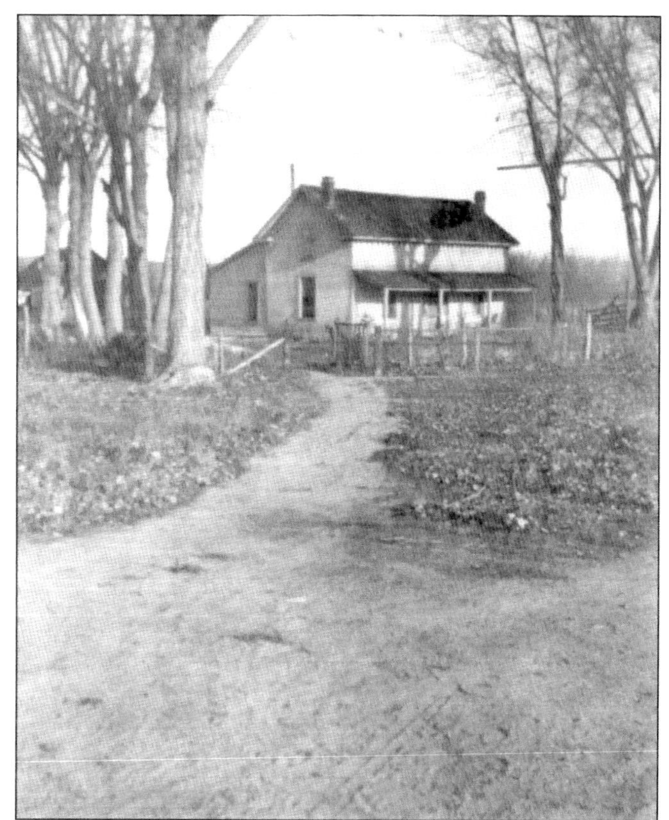

Dr. William Howarth's Farm at Plum Creek. The Howarth farm sat along Plum Creek on what is now the northeastern edge of present-day Roxborough. The bar between the trees at right was used for butchering stock. (Littleton Museum.)

Sterling Ranch. Land was granted to the Sterlings under a Civil War act in the mid-19th century. Their descendants owned the 2,200-acre ranch for a century. In 1970, the family sold the ranch to prominent Denver citizens Franklin and Joy Burns. In 2008, Sterling Ranch LLC principals Harold and Diane Smethills and Jack Hoogland closed on the property and announced plans to build a large residential development. These buildings will most likely be destroyed. (Tom Olkowski.)

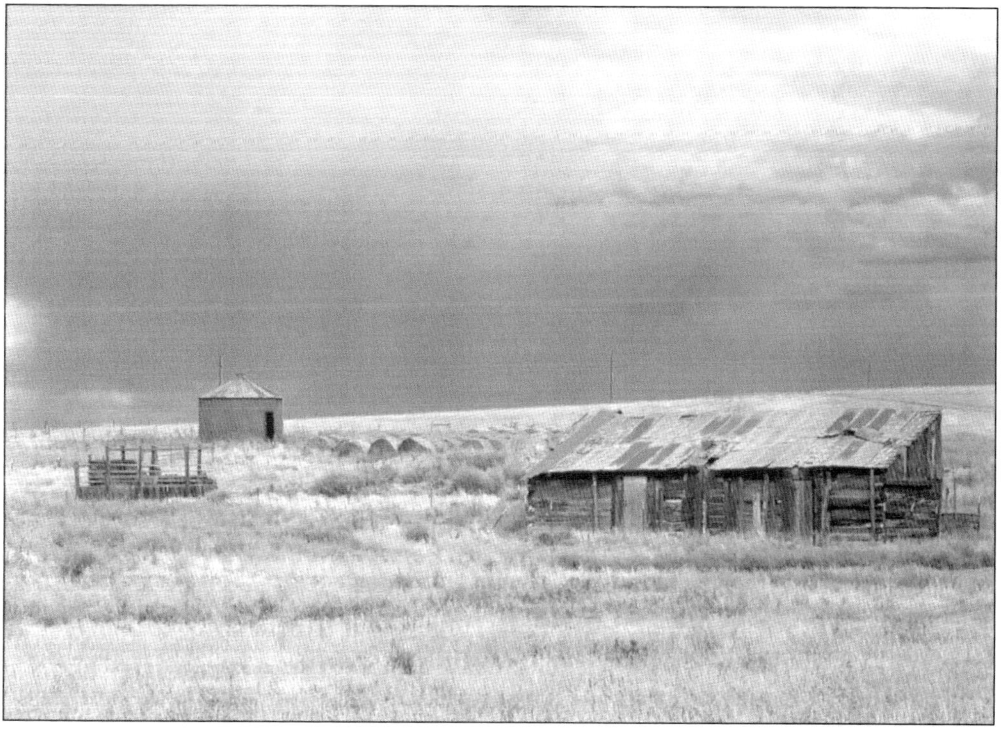

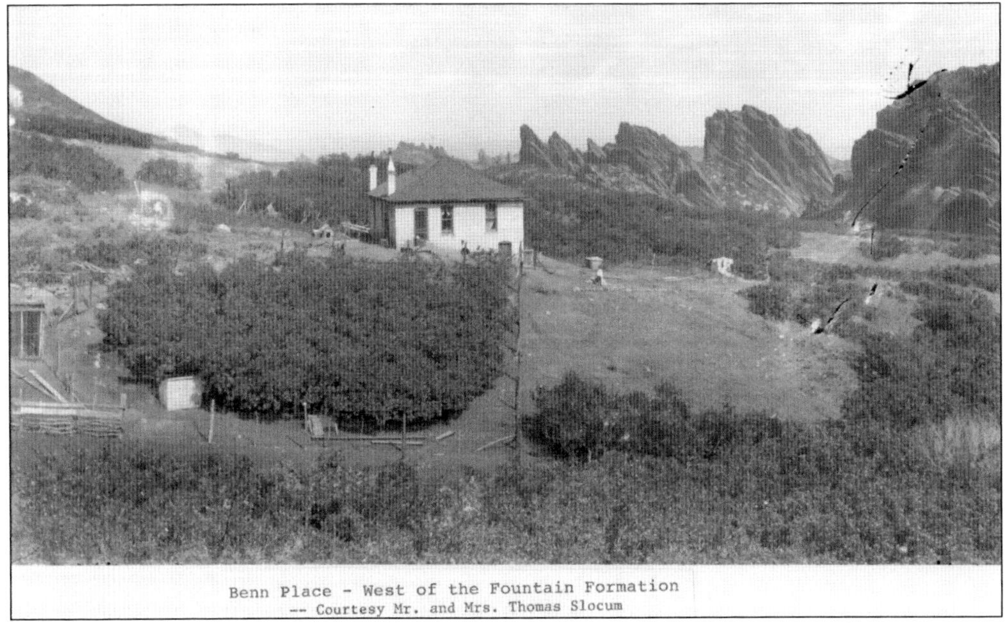

BENN PLACE. Joseph Benn homesteaded his land in the early 20th century. He and his wife, Hattie, purchased adjacent land in 1925 and built a home of silica brick. The 640-acre Benn ranch was located on the trail up the northwestern slope of Carpenter Peak. Some say remnants of Benn's building foundation can be found there. (Roxborough State Park.)

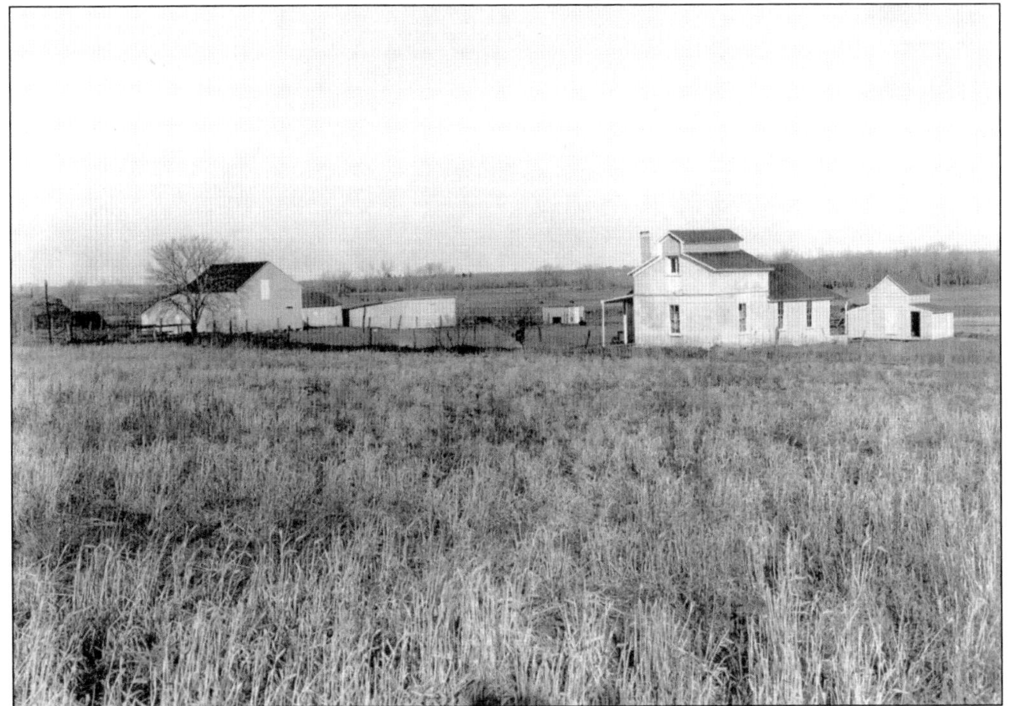

STRONG RANCH. This 1911 photograph shows the Strong ranch on the high plains north of Kassler. The soil did not support large farming operations, but prairie grasses made it an advantageous environment for raising cattle. (Denver Water.)

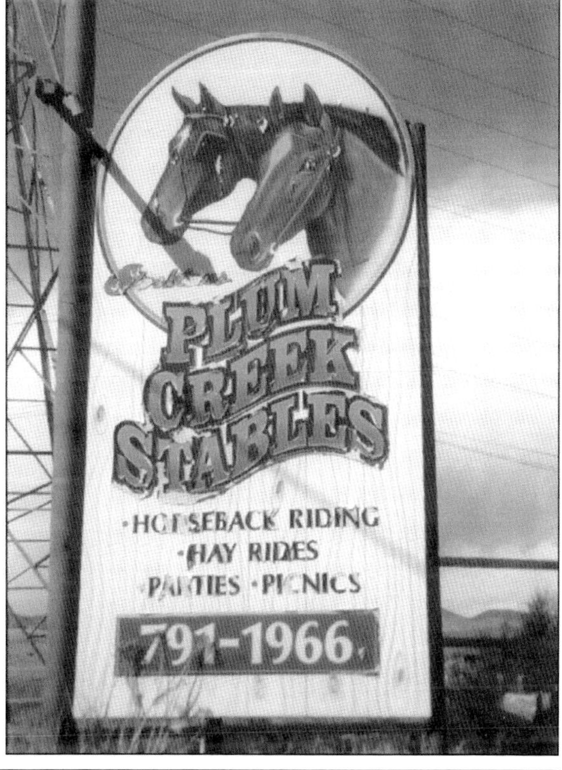

Stockton's Plum Creek Stables. This old homestead and ranch became a horse operation in the late 1950s that was owned by Deryl and Shirley Teel. The Hargrove family purchased it in the 1980s and developed it into what is now known as Stockton's Plum Creek Stables. In 1999, the Witt family purchased the operation and retained the Western environment and traditions. (Stockton's Plum Creek Stables.)

Branding Events. Branding stock has long been an annual event and is still done today. In this 2015 photograph, ranchers brand cattle on present-day Sterling Ranch. Not much has changed. (Tom Olkowski.)

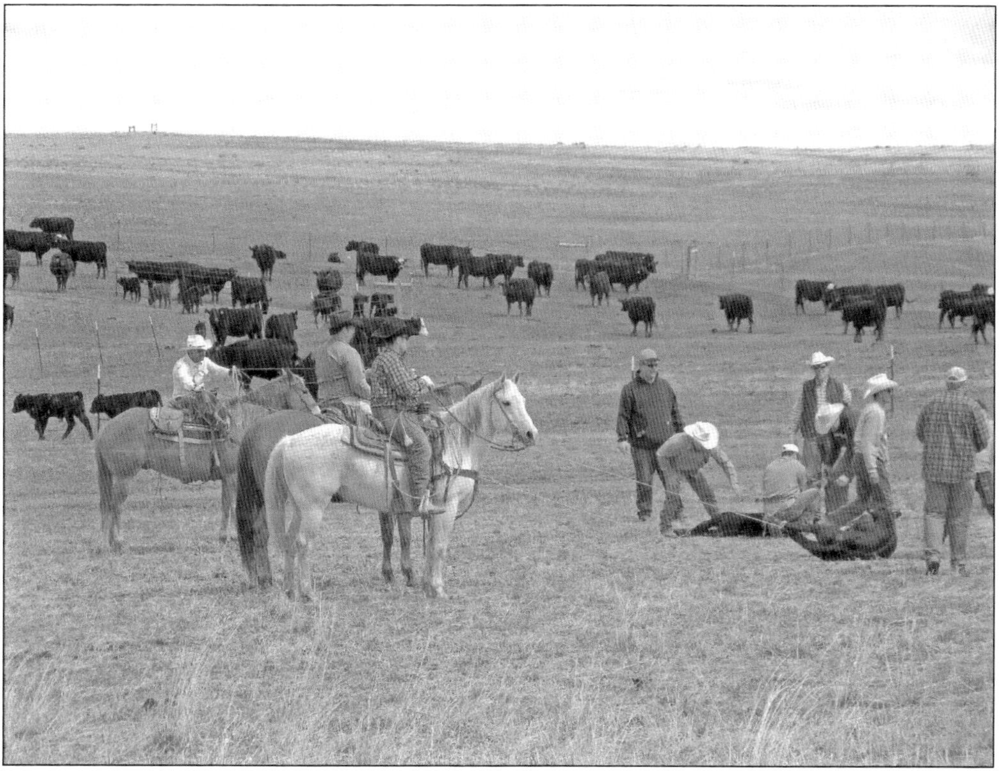

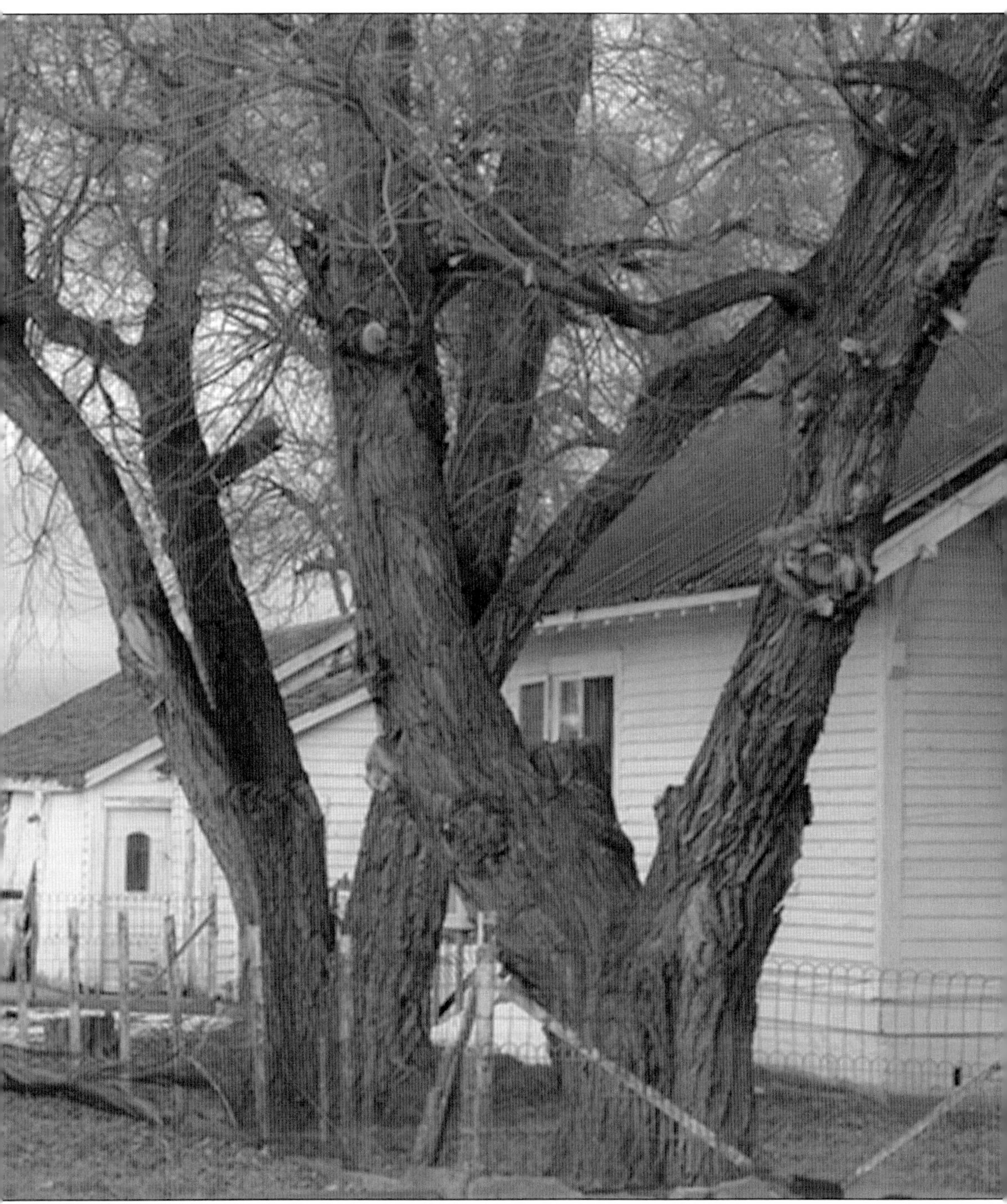

Rosendale Farm. Alice and Monte Rosendale built this farmhouse in 1919. The Rosendales constructed their home on land owned by Monte's father, Cornelius, who emigrated from Holland to start a dairy farm. Ten of Alice and Monte's eleven children were born in the 1,088-square-foot house near the Platte River. The Rosendales grew oats, wheat, corn, and barley, but most of the family's income came from their 45 cows. Ed Rosendale remembers: "There never was money to throw around but there was plenty to eat. We had no chance to fight; they kept us pretty busy."

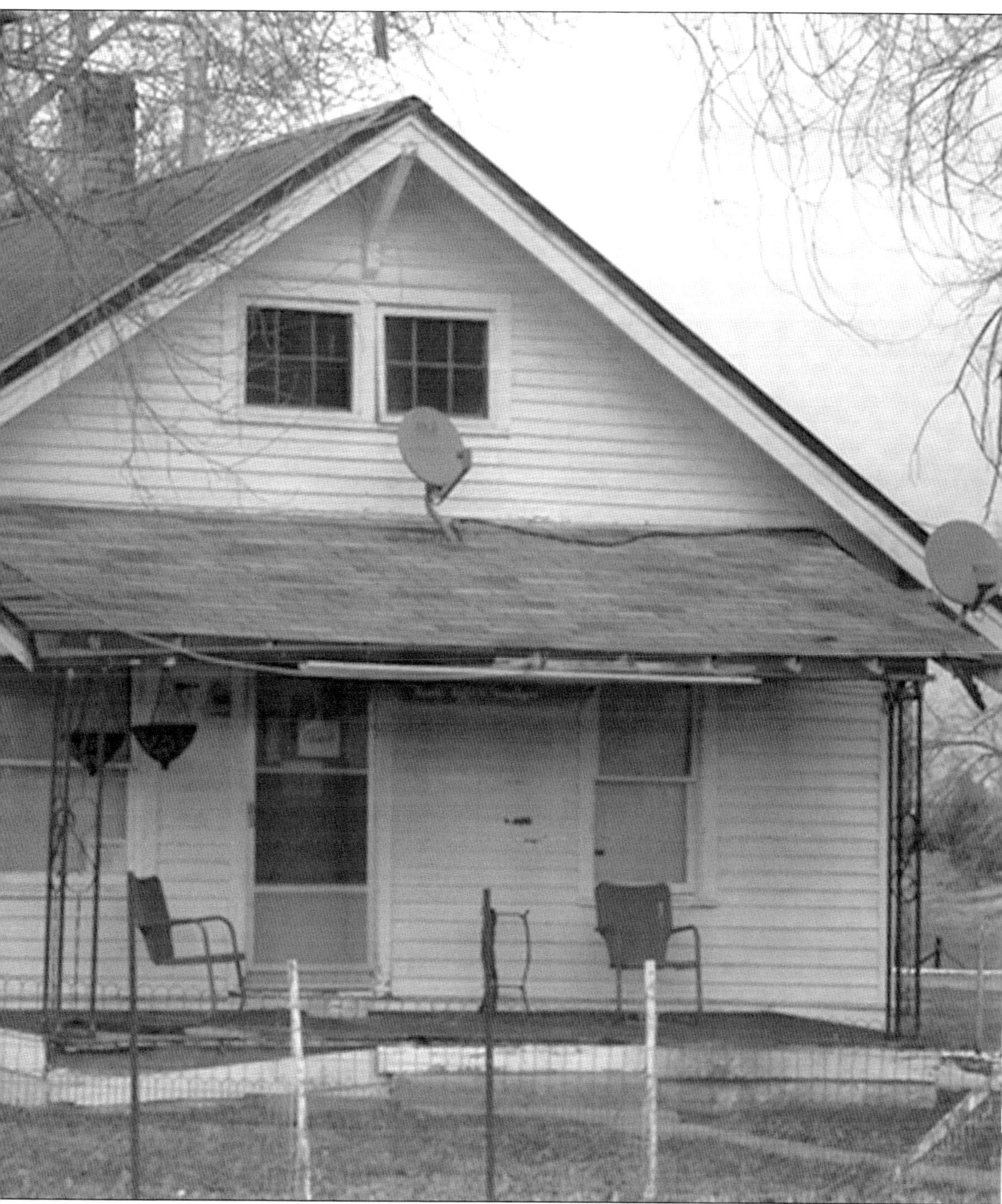

Ed's father's brand—a Lazy R with two quarter-circles—now marks Ed's own livestock. The Army Corps of Engineers purchased hundreds of acres from the Rosendales in the 1960s to build Chatfield Lake. The farm (and its nearly-100-year-old farmhouse) is now owned by Anthony and Brenda Schaefers. Brenda is a descendant of the Woodward and Myrick families; her great-grandparents lived and worked in Silica and Kassler. (Tom Olkowski.)

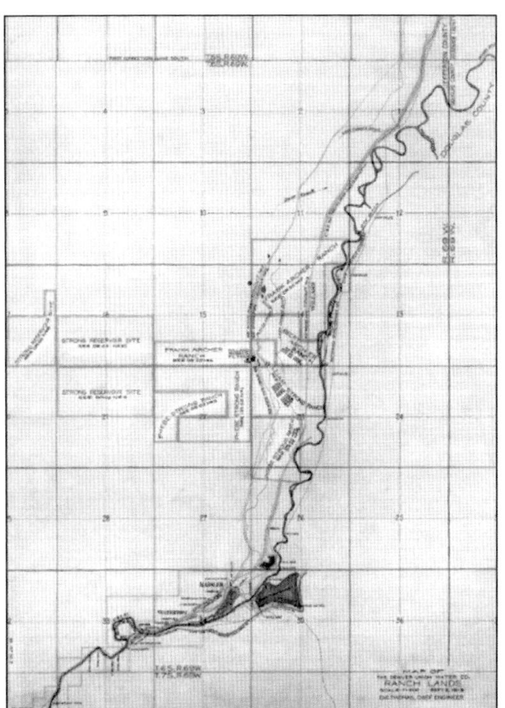

The Great Western Sugar Company. Agriculture was always a major source of income for local growers. North of Kassler, locals grew large fields of beets and sold them to the Great Western Sugar Company, a dominant producer of beet sugar for over 60 years. Beets were harvested, loaded onto trains, and shipped to Denver, where they were processed and made into pure sugar. (Denver Water.)

The Glenn L. Martin Company. This photograph was taken during the first decade of the Martin Company. Constantine Verdos owned 4,500 acres along the Platte River; the Martin Company purchased these plus thousands of additional acres in the mid-1950s for its Titan missile engine plant. Old-timers say that Verdos did not want to sell to a company that made weapons, so he sold it to another party, who then sold it to Glenn Martin. (Littleton Museum.)

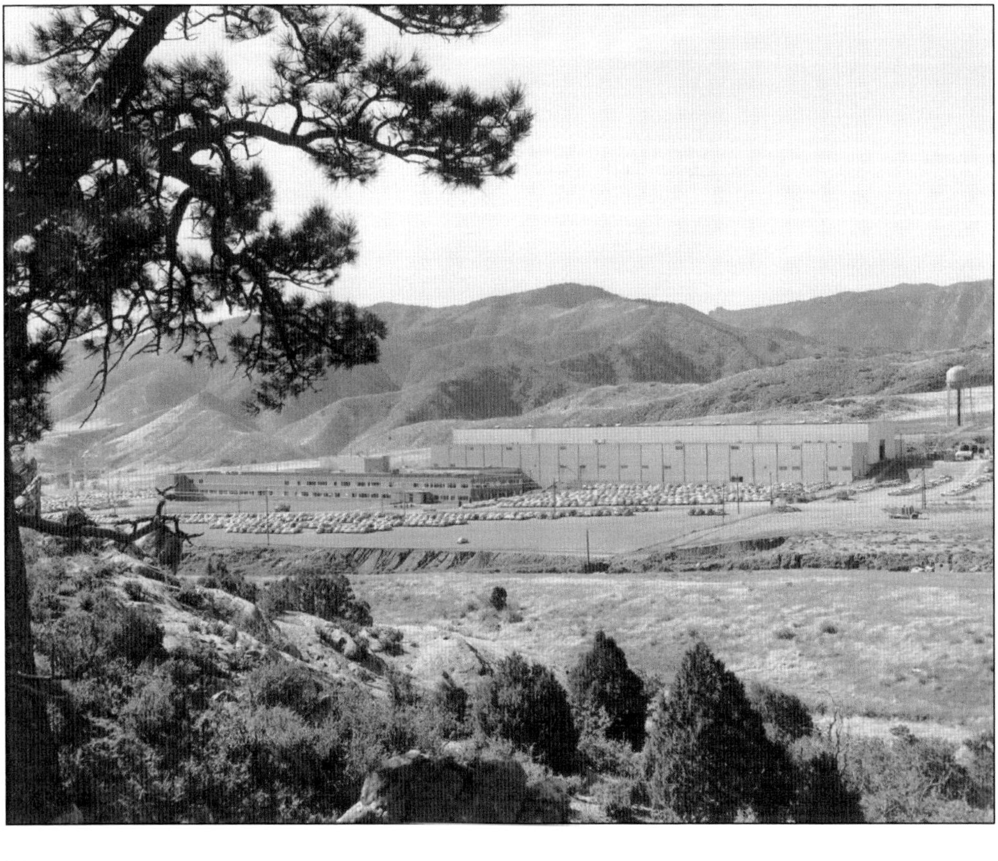

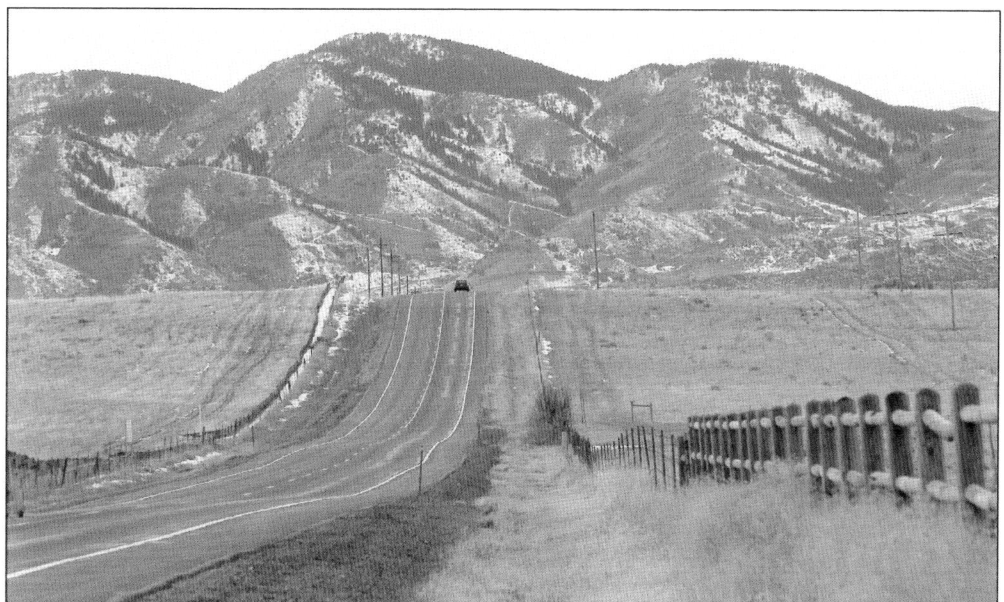

Waterton and Titan Roads. New roads were needed to transport the Martin Company's Titan rocket engines. In Jefferson County, a widened, paved road (now called Waterton Road) ran atop the county's dirt road through the middle of Kassler and across the river into Douglas County. Jones Road, named after a local dairy farmer, was excavated and heavily reinforced to carry heavy engines; its name was changed to Titan Road, shown in this image. (Tom Olkowski.)

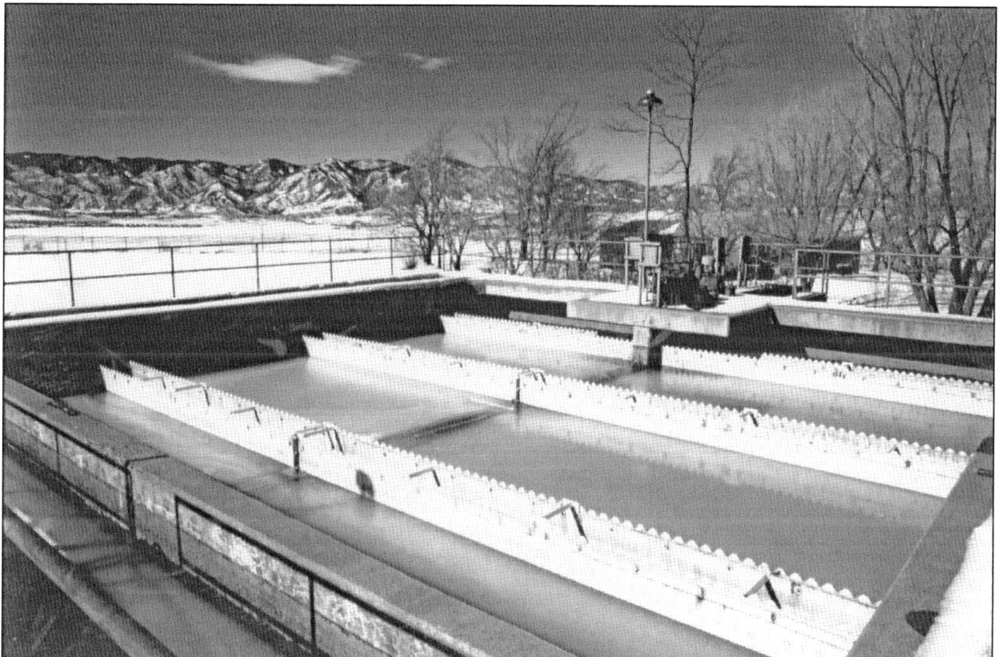

Roxborough's First Water-Treatment Plant. The Martin Company needed water—and lots of it. In 1958, Denver Water constructed the first water-treatment plant in the Roxborough area; it is still in operation. Due to increased residential growth over the last 65 years, construction began on a new water-treatment plant in 2015. (Roxborough Water and Sanitation District.)

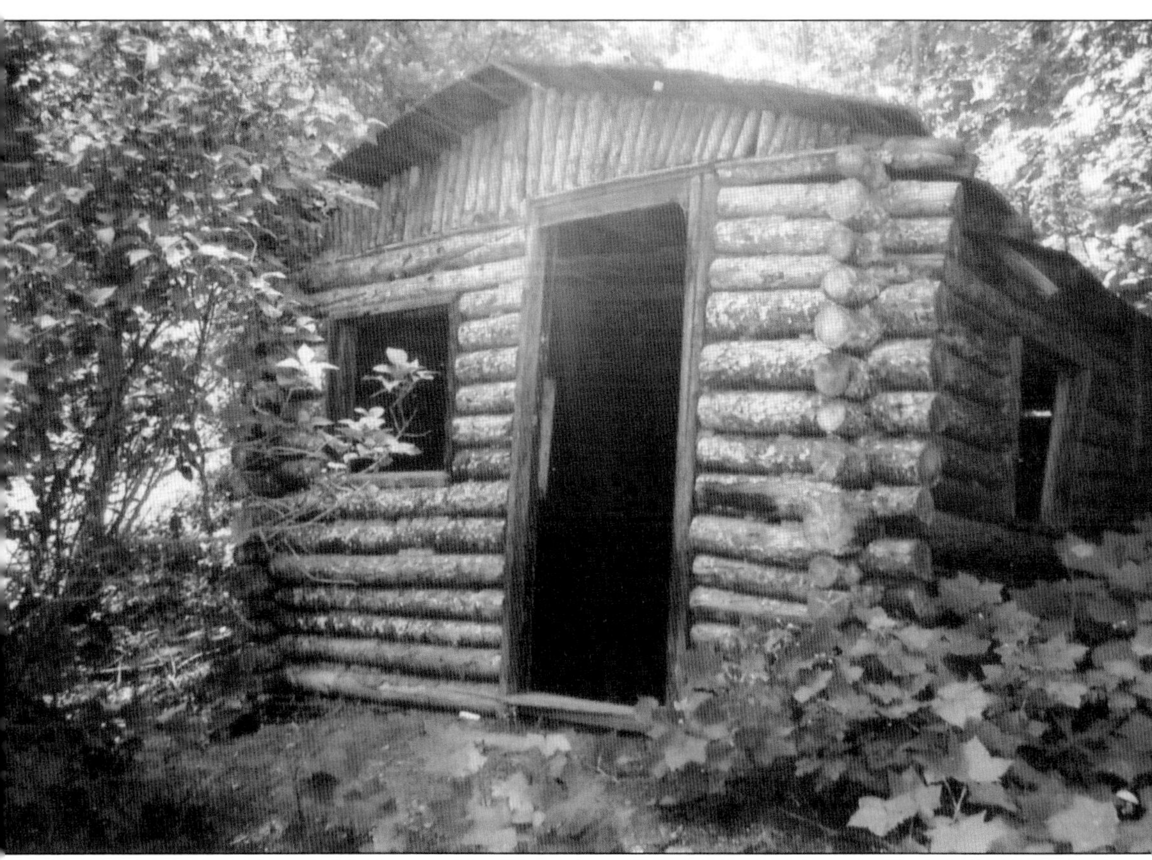

Prohibition Years. The Douglas County History Research Center notes in one of its summaries: "During prohibition, Roxborough's remoteness became a breeding ground for construction and operation of distilleries in and around the area." Old-timers say one such still was operated by Ada Thiele, better known as "Mountain Jeannie." This photograph shows a log cabin on Mountain Jeannie's Trail's End property. (Char Nauman.)

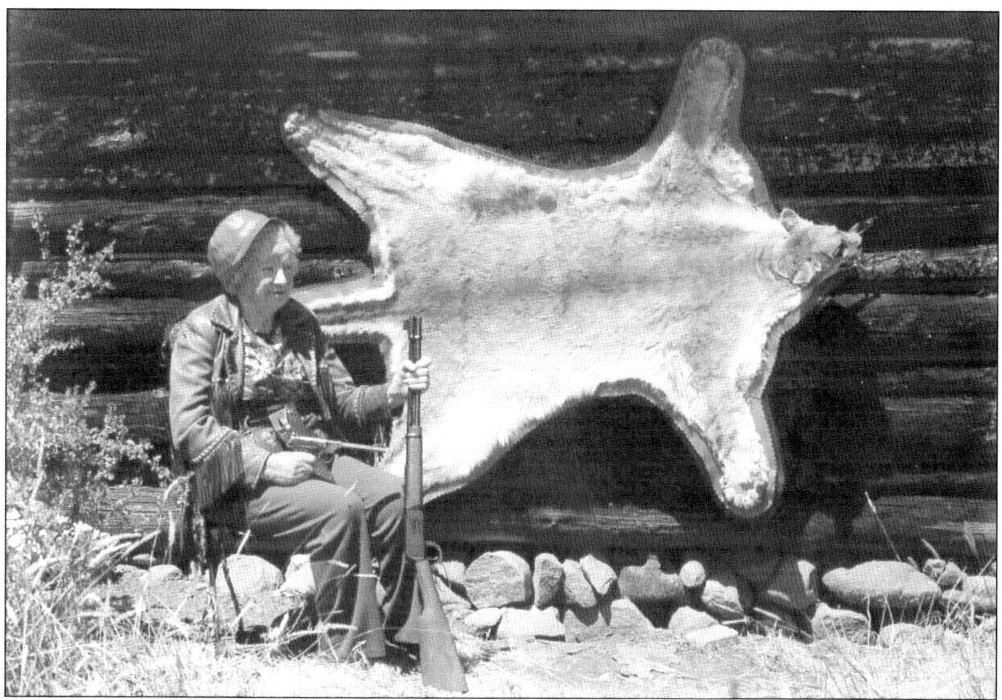

Mountain Jeannie's Trail's End. There were few amenities at Ada Thiele's home, Trail's End, high in the foothills. An underground spring supplied water. Thiele, better known as "Mountain Jeannie," took odd jobs throughout Roxborough and Littleton. When guests were invited to her home, they were expected to help out around the place. No one minded, as she always served up food (like fried rabbit and fresh vegetables from her garden), home-brewed drinks, and entertaining stories. (Melanie Grothe.)

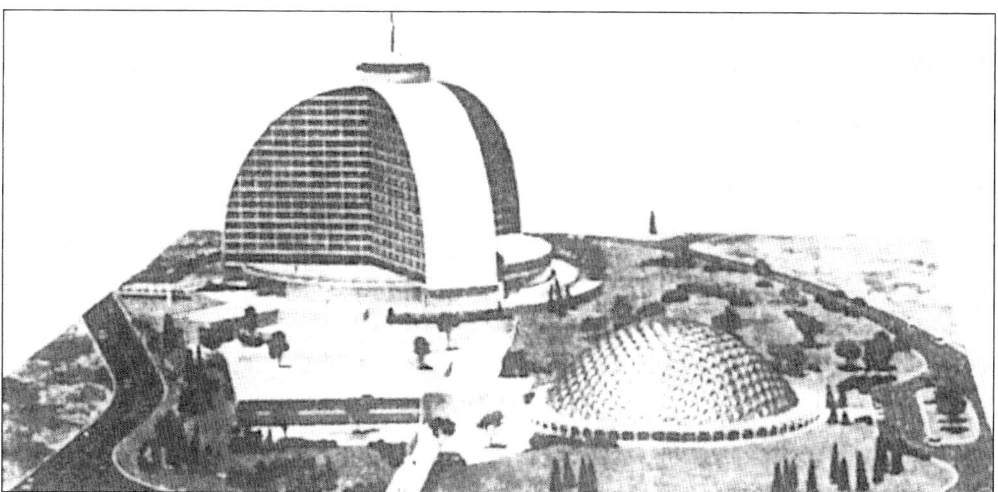

Another Dream. The May 18, 1962, issue of the *Littleton Independent* reports that Paul Rush proposed building a 21-story, 500-room resort hotel and an auditorium that could seat nearly 6,000 people. It would be constructed on the Ringenbergs' old Willow Creek Ranch, located three miles south of the Martin Company plant, and would face northward toward the gigantic red rocks in Roxborough Park. Like many others planned before it, this resort never materialized. (Littleton Museum.)

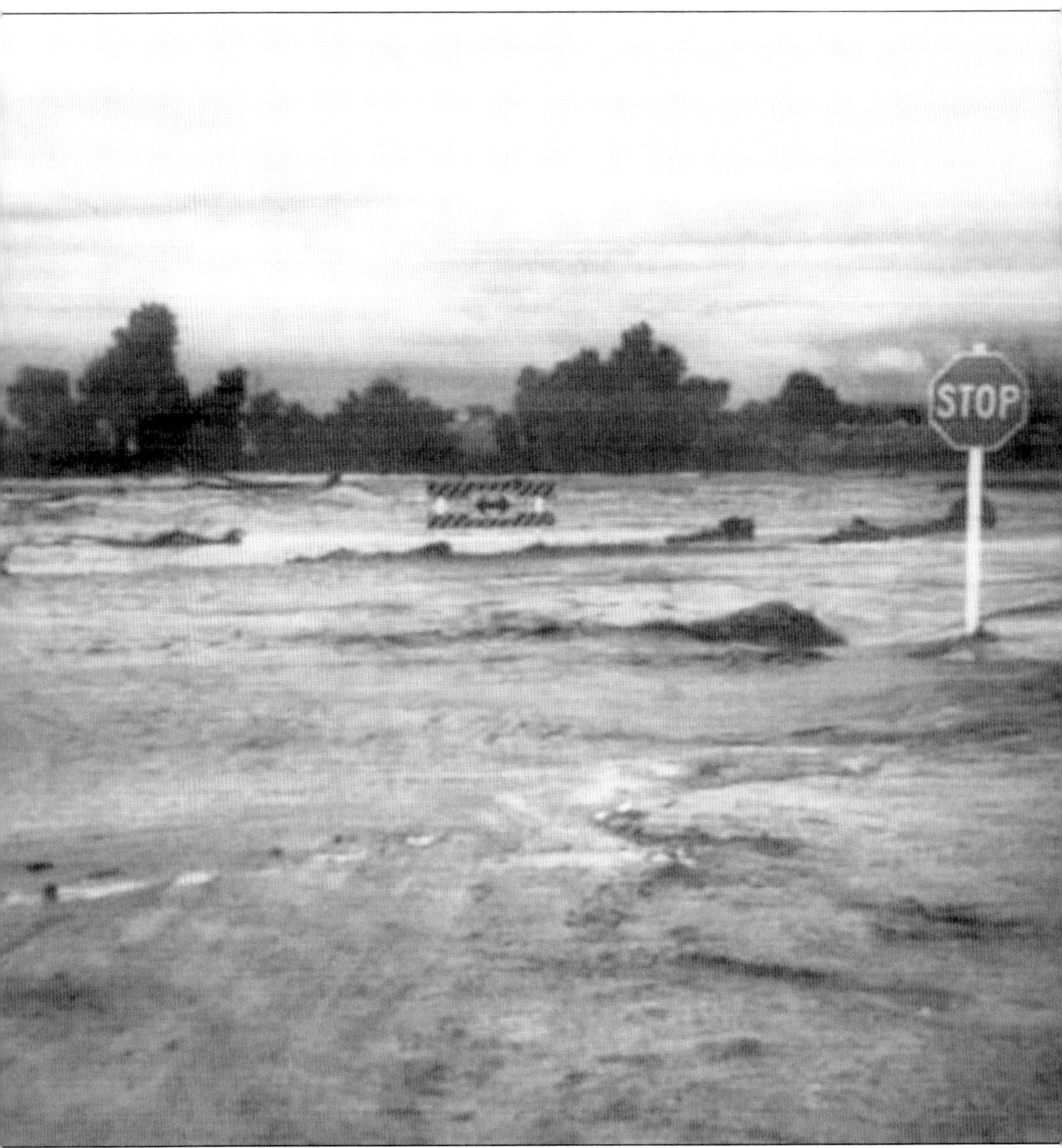

The Flood of June 16, 1965. After rain fell for a week in Douglas County, a slow-moving thunderstorm occurred east and south of Roxborough, flooding Plum Creek. The surging water merged with Cherry Creek and the South Platte River, wreaking havoc on the South Platte valley and creating the worst flood in Denver's history. Plum Creek was impassable for weeks after the storm, which prevented Roxborough residents from traveling east. As a result of the flood, construction on Chatfield Dam began in 1967. It was finished in 1975. (Douglas County History Research Center.)

Seven

Living the Roxborough Dream

For one early homesteader, Roxborough's sandstone monoliths were simply "a pile of rocks." For other pioneers, the region was filled with opportunity. For Henry Persse and other dreamers, Roxborough was paradise—a geographical wonder where they would create spectacular resorts.

An aspiration to build a magnificent resort resurfaced in 1967, when Eagle Development Corporation purchased an option on the Helmers' 3,200-acre ranch. In 1970, the option was picked up by Woodmoor Corporation, which announced plans to build exclusive residential and recreational communities. Hundreds of lots were sold. Buyers built dream houses. Everything came to a halt in 1974, when overextended Woodmoor filed for bankruptcy. Parcels of land were broken off and sold. By 1979, courts cleared legal obstacles, and a group of creditors committed additional funds to complete the infrastructure and repair a golf course overrun with weeds and cattle.

As legal wrangling continued through the 1970s, the State of Colorado dreamed of creating a park that had been visualized decades earlier. In 1975, the state purchased 500 acres. Roxborough State Park consists of close to 4,000 acres today.

After the Woodmoor bankruptcy in 1974, land east of the hogback was sold. Developers planned 2,750 homes in Roxborough Village (to the east of the Roxborough Park residential area) until a collapse in the economy decreased development. Its infrastructure was 65 percent complete and build-out less than 1 percent. In 1975, the water district filed for bankruptcy. When the housing market revived, development resumed until the market collapsed again. The water district filed for bankruptcy, and residents' taxes increased dramatically. Eventually, the water district recovered, residents resolved tax issues, and Roxborough Village became a stable, vibrant community.

At the beginning of the new millennium, developers' dreams sounded oddly familiar. Investors purchased the Slocum Ranch, a pioneer homestead nestled in Roxborough's foothills. Plans included a gated community with a private golf course. Buyers purchased lots, and owners began building homes. By 2008, a depressed economy collapsed the housing market. As with Roxborough Park and Roxborough Village decades before, investors defaulted on loans. Today, legal, financial, and water issues are being resolved and new homes are being built.

In 2015, Roxborough retains a small-town ambiance, with Roxborough Elementary School and Roxborough Marketplace serving as cornerstones for its 10,000 residents. Two housing developments are on course to build 14,000 homes within the area's 80125 zip code, quadrupling Roxborough's population. Roxborough's ageless, stunning geology will not change, but the visions of these new dreamers will alter the landscape forever.

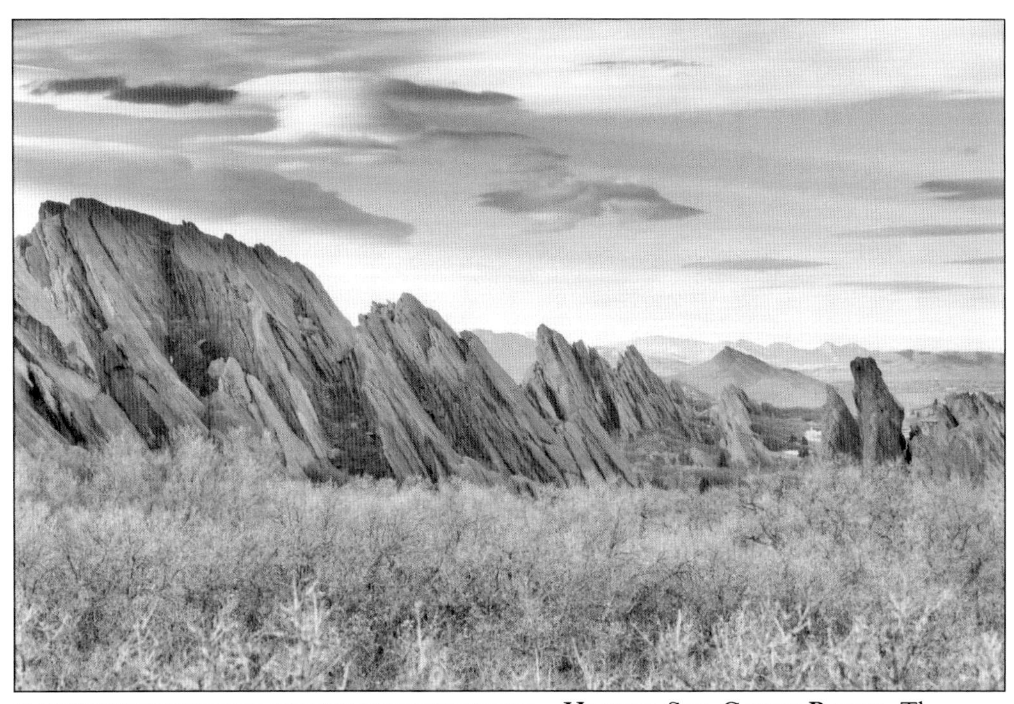

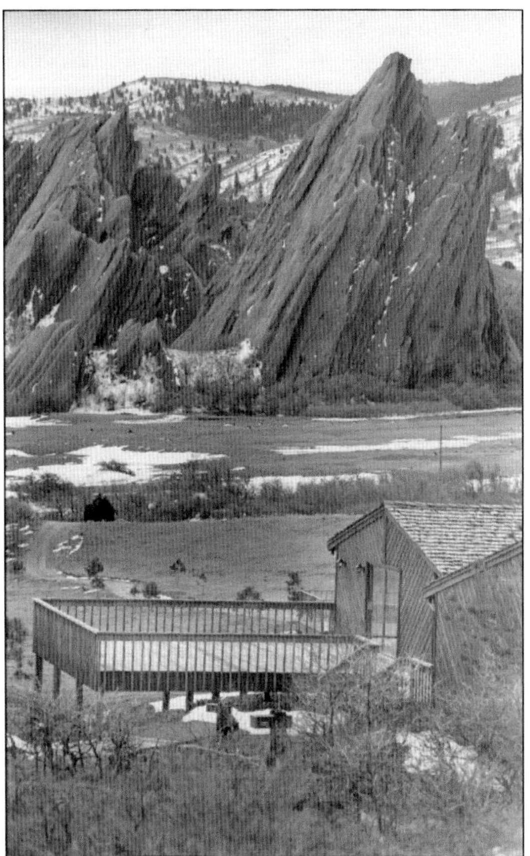

Helmers Sell Cattle Ranch. The Helmer brothers Toney and George, along with sister Cecelia "Cel," first sold an option to the Eagle County Development Corporation in 1967. By 1970, it was the Woodmoor Corporation that purchased the land. The *Denver Post* reported in September 1970 that Woodmoor placed an option on thousands of acres, some of which included Roxborough Park's spectacular red rock formations for which Roxborough was so well known. The purchase price was reported to be $4.1 million. (Lance W. Moreland.)

Woodmoor Advertises Roxborough as a "Peaceful Co-existence between Man and Nature." For more than a century, entrepreneurs dreamed of creating an outstanding resort in Roxborough. Woodmoor Corporation envisioned a community with 6,400 houses, a 70-acre lake, a golf course, and an equestrian center. A program was created to sell lots in a similar way to lots sold in Florida. Lots were advertised as having electricity and underground water and sewer. Pictured is Woodmoor's sales office. (Ed and Nancy Bathke Collection.)

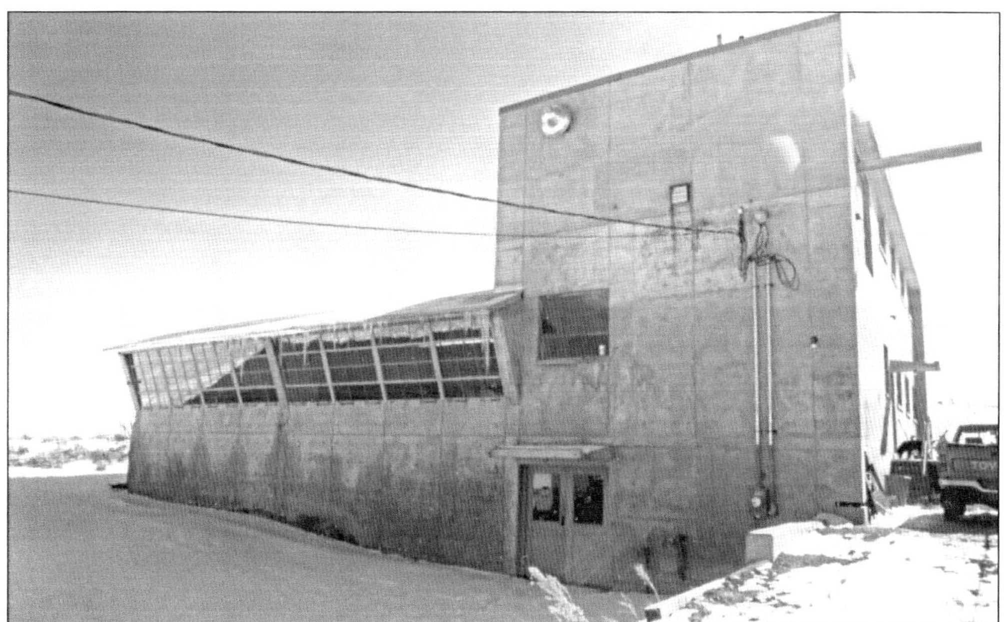

Water! Roxborough Park Metropolitan District Formed. Woodmoor began building the community's infrastructure, and in January 1972, eleven electors formed the Roxborough Park Metropolitan District to furnish water, sewer, and fire protection to the 3,200 acres of the former Helmer Ranch. In February 1972, the district contracted with Aurora for 3,100 feet of water and the purchase of a water-treatment plant. Pictured is the 1950s water-treatment plant. (Roxborough Water and Sanitation District.)

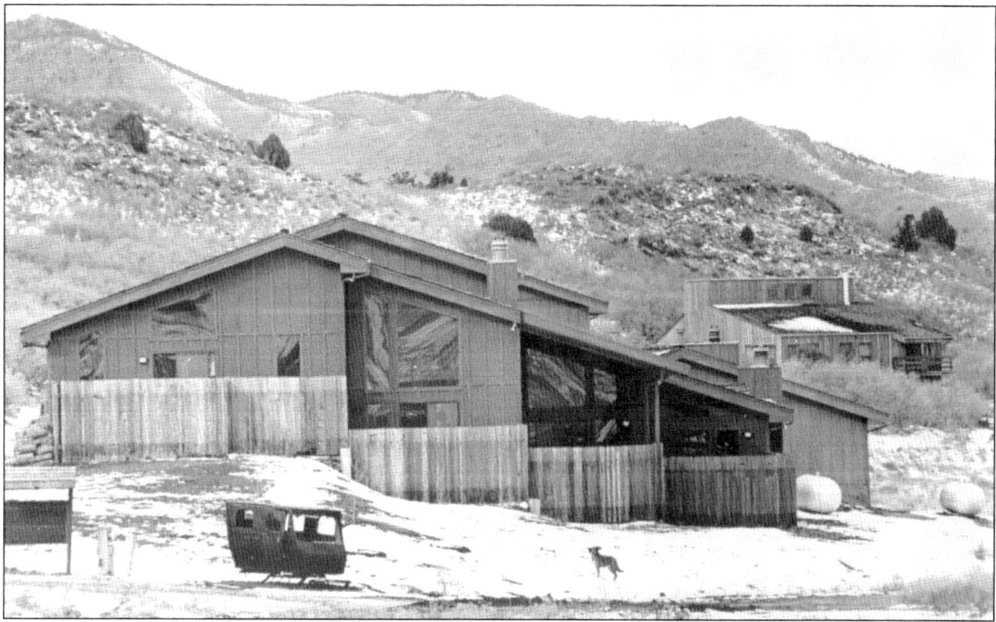

Roxborough Park Residential Community's First Residents. The cluster homes shown in this photograph were built in 1973. Jeanne and Dick Lamar purchased the first home and lived there until their custom home could be built in a not-yet-developed area. Rampart Range Road, which led into the development, was unpaved. (Ed and Nancy Bathke Collection.)

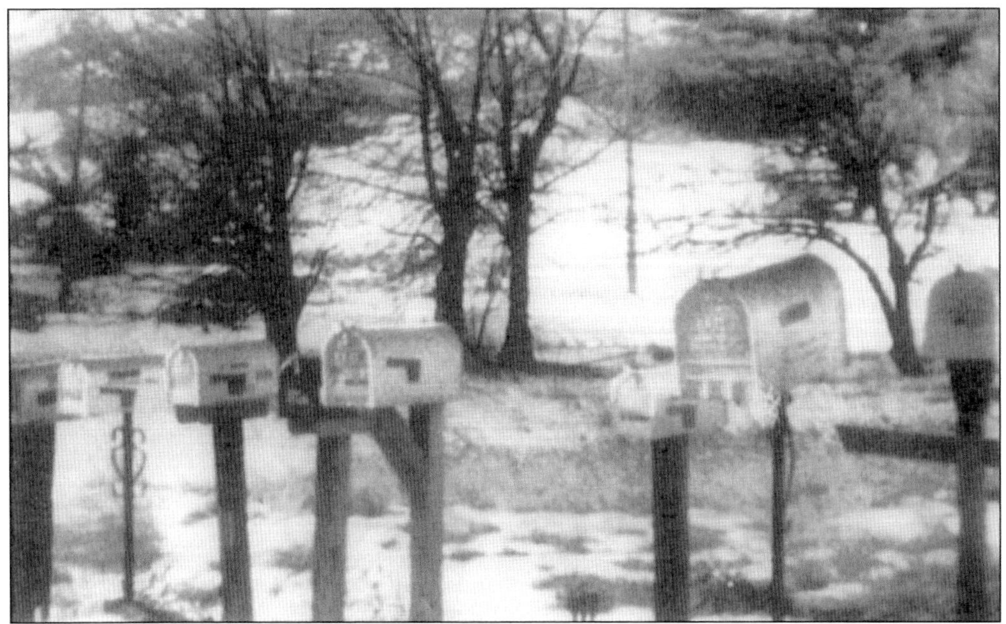

ROXBOROUGH PARK'S FIRST MAILBOXES. These mailboxes belonged to Roxborough Park's first residents: Dick and Jeanne Lamar, John and Bonnie Hartman (and their son, Jason), Butch and Jean Thomas, Don and Joyce Selbie, Tom Hobbs, and Merle and Char Nauman (and their daughters, Cathy and Cindy). Because of Roxborough Park's remote location, the few residents depended upon each other for basic needs. (George and Marilyn Bostwick.)

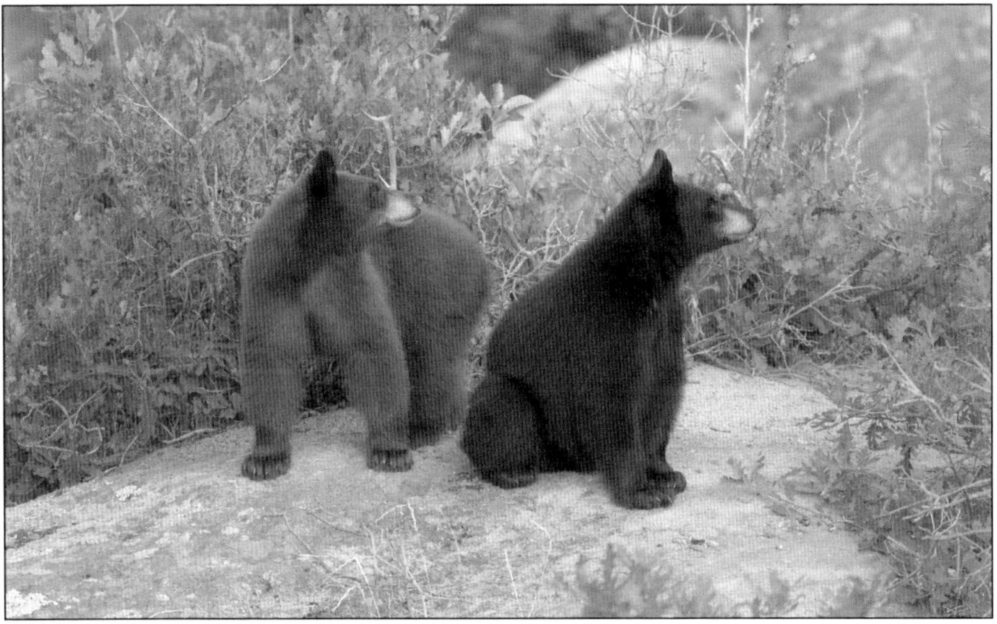

WILDLIFE. Despite Roxborough's remoteness, people chose to live there because of the area's natural beauty. Its proximity to Pike National Forest allowed residents to watch wildlife in its native habitat. Roxborough Park (not to be confused with Roxborough State Park or Roxborough Village) streets were given names like Twin Cubs, Puma Trail, Elk Rest, and Fox Paw Trail. (Lance W. Moreland.)

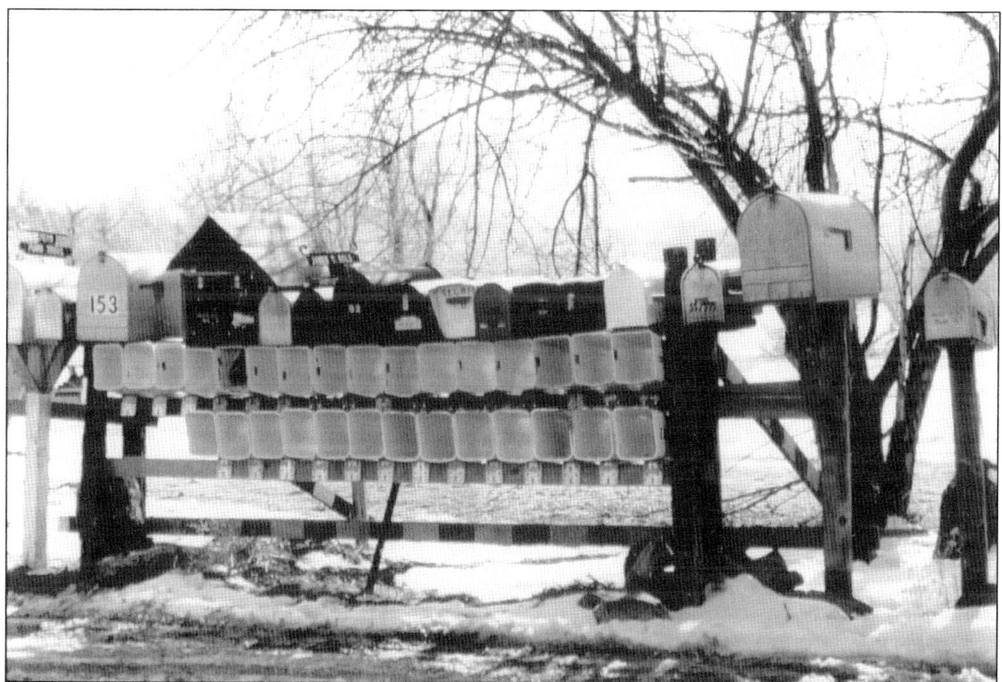

MORE RESIDENTS MOVE IN, 1973. The first mailboxes were built under the Helmer family's apple tree. The two bottom rows were slots for newspapers. Growth continued until Woodmoor Corporation began experiencing financial difficulties. (Ed and Nancy Bathke Collection.)

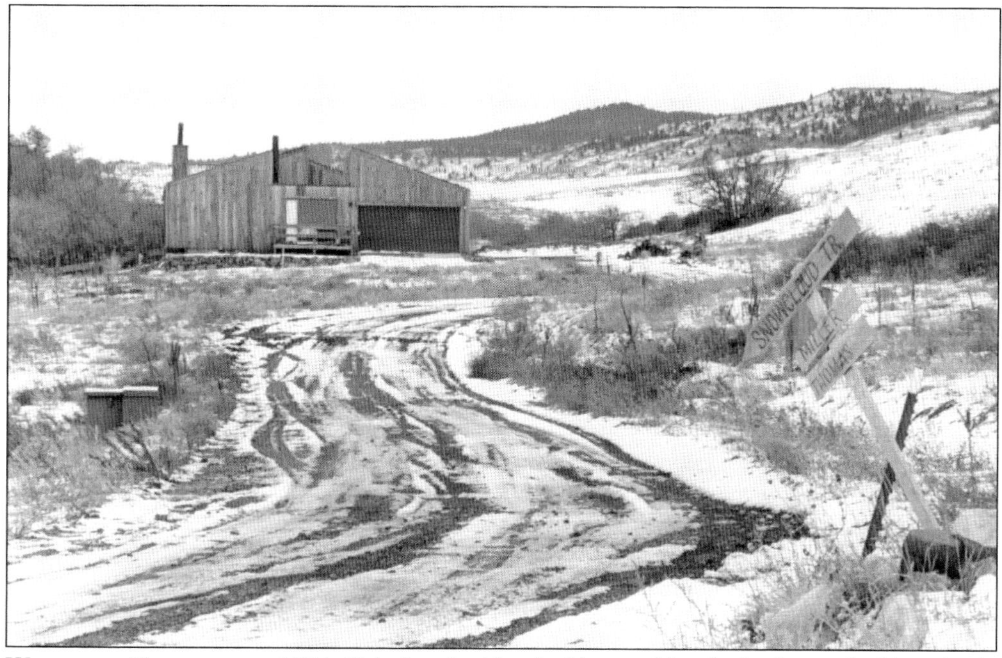

WOODMOOR BANKRUPTCY, 1974. Eight hundred lots had been sold and a few homes had been built. Soon, another Roxborough resort dream evaporated when the Woodmoor Corporation declared bankruptcy in January. Eventually, only 800 acres remained, and they were all west of the hogback. The remaining 2,400 acres were sold off in pieces. (Ed and Nancy Bathke Collection.)

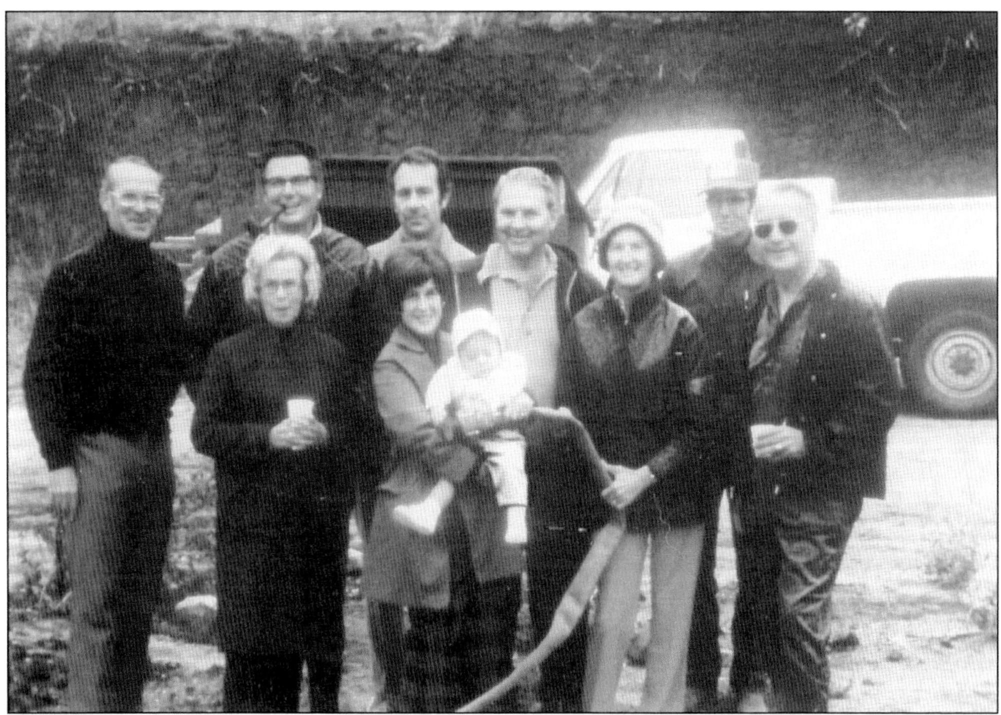

Roxborough Park's Volunteer Fire Department. In 1974, Roxborough Park volunteers formed the Roxborough Fire Department and conducted their first fire drill later in the year. Pictured are, from left to right, (first row) Joyce Selbie, Bonnie Hartman (holding her son Jason), and Jeanne Lamar; (second row) Tom Hobbs, Don Selbie, Jon Hartman, Butch Thomas, Otto Haney, and Elmo Duvall. (West Metro Fire and Rescue Department.)

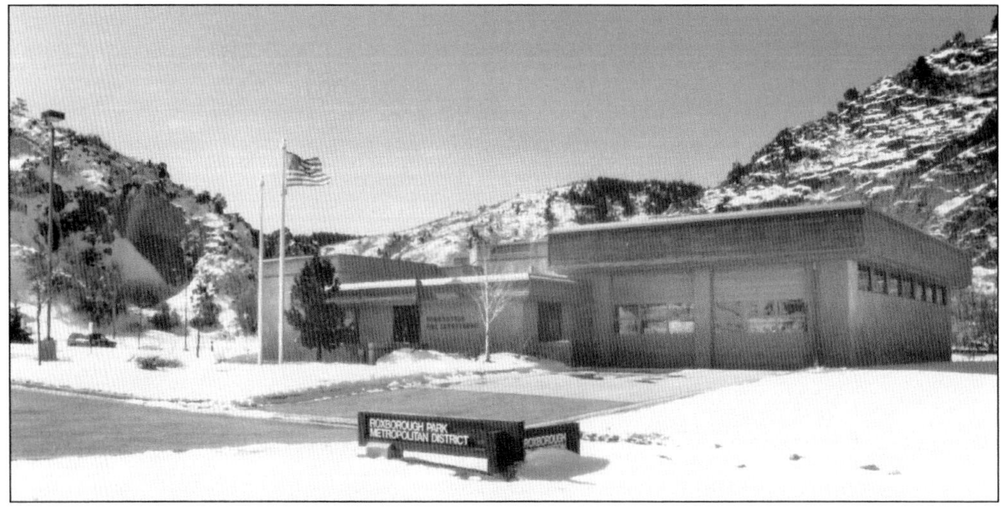

Saving the Dream. The Roxborough Park Property Owners Association was formed to insure the interests of residents and property owners during the bankruptcy proceedings. Otto Haney, Bill Leipold, Paul Willoughby, Dick Thomas, and Butch Thomas were leaders in this effort. The association went to court to acquire additional loans to continue development and improvements. Years later, the structure in this photograph was built for the Roxborough Park homeowners' association and fire station. (West Metro Fire and Rescue Department.)

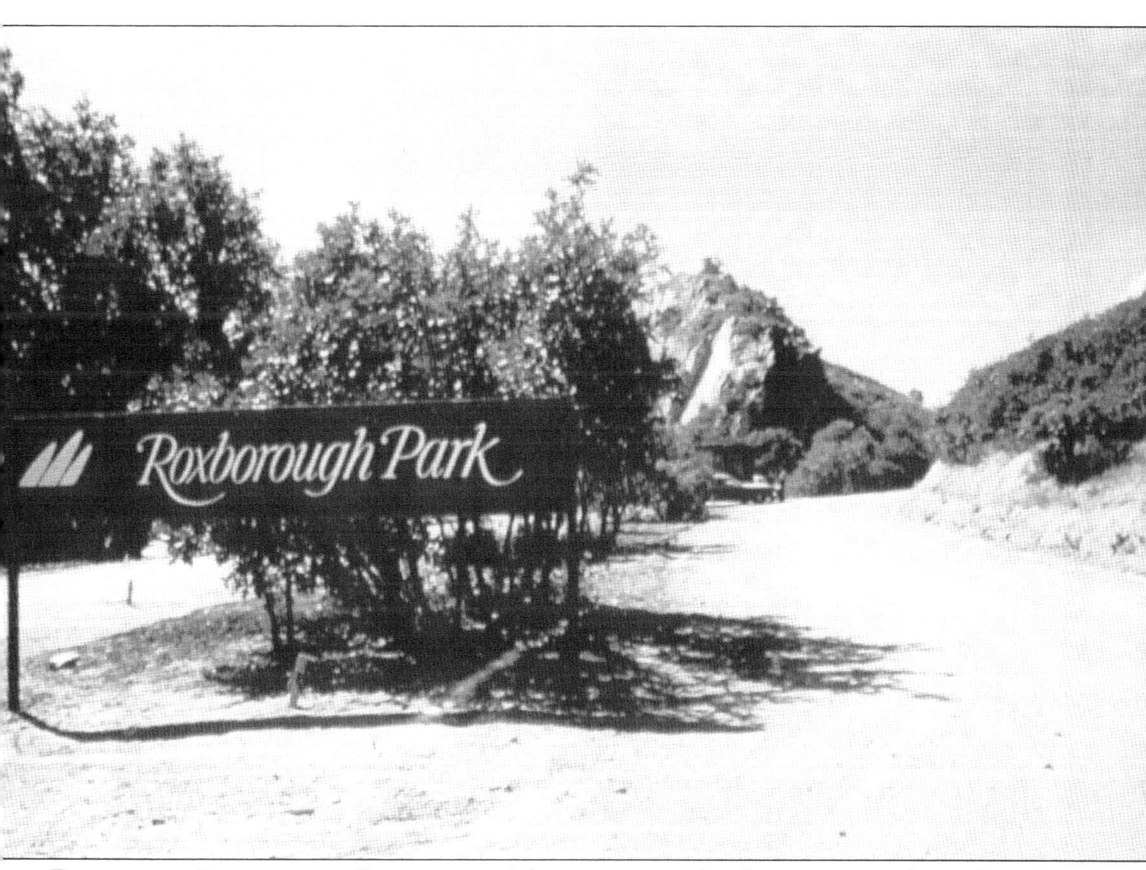

Roxborough Development Corporation. This sign appeared at the entrance to the residential community Roxborough Park. The road cut through what had been the tow n of Silica and the Helmer Ranch. Roxborough Park's founders struggled in trying to save Roxborough Park. It was only after district court judge Richard Matsch pressured Woodmoor Corporation's major creditors that Brad Wolff, a consultant to Princeville (one of Woodmoor's creditors), convinced the largest creditors to loan an additional $2.5 million to the newly formed Roxborough Development Corporation. That action saved the community from bankruptcy. In 1979, construction began again in Roxborough Park. (Ed and Nancy Bathke Collection.)

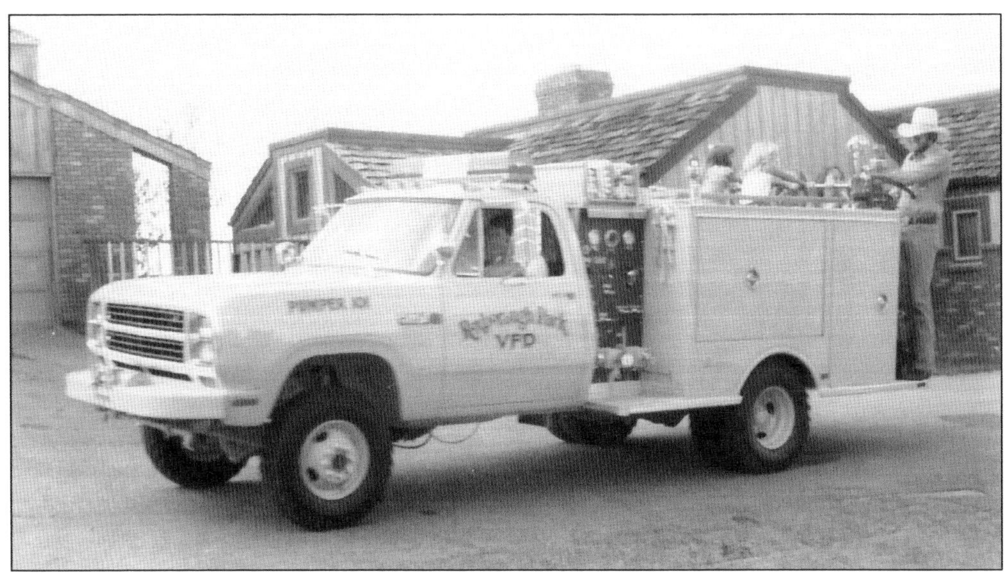

Roxborough Park's First Fire Truck. In 1980, Roxborough residents were able to purchase a 250-gallon pumper truck, hire a consultant, and train their all-volunteer "department." In this photograph, fire chief Gene Abair is in the driver's seat. The others are unidentified. Roxborough's first fire commissioner was Bill Leipold. The first fire chiefs were Abair, Dick Wehrman, Tadd Spicer, Bob Rinne, and Pat Plampin. (West Metro Fire and Rescue Department.)

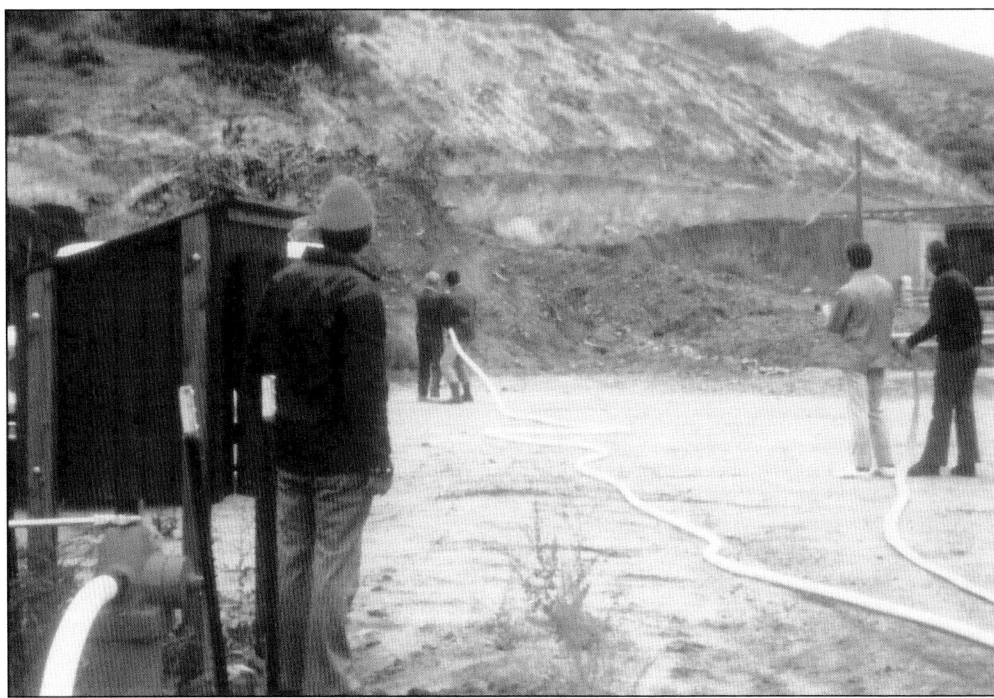

Wooden Boxes. Wooden boxes, built to house 750 feet of new fire hose, were located close to fire hydrants near occupied homes. This photograph shows two unidentified women doubling up to control the hose in case the water was turned on. The others in the picture are also unidentified. (West Metro Fire and Rescue Department.)

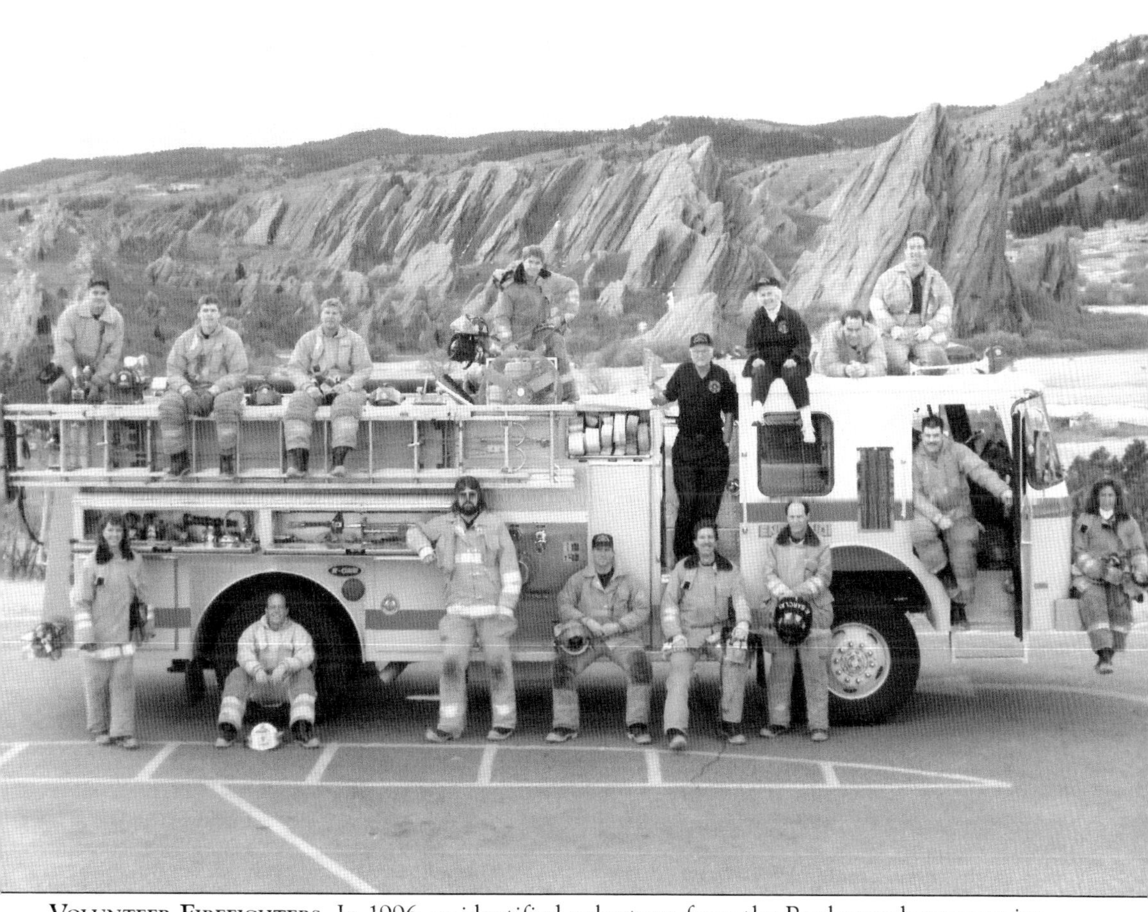

Volunteer Firefighters. In 1996, unidentified volunteers from the Roxborough community met in the parking lot overlooking Arrowhead Golf Club. Professionals from the West Metro Fire and Rescue Department took over from the volunteers in 2000, almost three decades after volunteers answered their first call. (West Metro Fire and Rescue Department.)

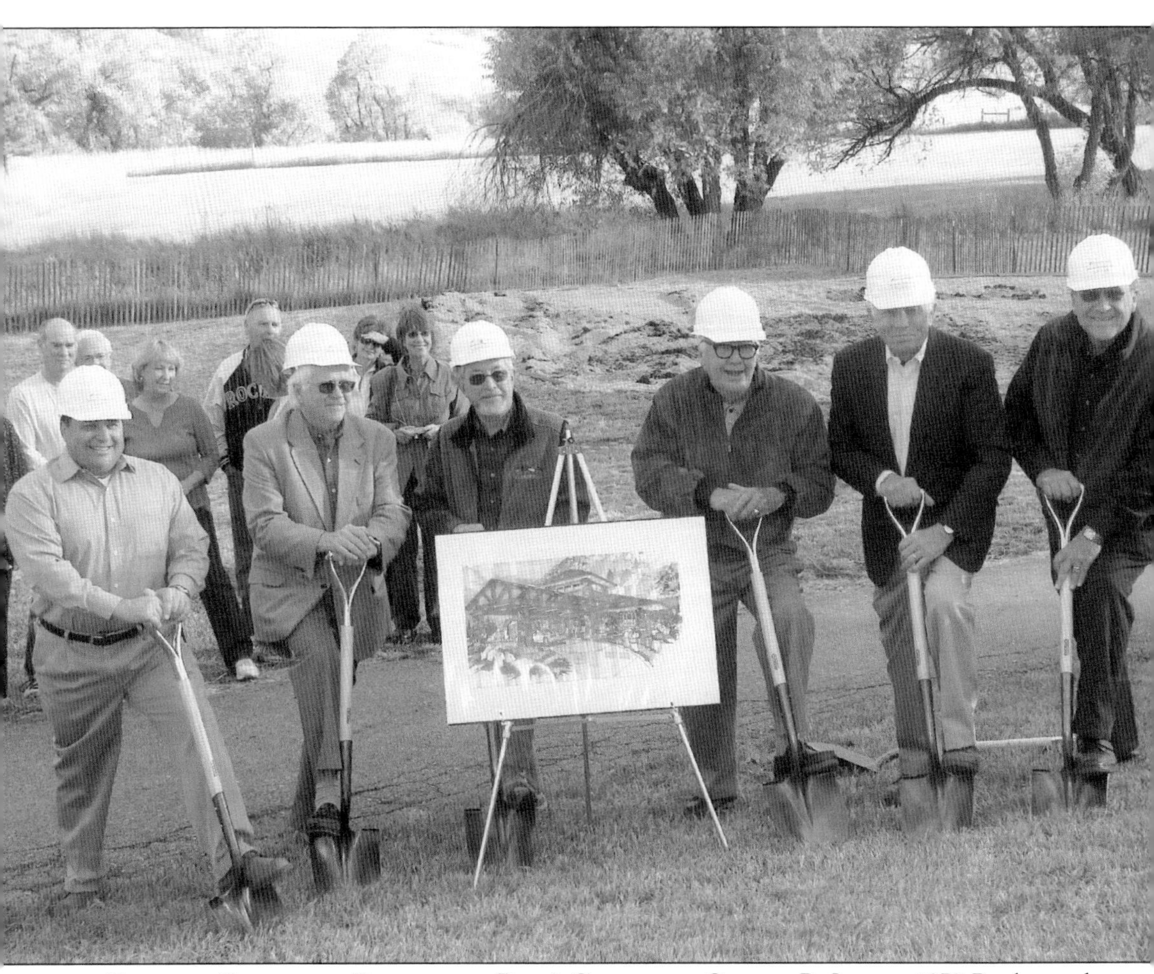

Breaking Ground for Roxborough Park's Community Center. By January 1979, Roxborough Park's legal and financial problems were largely resolved, and construction once again began—the first since the bankruptcy five years earlier. Almost 20 years later, on October 15, 2007, Roxborough Park Foundation board members broke ground for Roxborough Park's Community Center. Pictured in the foreground are, from left to right, unidentified, Lloyd Whittall, Herb Livingston, Otto Haney, Neil Schilmoeller, and Greg Liptak. Those in the background are unidentified. (Greg Liptak Collection.)

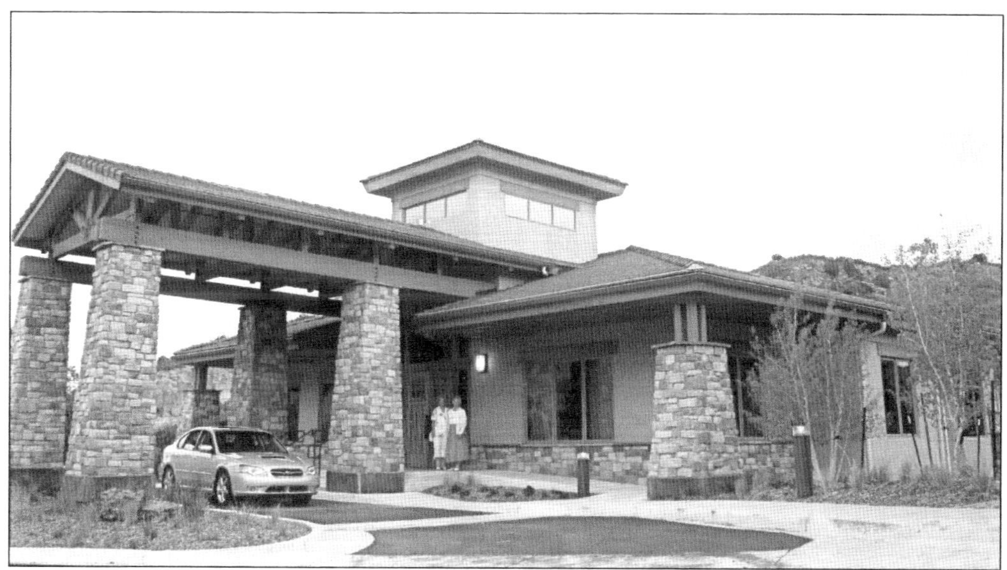

Finished Community Center. In 1979, Brad Wolff was quoted in the *Douglas County Town and Country Squire:* "We honestly think Roxborough Park will be the most beautiful spot in the world when we are finished [with all the legal problems.]" Within 30 years, the community grew from 6 homeowners to 970. Currently, 2,200 residents call Roxborough Park home. In this image, two unidentified people stand in the portal of the new Roxborough Park Community Center validating Wolff's claim. (David and Pam Irwin.)

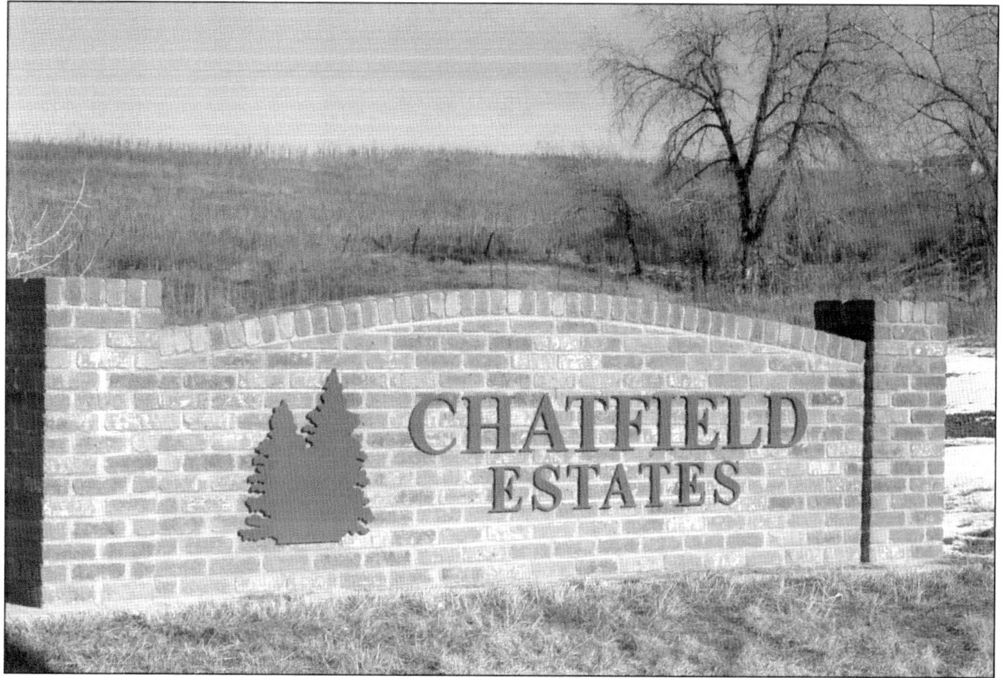

Chatfield Estates. Chatfield Acres Estates and Chatfield Estates East were built in the early 1970s on Roxborough's eastern border. Approximately 80 homes, each on a few acres and using wells for water, were built on a high ridge overlooking Platte Valley, Chatfield State Park, and the Rocky Mountains to the west. (Tom Olkowski.)

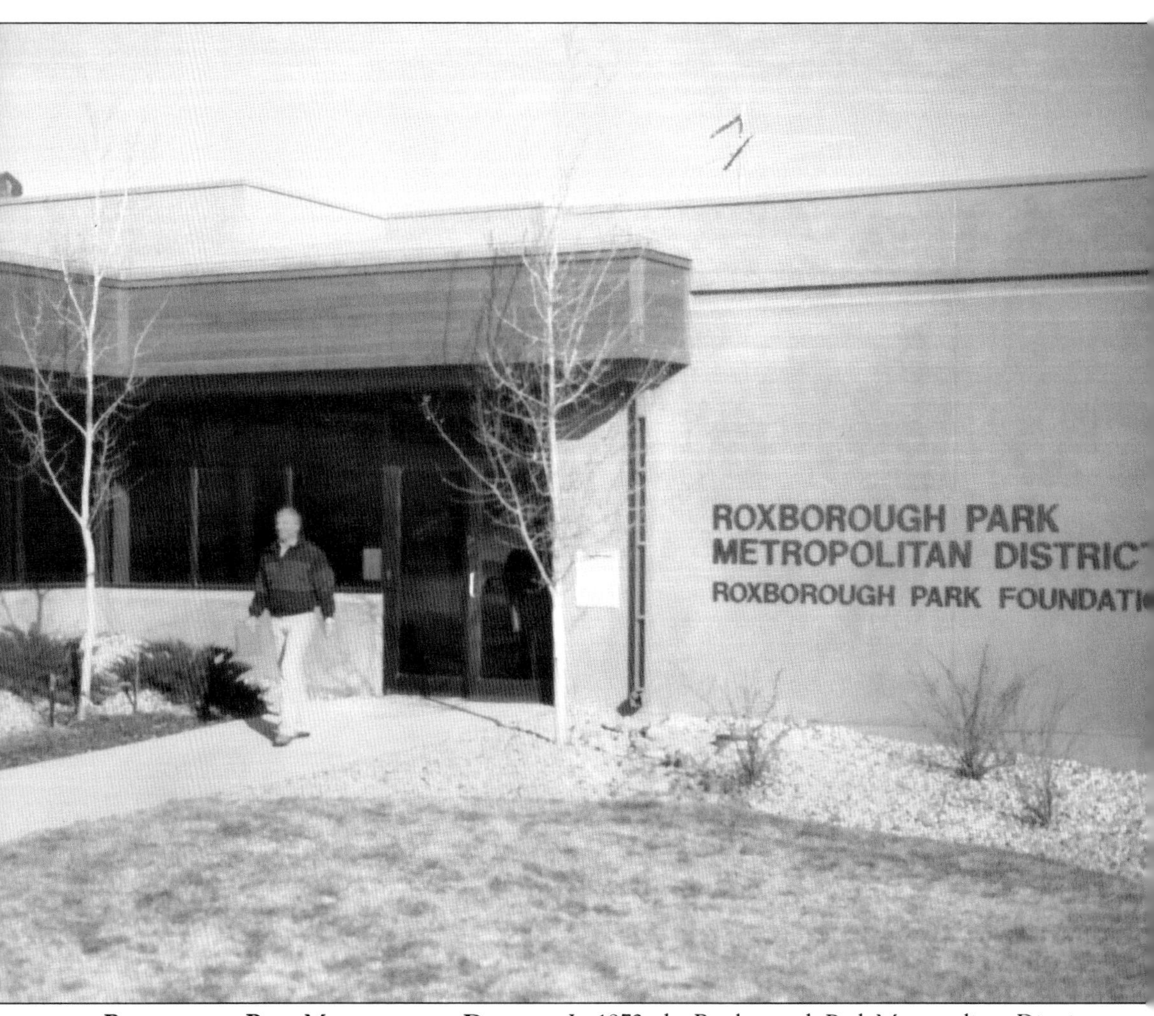

ROXBOROUGH PARK METROPOLITAN DISTRICT. In 1972, the Roxborough Park Metropolitan District was formed to provide community water, sewer, and fire protection services to Roxborough Village homes. The district planned for groundwater wells, but test wells could not provide an adequate water supply, so the district entered into a 25-year water lease contract with the City of Aurora. In this photograph, district director Larry Moore is in front of the building. (West Metro Fire and Rescue Department.)

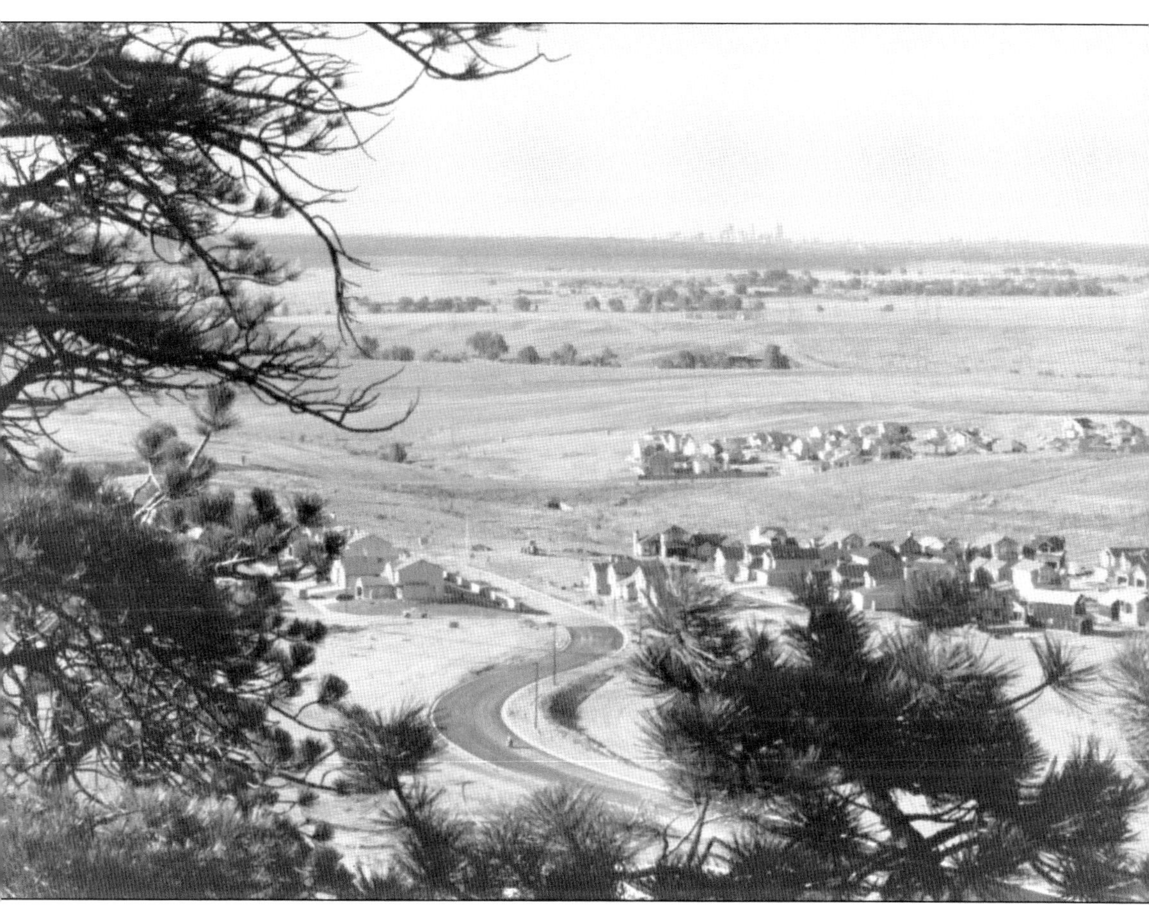

ROXBOROUGH VILLAGE CONSTRUCTION. This photograph was taken in 1987 from high on the Dakota Hogback looking north over Roxborough Village West. The city of Denver's skyline about 25 miles to the north is visible in the background. The winding road is Village Circle West. (Prysby family.)

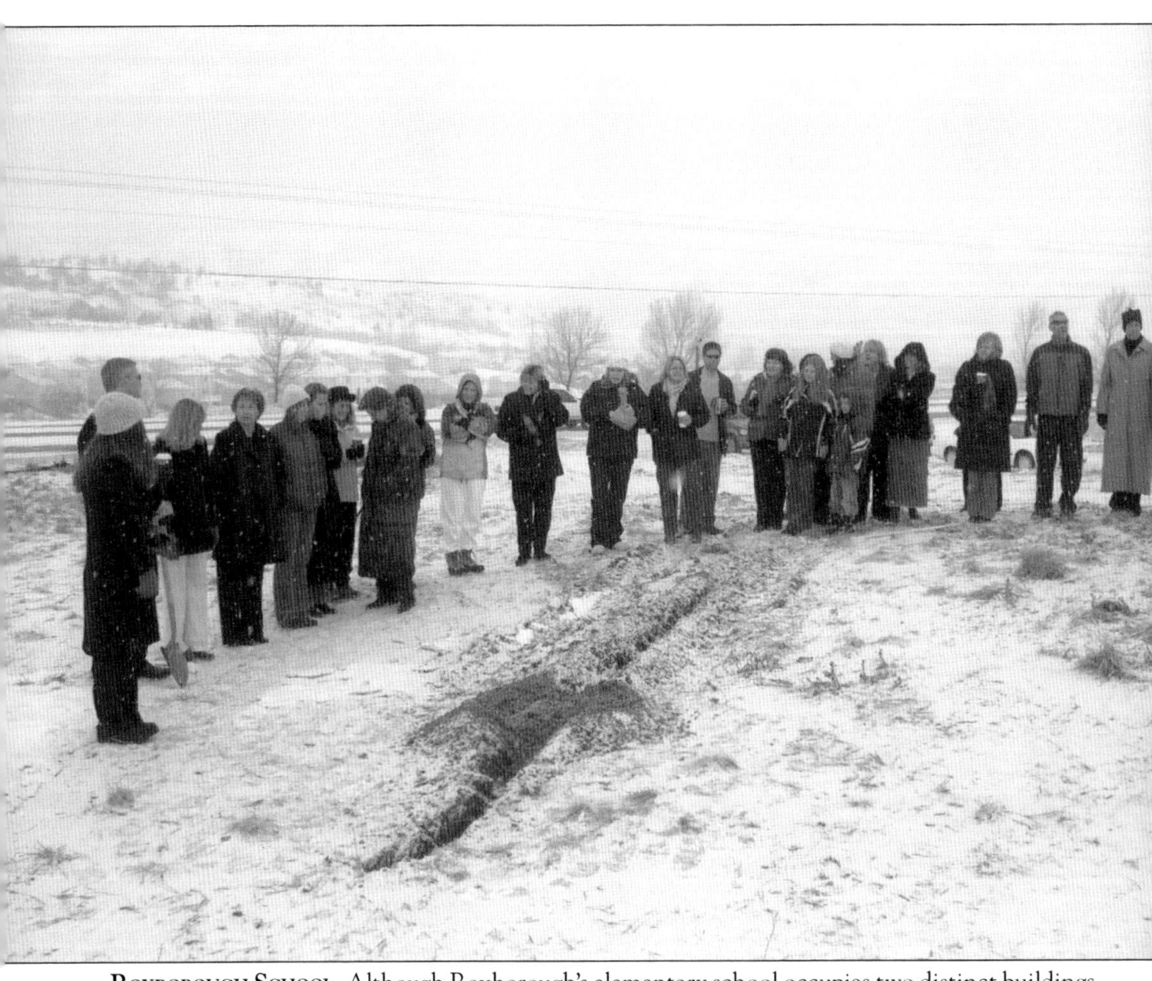

Roxborough School. Although Roxborough's elementary school occupies two distinct buildings, called Roxborough Primary and Roxborough Intermediate, the community considers them as one elementary school. Both are located in Roxborough Village. Roxborough Elementary, located in Village West, was built first and included grades one through six. As the community grew, another school was needed. This photograph shows unidentified people at the intermediate school's ground-breaking ceremony. (Ed Yeats.)

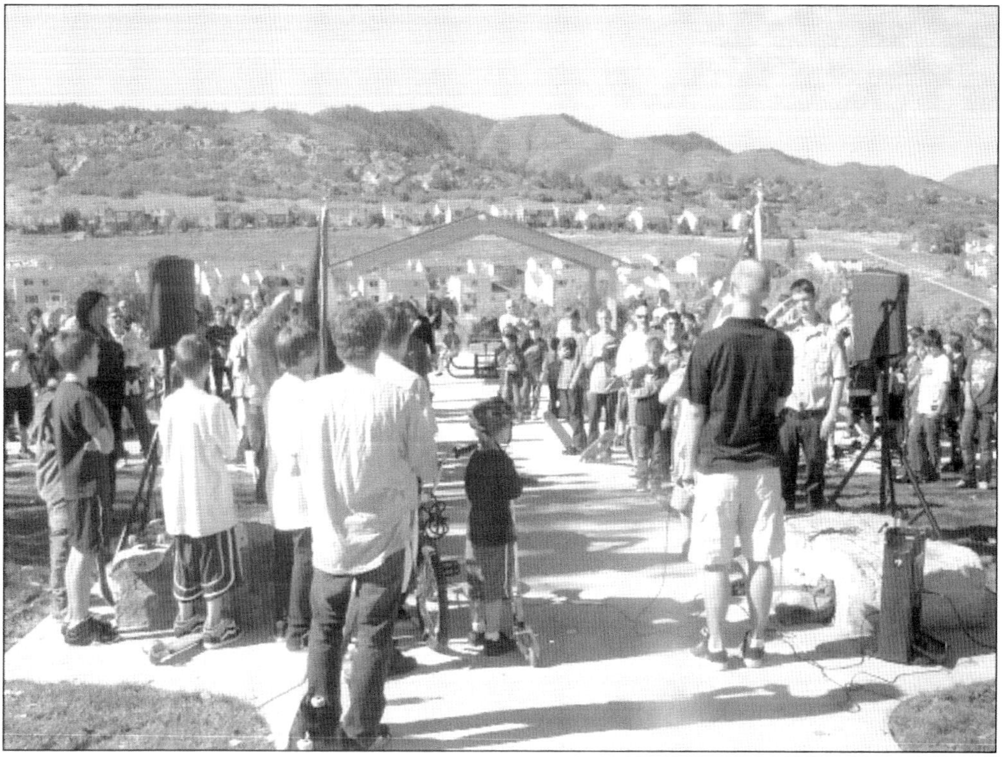

Skate Park Dedication. This photograph was taken in October 2009 at the opening of Roxborough Village's skate park and is typical of the hundreds of well-attended activities at the park each year. The Boy Scouts are presenting the colors in this image. (Ed Yeats.)

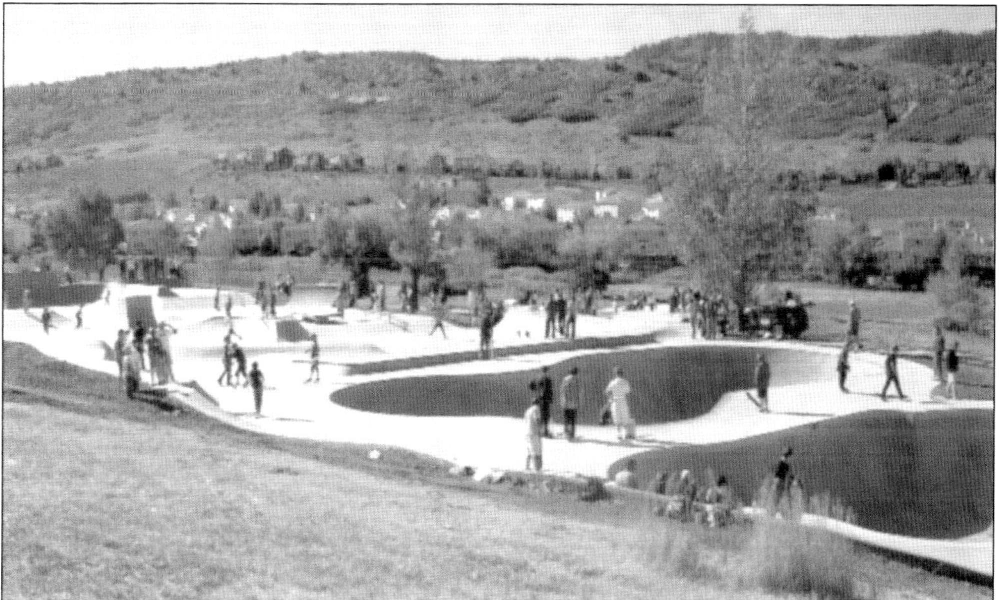

Roxborough's Skate Park. Residents came together to build a skate park for the area's children and teenagers. It is used almost daily by people of all ages and is consistently named as one of the top skate parks in Colorado. (Ed Yeats.)

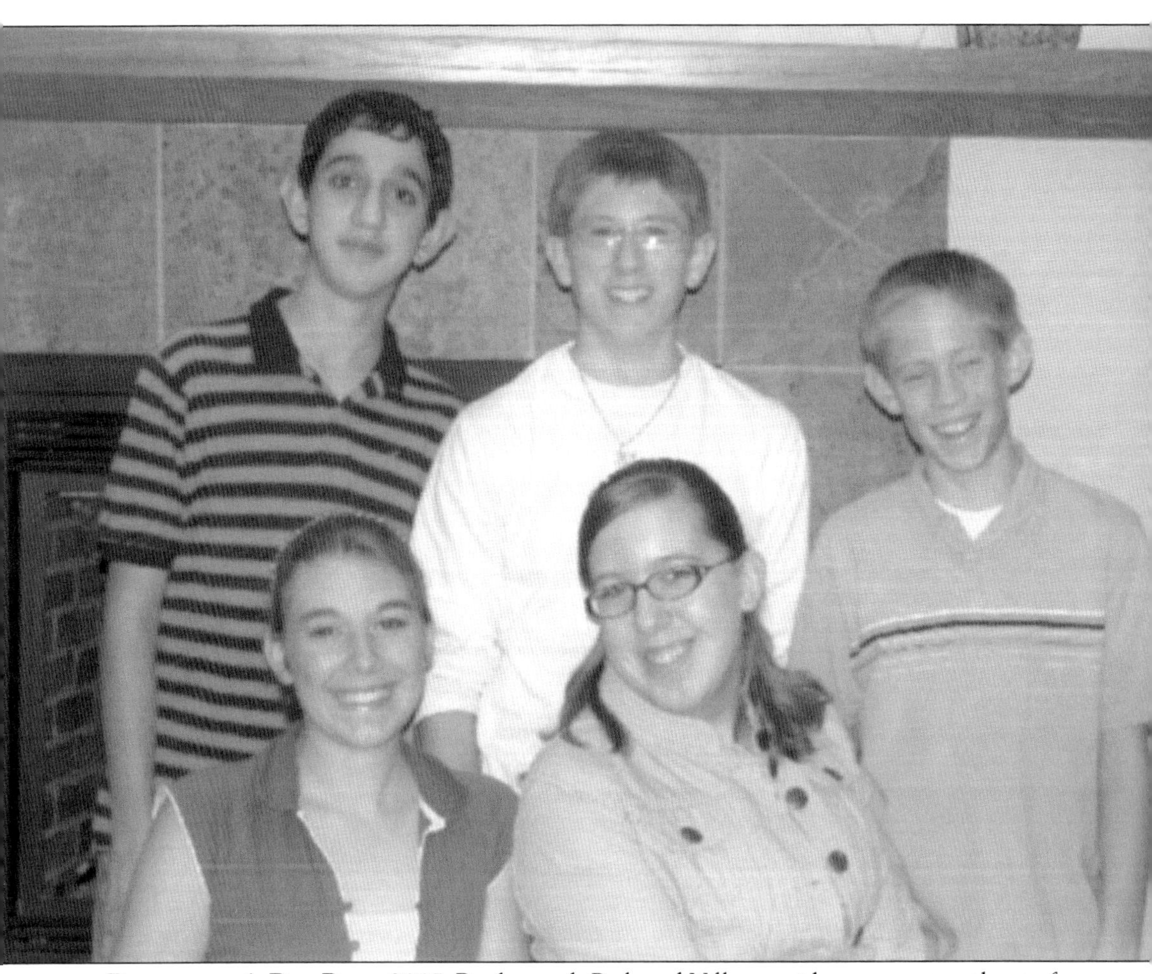

Roxborough's Rat Pack. 2007. Roxborough Park and Village residents came together to form a community group for teenagers. Rat Pack members are active in the community in a variety of ways. Pictured are a few of the original members. They are, from left to right, (first row) Kassie Prysby and Hanna Trainor; (second row) Hisham Amery, Evan Giacchino, and AJ Wilkerson. (Ed Yeats.)

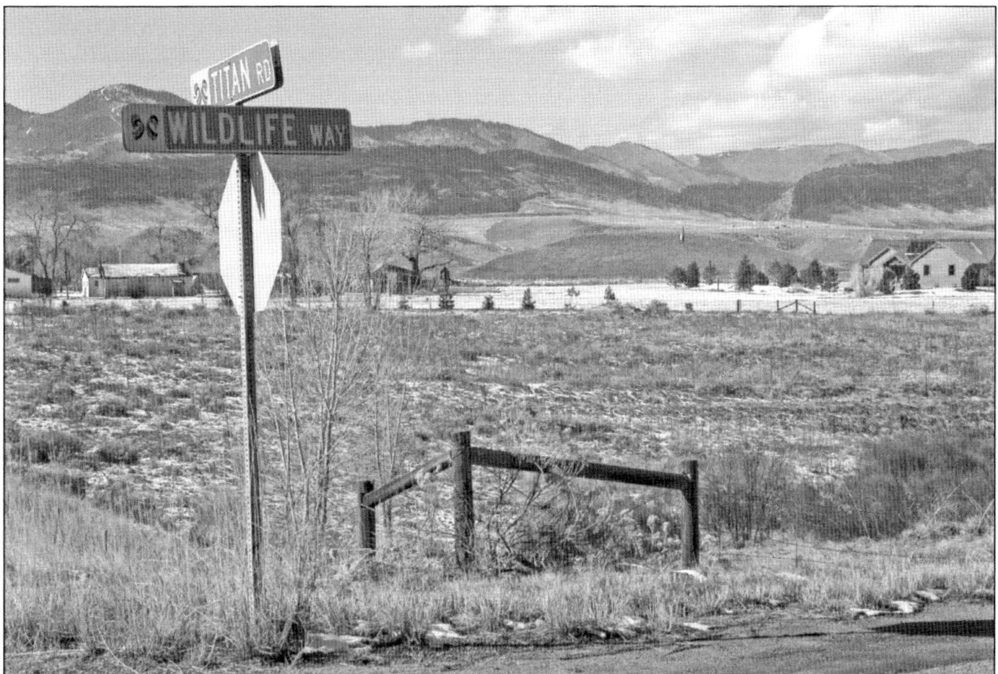

Times Are Changing. For most of the 19th and 20th centuries, Roxborough has been an area of large ranches, farms, and wide-ranging vistas. From the mid-1950s through the 1960s, small communities like Sunshine Acres, View Ridge, and Plum Creek Acres were developed. Many of their residents value the rural ambiance. Within the next few years, thousands of homes will be built within Roxborough's 80125 zip code that will have an impact on these areas. (Tom Olkowski.)

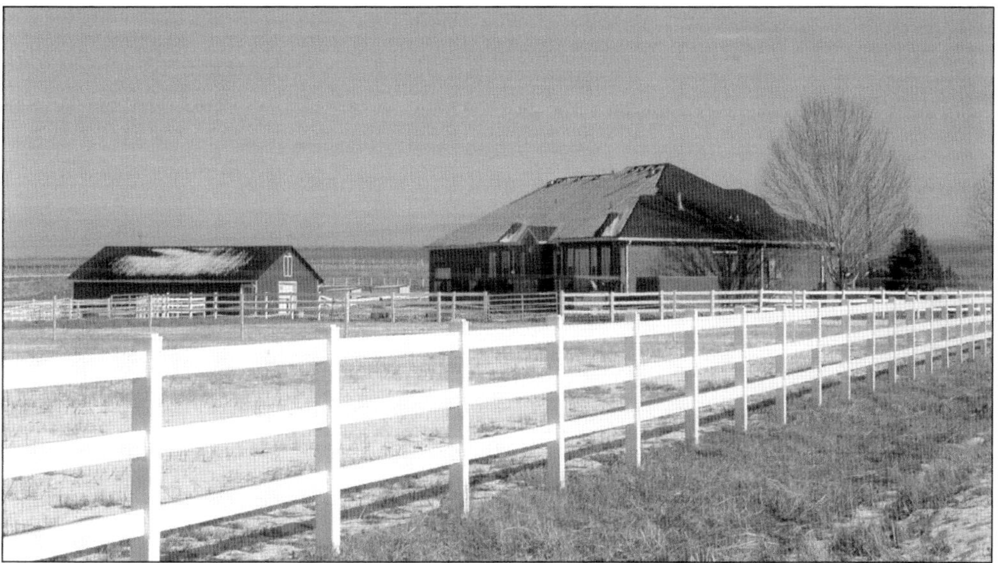

Hobby Farms. Hobby farms are small farms that are usually not a prime source of income. Because these farms are often part of a semirural lifestyle, they have dotted Roxborough's landscape for more than 50 years. Some are zoned for a few horses, while others might provide a small side income. Although scores of hobby farm owners live within Roxborough's 80125 zip code, they often identify as Littleton residents. (Tom Olkowski.)

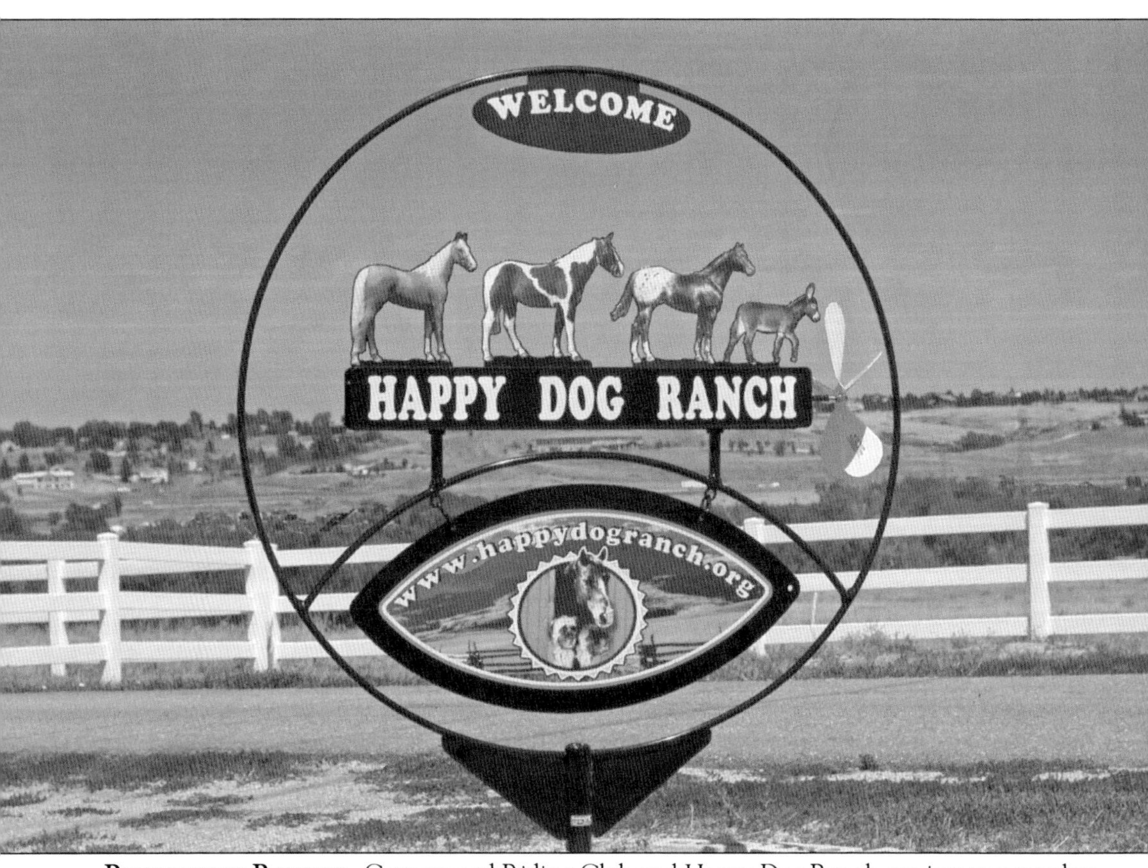

Roxborough Ranches. Cottonwood Riding Club and Happy Dog Ranch are just two ranches on Roxborough's high plains. A dozen or more ranches offer a variety of programs ranging from educational, vocational, and therapeutic activities to participation in an international polo club. (Tom Olkowski.)

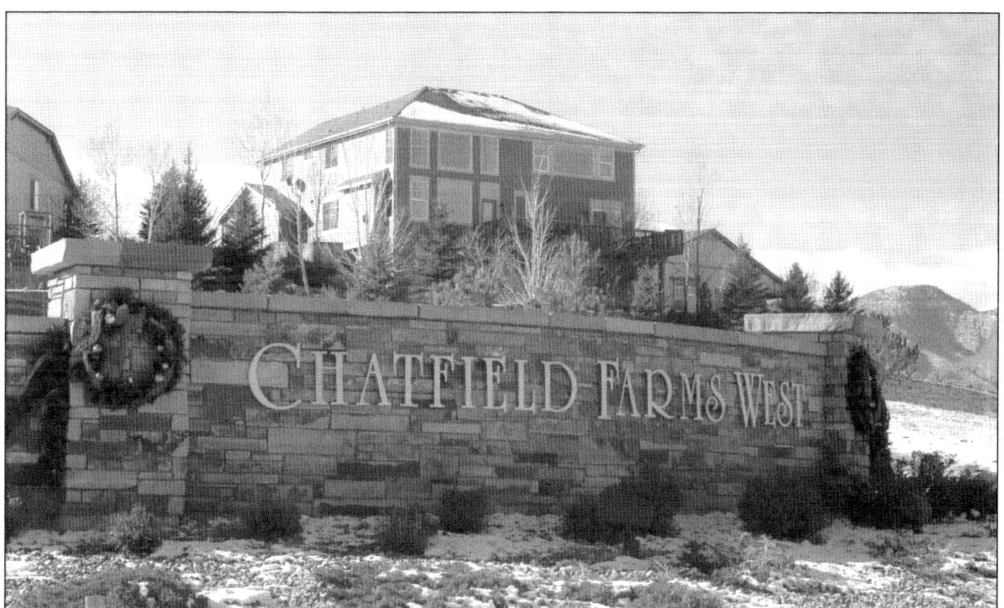

Chatfield Farms, Chatfield Farms West, Arrowhead Shores, Blue Mesa. Several large residential communities were built in Roxborough over the past 15 years, adding hundreds of new homes and families to Roxborough. Fortunately, these neighborhoods did not experience the devastating financial problems of previous developments. (Tom Olkowski.)

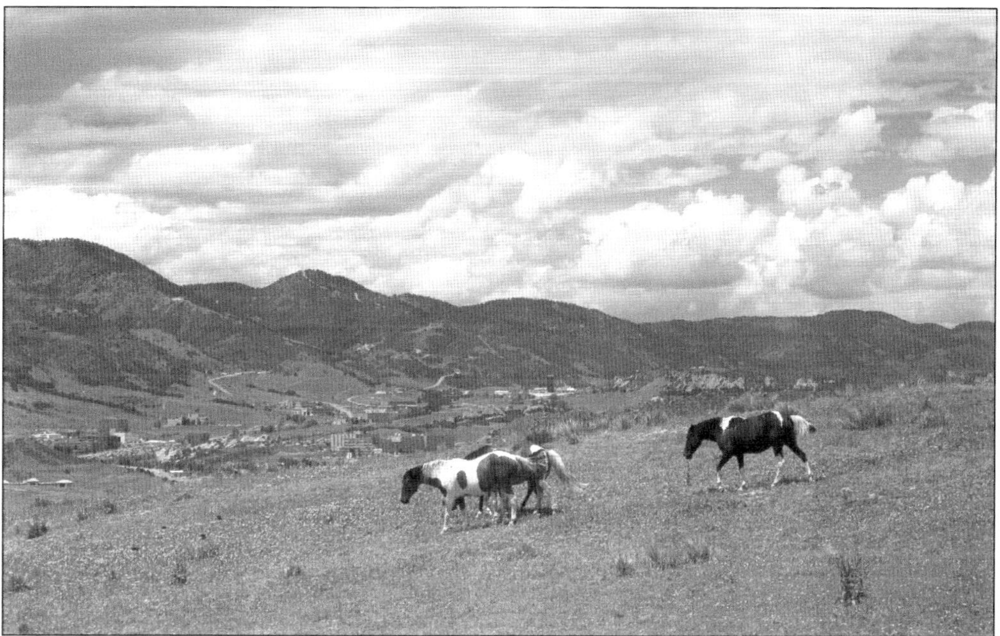

Glenn L. Martin Airplane Company (Now Lockheed Martin). This photograph was taken from a high open ridge overlooking the Lockheed Martin plant. Over the past six decades, when it went from building Titan missile engines to space vehicles, Glenn Martin's company changed names a few times. As Lockheed Martin, it was recently awarded a contract to build the next-generation spacecraft *Orion*, which will transport crews into a new era of space exploration. (Tom Olkowski.)

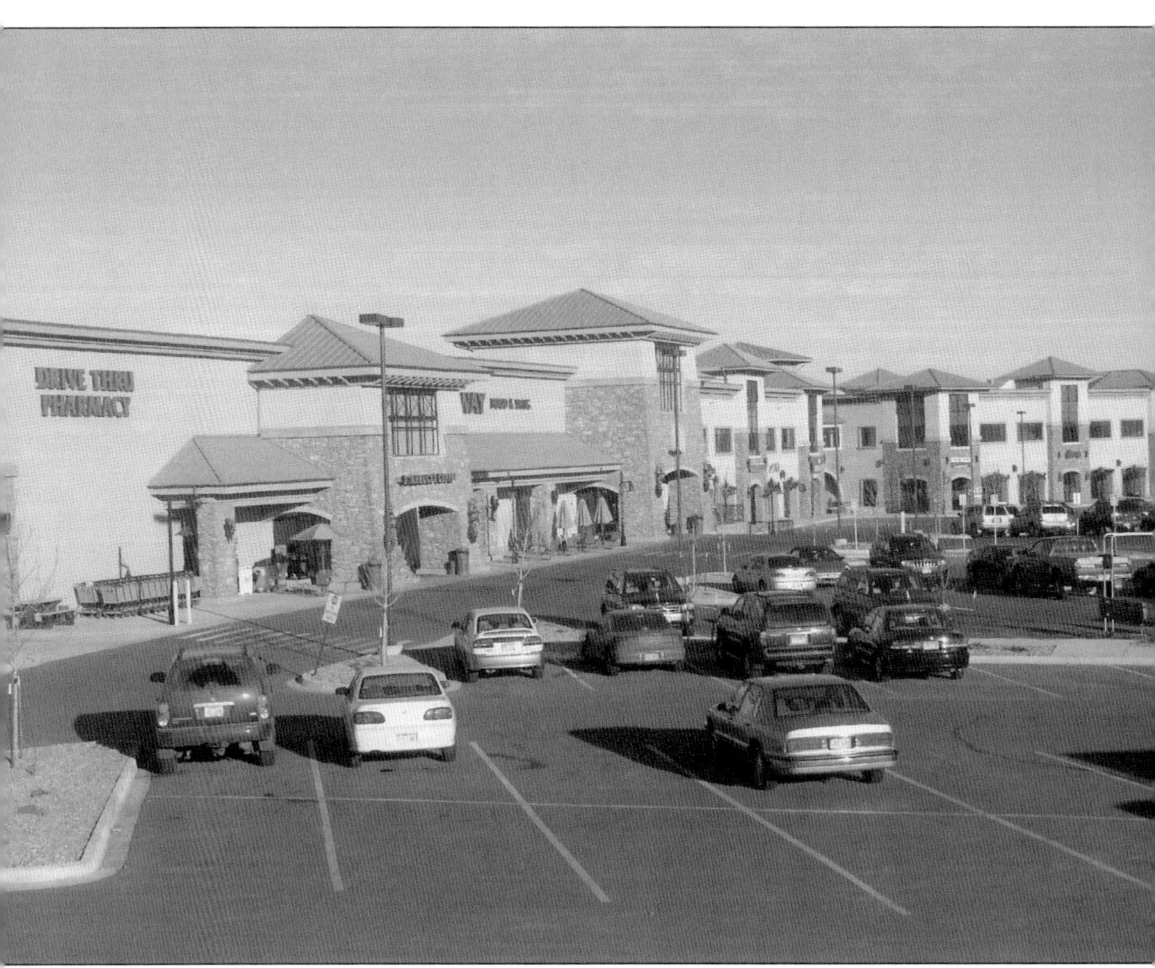

Roxborough Marketplace, 2004. Through the last half of the 20th century, only one small store, Loaf and Jug's gas station and convenience store, served Roxborough's rural and few residential communities. As Roxborough's population grew, a small, grocery-anchored shopping center was built at Waterton and Rampart Range Roads and a post office was placed in the Safeway convenience store. About 8,700 cars pass by daily. (Ed Yeats.)

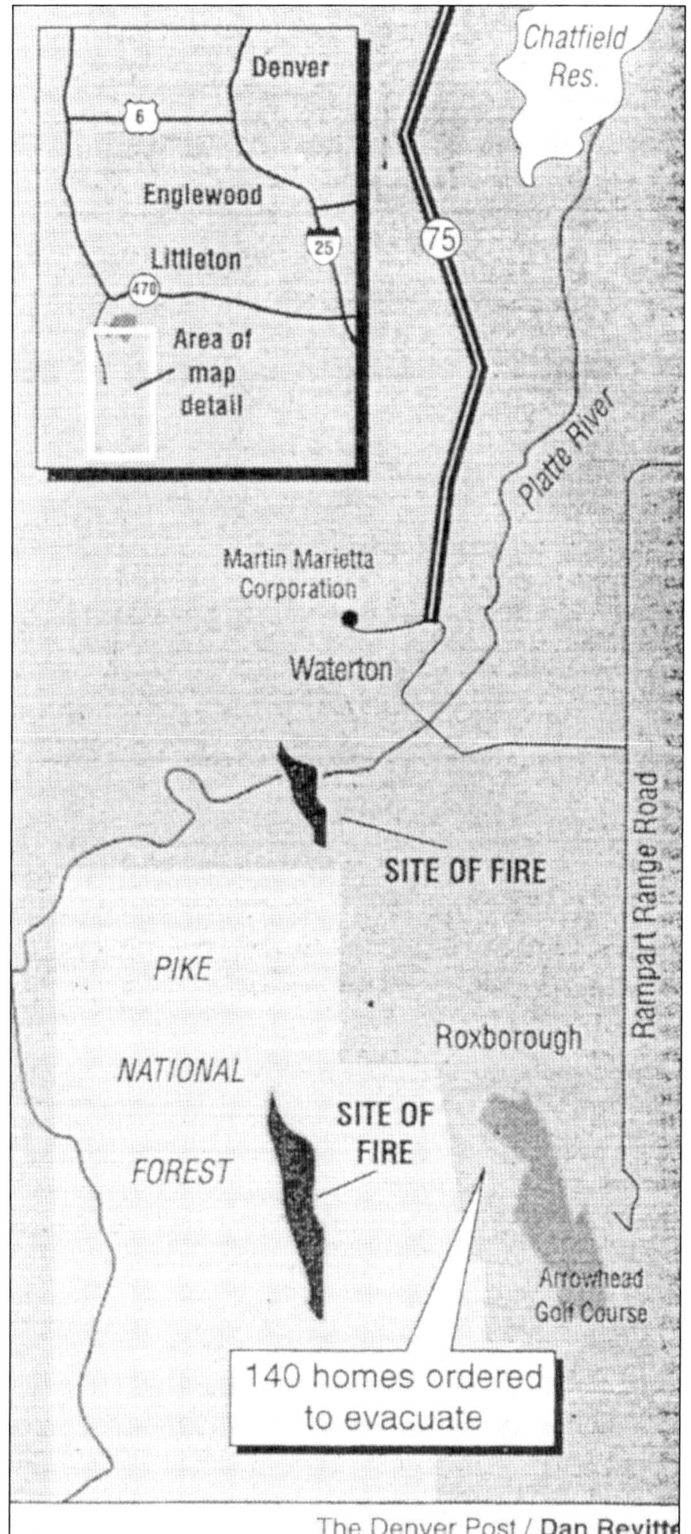

FIRE! At the beginning of the 21st century, Colorado experienced a severe multiyear drought. Arid and windy Roxborough was tinder-dry. Colorado's worst wildfire, the Hayman fire erupted in 2002 and quickly raced through Pike National Forest. At one point, it was seven miles away from Roxborough, moving at one mile per hour. Residents were evacuated. The fire scorched 138,000 acres and took one life. Fortunately, favorable winds blew the flames away from Roxborough. (West Metro Fire Department.)

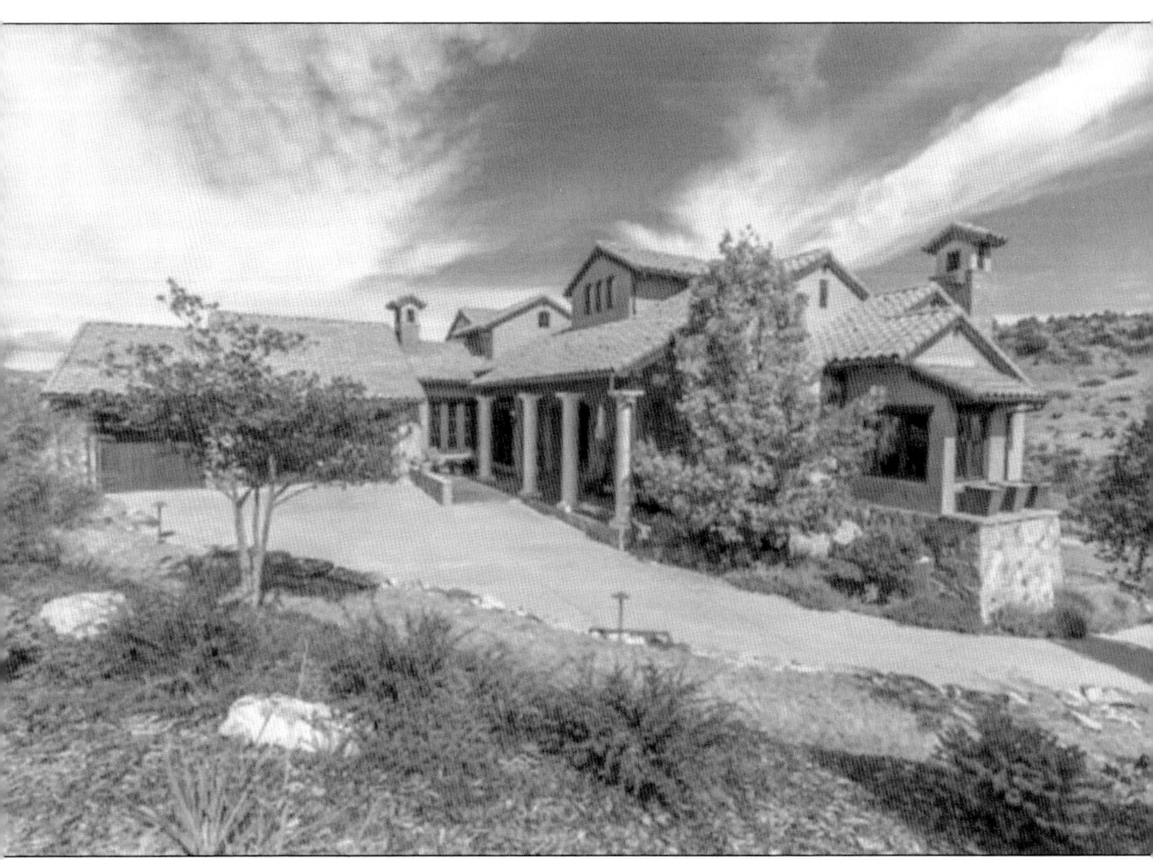

The Ravenna Dream. At the start of the 21st century, much like dreamers in Roxborough had done for the hundred years before them, developers obtained a large ranch that had once been a 1850s homestead. Plans included million dollar homes sited throughout the exclusive residential community that would sit on foothill slopes overlooking the valley. An exceptional members-only golf course, magnificent clubhouse, and private access to the South Platte River for fishing were included in the plans. (Ravenna Golf.)

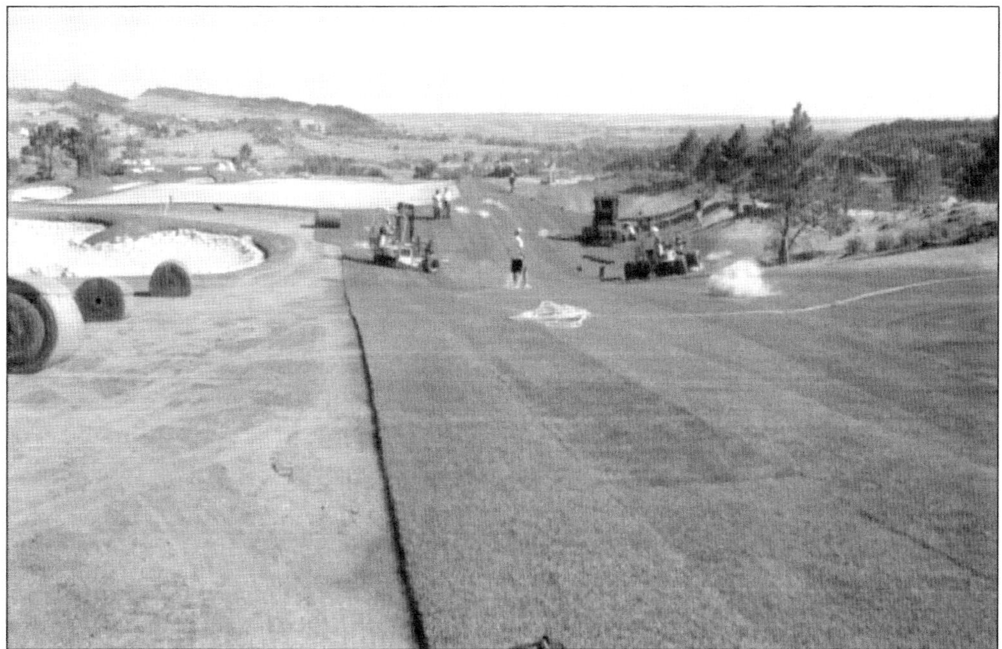

Ravenna Dream Shattered. In January 2011, the *Denver Post* reported upscale Ravenna was in trouble. "The clubhouse, pool and tennis courts were never built, some of the roads are crumbling and with just two dozen homes built, the Ravenna development . . . feels like a ghost town." In a depressed real estate market, River Canyon Real Estate Investment LLC was unable to develop the 636 acres near Waterton Canyon and defaulted on its loans. (Ravenna Golf.)

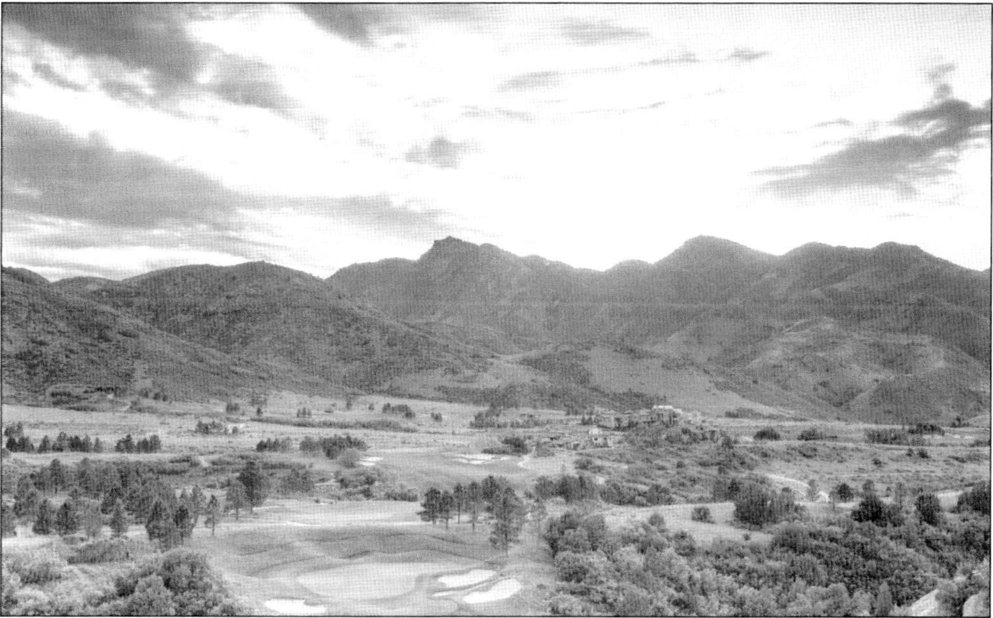

Ravenna Renewed. A financial crisis decimated the real estate market throughout the 21st century's first decade, but, as the economy improved, Ravenna's homeowners and investors were able to return to a vision of building an exceptional community. Although there are still challenges ahead, new homes were built in 2015. (Ravenna Golf.)

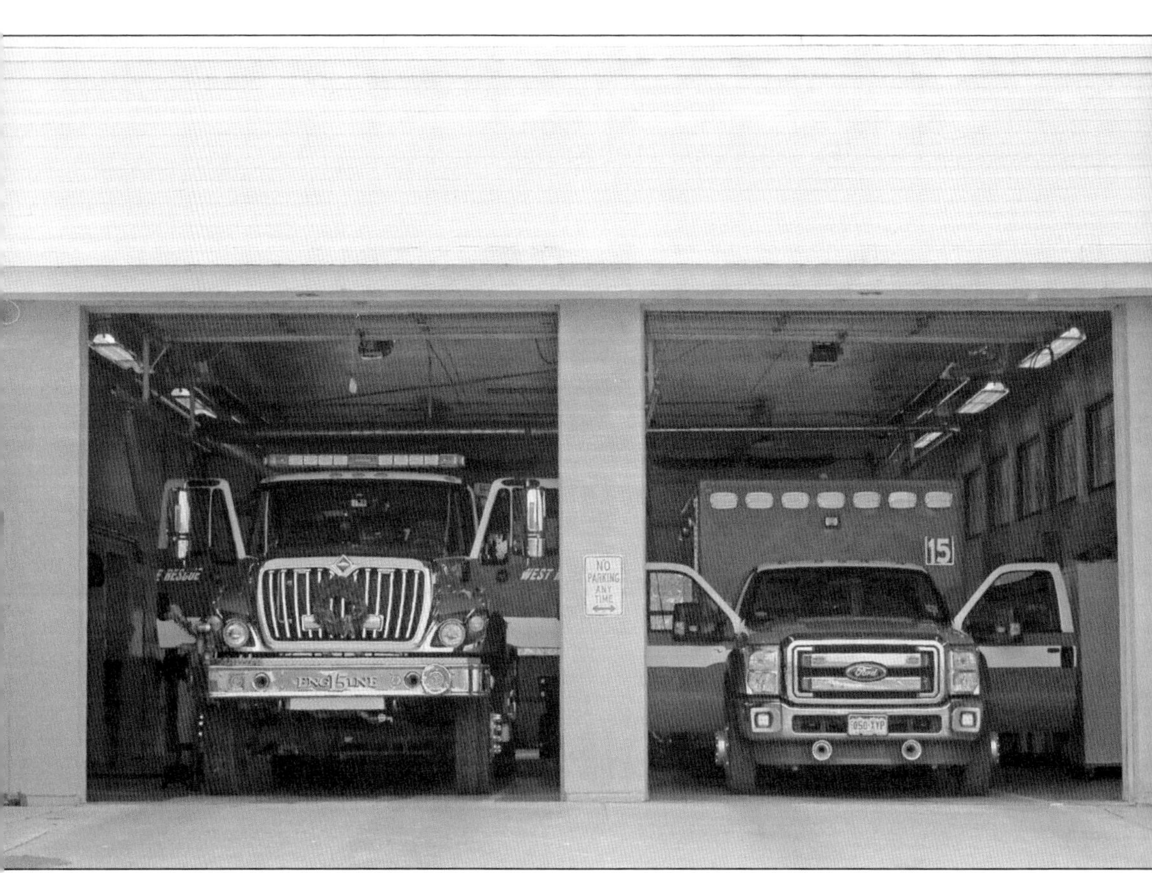

West Metro Fire and Rescue. In 2000, residents voted to accept West Metro Fire and Rescue as the full-time professional service provider for the Roxborough community. Roxborough's West Metro Fire and Rescue Department Station No. 15 is pictured here. The fire station was built on land where the mining town of Silica once stood. (Tom Olkowski.)

Eight

Surrounded by Natural Beauty

Surrounded by an abundance of natural beauty, Roxborough's 80125 zip code's 42.13-square-mile area is an exceptional place to live. Residents and visitors commonly see elk, whitetail deer, foxes, coyotes, mountain lions, and black bears. Pike National Forest and the Rocky Mountains lay to the west, and Roxborough State Park is to the south. Chatfield State Park runs along Roxborough's northern boundary. Three sharp-ridged hogbacks rise along the base of Roxborough's foothills. The spectacular Fountain Formation—with its soaring 60-degree, 68-million-year-old red rocks—is part of the same ageless creation as the more public and well-known Red Rocks Park and Garden of the Gods. In the heart of Roxborough's high plains, Sharptail Ridge is managed with Open Space funds. Arrowhead Golf Club's 18-hole course is one of the most scenic public courses in Colorado.

Along the South Platte River, Waterton Canyon can be walked or biked to Strontia Dam, located six and a half miles above the trailhead. The High Line Canal's path takes hikers and equestrians through open fields and neighborhoods for 66 miles toward Denver's northern suburbs. The nationally known Colorado Trail can be reached from Roxborough State Park's ancient Carpenter Peak or through Waterton Canyon. The long-distance trail runs 486 miles from the mouth of the canyon to Durango. Its highest point is 13,271 feet, and most of the trail is above 10,000 feet.

In 2010, the US Census showed 9,099 people (living in 3,312 households) and 1,328 families living in Roxborough, but within the next 20 years, the area's population will multiply quickly as Shea Homes and Sterling Ranch developers begin building large communities in what is sometimes called the Chatfield Valley. In the early 1970s, Woodmoor Corporation, which was planning a 3,000-acre development in Roxborough, published a newsletter proclaiming Roxborough's beauty and uniqueness: "Such land is rare. To preserve and protect its natural beauty, yet permit the environment to be shared by all, becomes the challenge and the responsibility." Almost 50 years later, these words are more relevant than ever before.

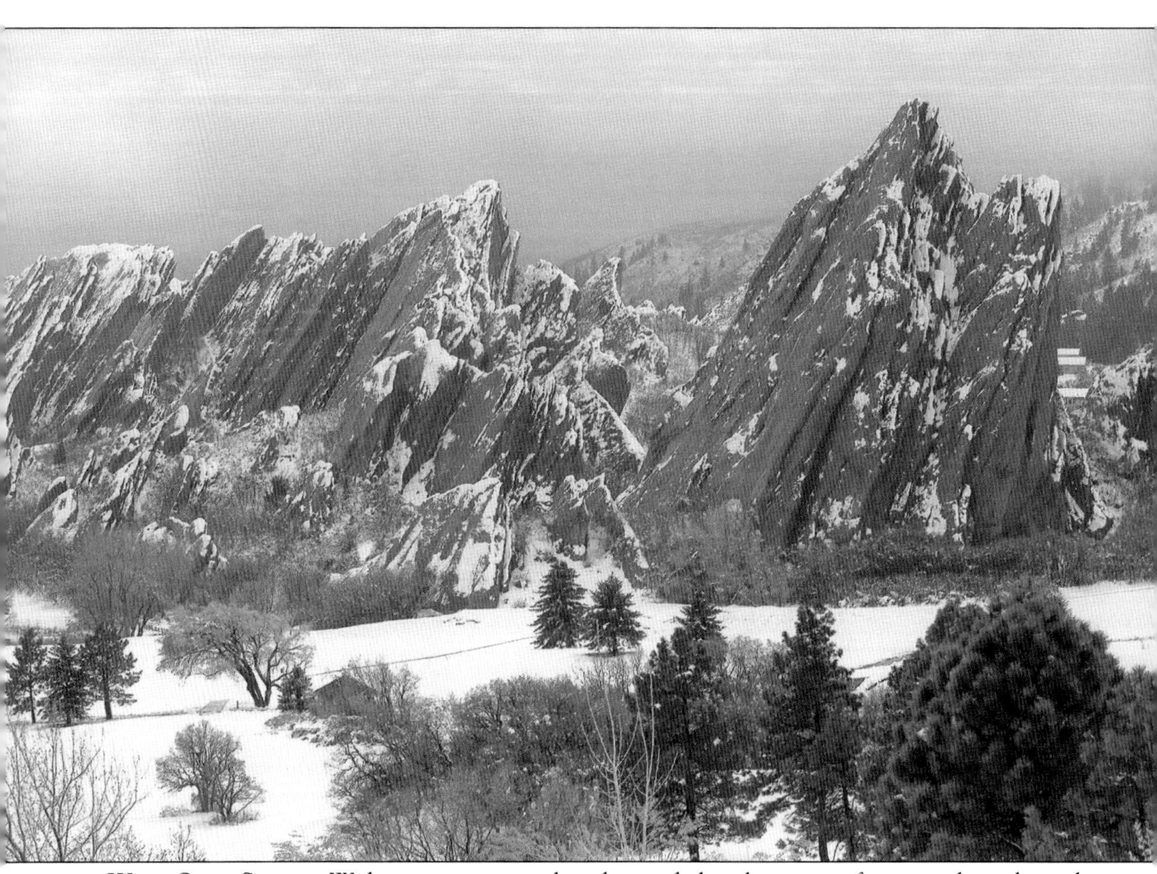

Wide-Open Spaces. Wide-open spaces, a big sky, and the changing of seasons have brought thousands to the West. This photograph captures the spectacular beauty of snow on the Fountain Formation's red rocks that are found in Roxborough State Park and Roxborough Park's residential community. (Tom Olkowski.)

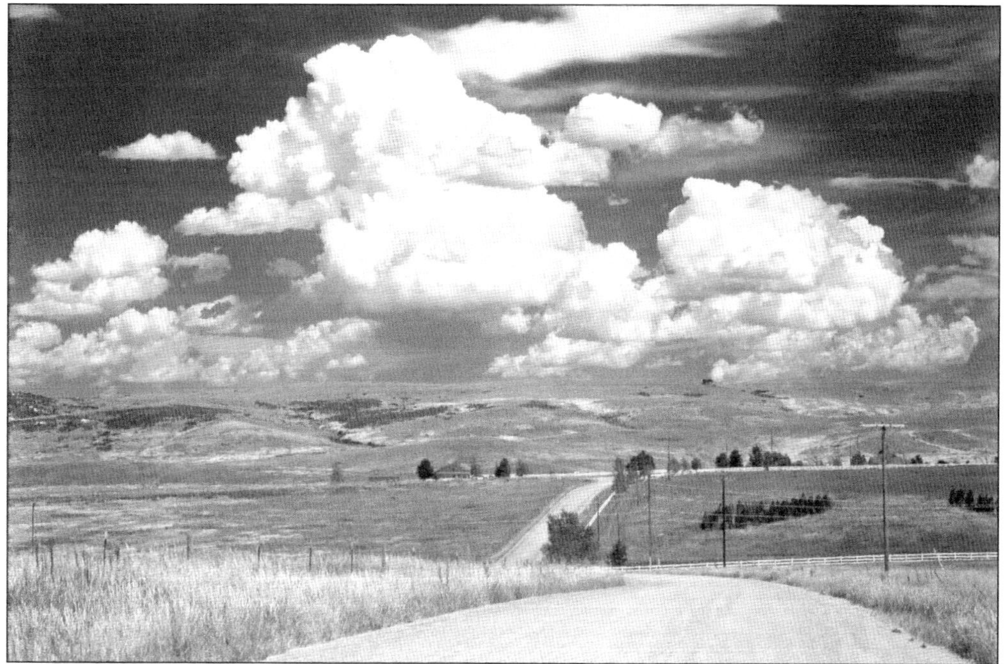

Open Road and Clouds. Roxborough is marked by high grassy plains, small farms and ranches, and open unpaved roads. It has maintained its rural appearance for many years, but with projected population growth, these open roads will be paved and the scene will change dramatically. (Tom Olkowski.)

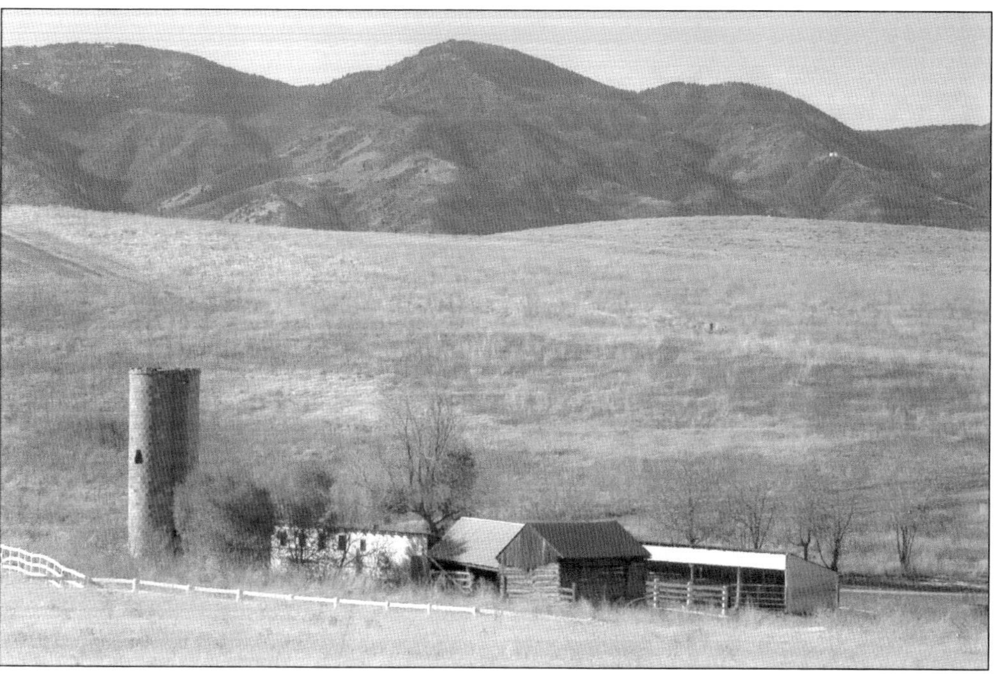

Homestead, Silo, and Mountains. An old homestead, barn, and silo reflect the rugged and often lonely life farmers faced in the unforgiving West. Difficulties and distances required early pioneers—and those who followed them—to rely on each other. (Tom Olkowski.)

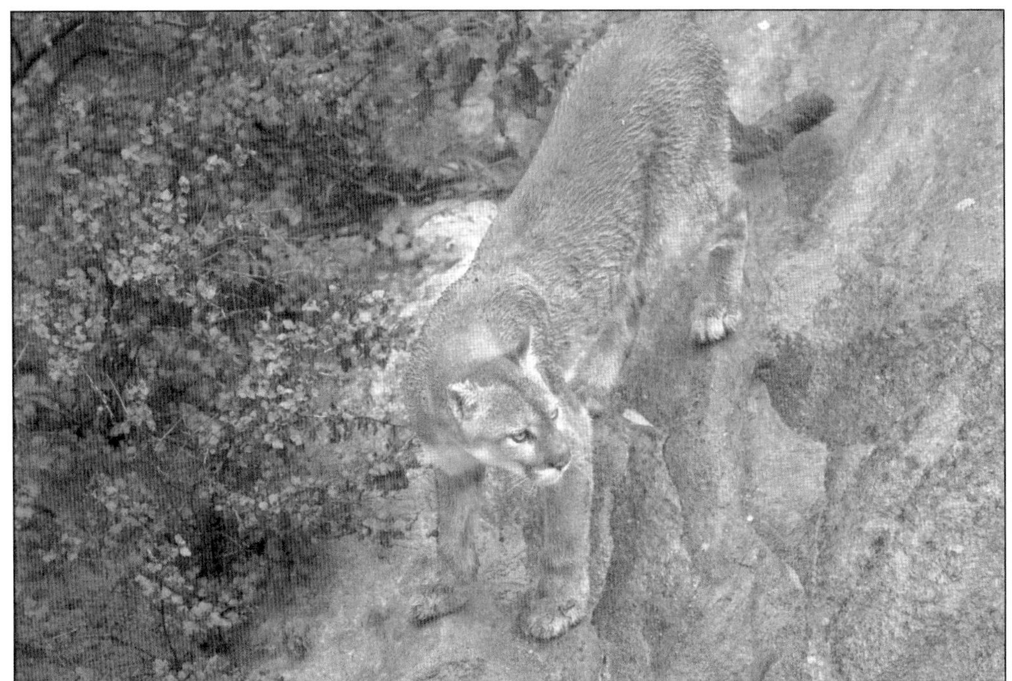

Mountain Lion. Scrub oak cover, a rugged rocky terrain, and an abundance of deer create an ideal habitat for mountain lions. Wildlife experts caution people to be constantly aware that bears and mountain lions share their environment. (Lance W. Moreland.)

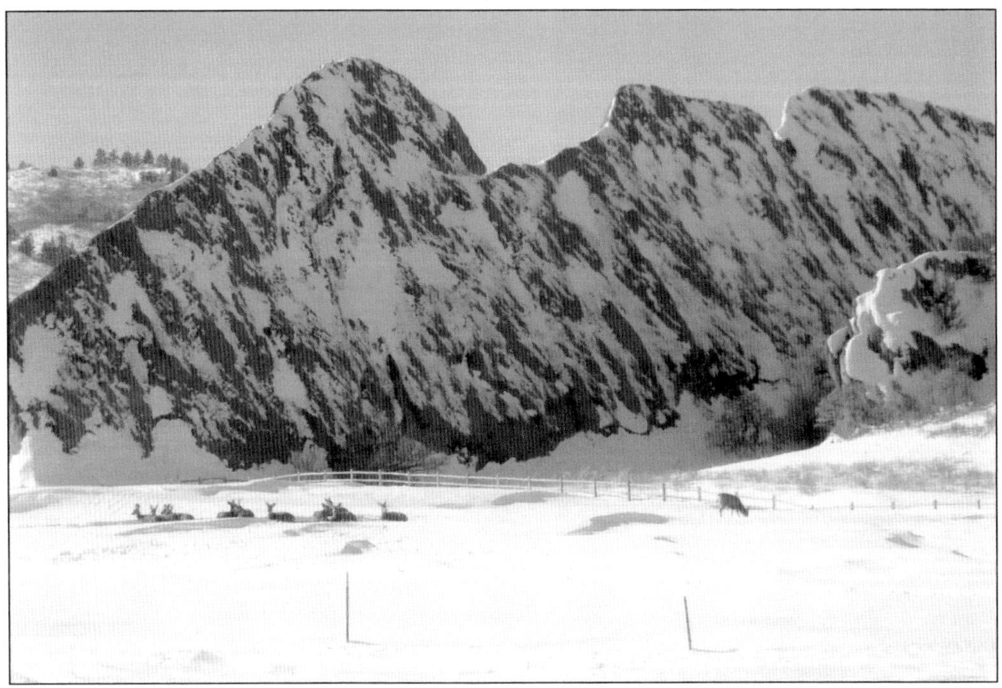

Red Rocks Powdered with Snow. Whitetail and mule deer living in Roxborough State Park and among residents in Roxborough Park are generally unafraid of people and vehicles. (Tom Olkowski.)

PIKE NATIONAL FOREST. Pike National Forest was designated a national forest in 1906. Its 1,106,604 acres cover five Colorado counties. At the edge of the forest, the 7,200-foot-high Carpenter Peak is a familiar sight to residents and visitors. This photograph was taken from Carpenter Peak and the view looks down on homes in Roxborough Park's Stonehenge area. (Prysby family.)

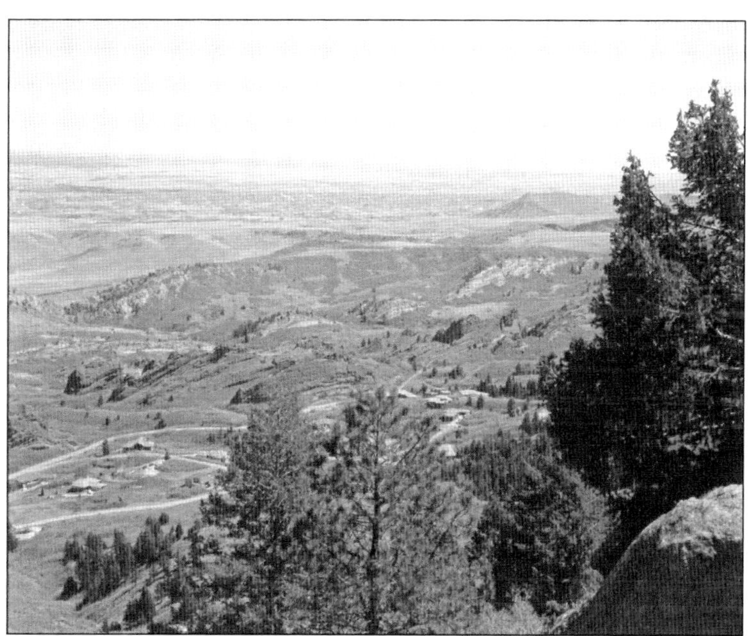

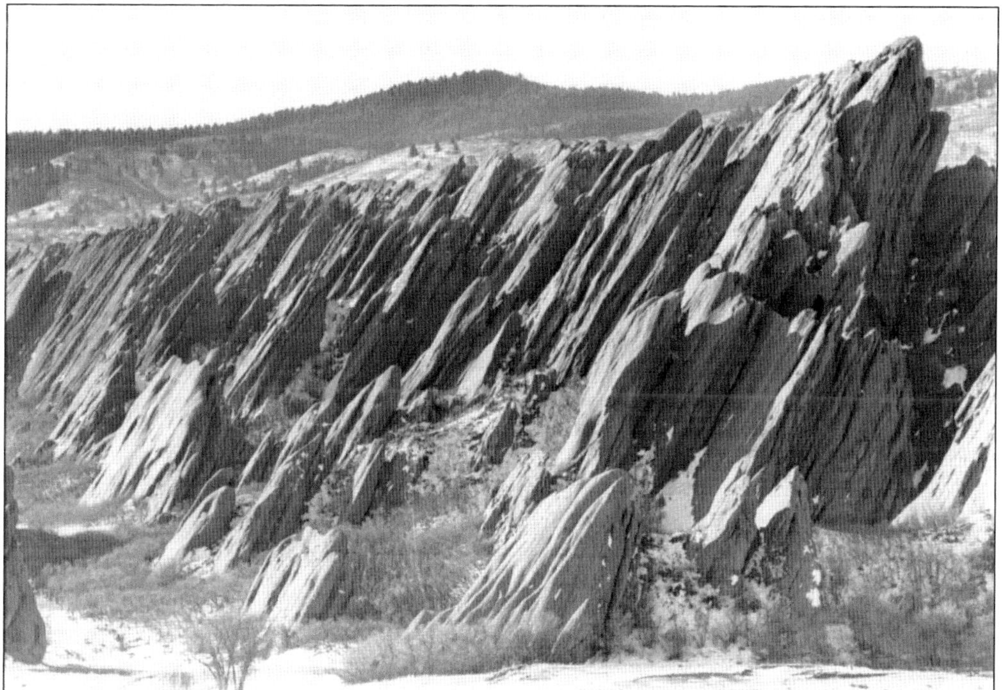

FOUNTAIN FORMATION'S RED SANDSTONES. The ancient red sandstones of the Fountain Formation are older than the Rocky Mountains and have been called "timeless," "translucent," "frozen red fountains," and "bony pieces of some prehistoric animal buried just beneath the surface." (Ed and Nancy Bathke Collection.)

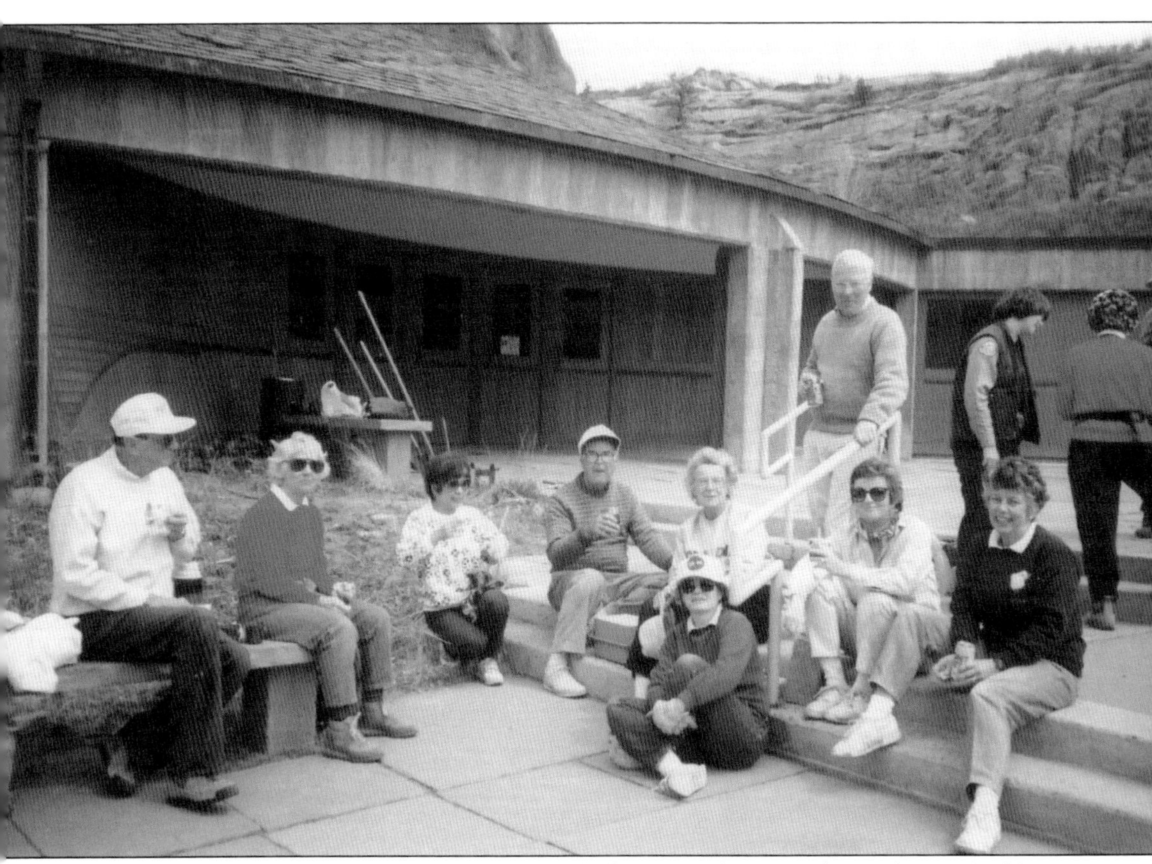

Roxborough State Park Visitors. Unidentified visitors relax at Roxborough State Park's visitor center, where, in 1878, John Smiles homesteaded the land. The hikers are resting after a visit to Henry Persse's Roxborough's stone house. In 1910, Denver mayor Robert W. Speer suggested that Roxborough's inspiring 60-degree monoliths become part of Denver's city parks, but his effort was unsuccessful. (David and Pam Irwin.)

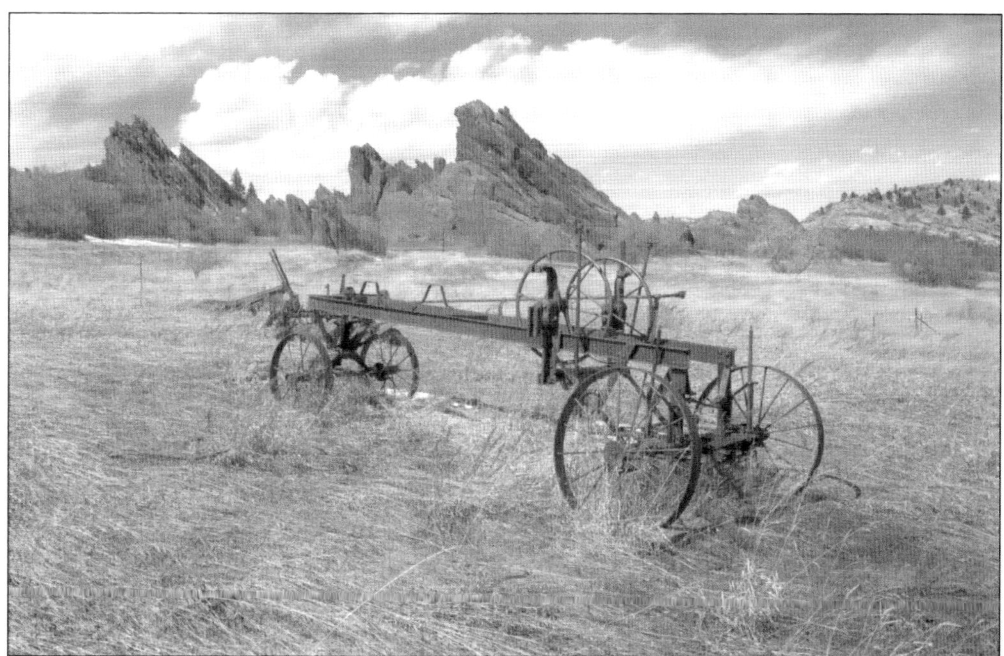

Ranch Equipment at Roxborough State Park. In 1925, the City of Denver offered Toney Helmer $21,000 for the land that included the Fountain Formation's red rocks, but the offer was $2,000 less than his asking price. The equipment shown in this photograph was left in the park and probably belonged to the Helmer brothers Toney and George. (Lance W. Moreland.)

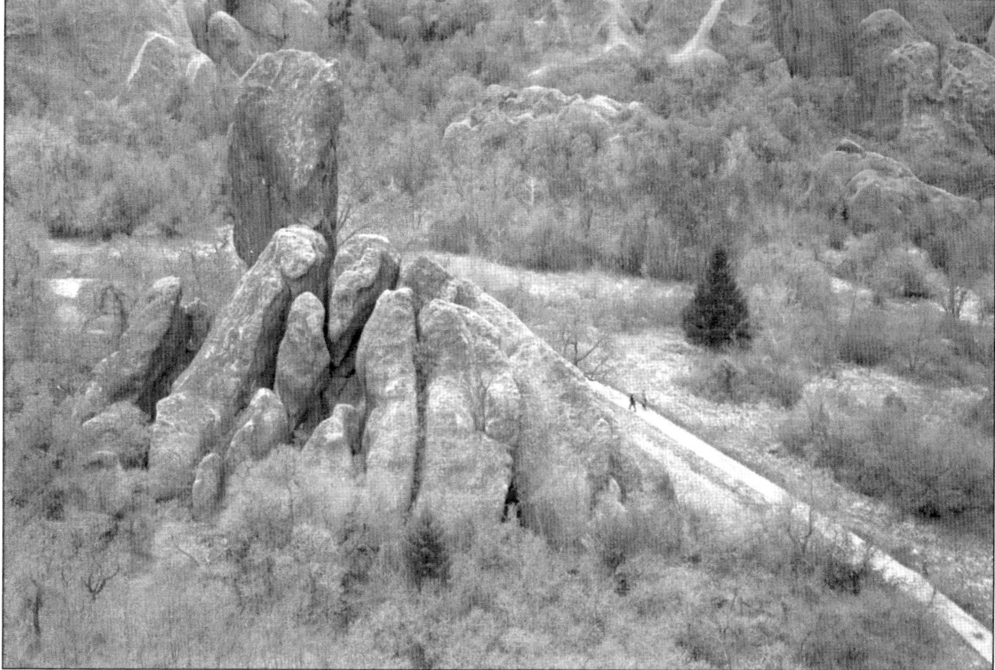

Roxborough State Park Vista. Roxborough State Park has miles of trails, ranked from easy to difficult. This photograph was taken from a high spot overlooking a popular trail. Unidentified hikers are pictured. (Lance W. Moreland.)

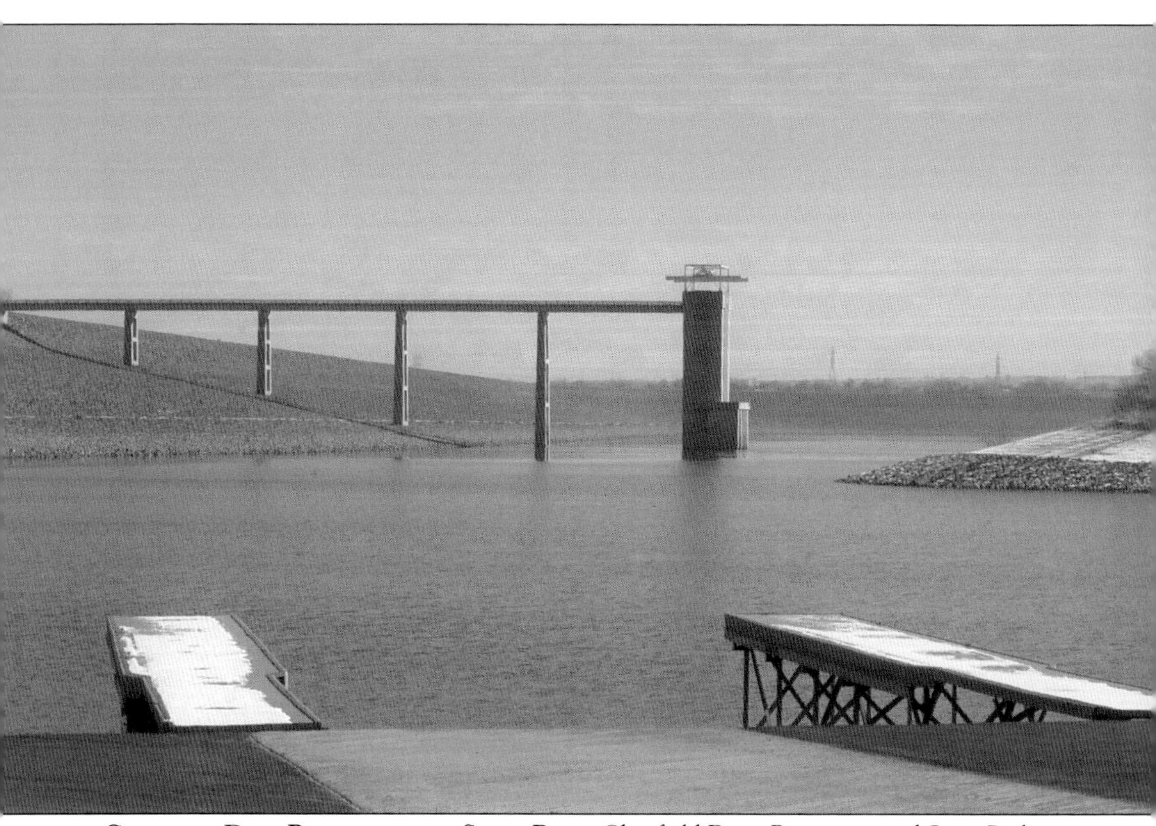

CHATFIELD DAM, RESERVOIR, AND STATE PARK. Chatfield Dam, Reservoir, and State Park carry the name of Union lieutenant Isaac W. Chatfield, who purchased 720 acres there in 1870 and farmed it until he moved in 1879. The dam was built on the South Platte River by the Army Corps of Engineers in 1975 as a response to one of Colorado's greatest natural disasters, the 1965 flood. Denver Water stores water behind the dam. The Corps of Engineers leases the land around the lake to the state. (Tom Olkowski.)

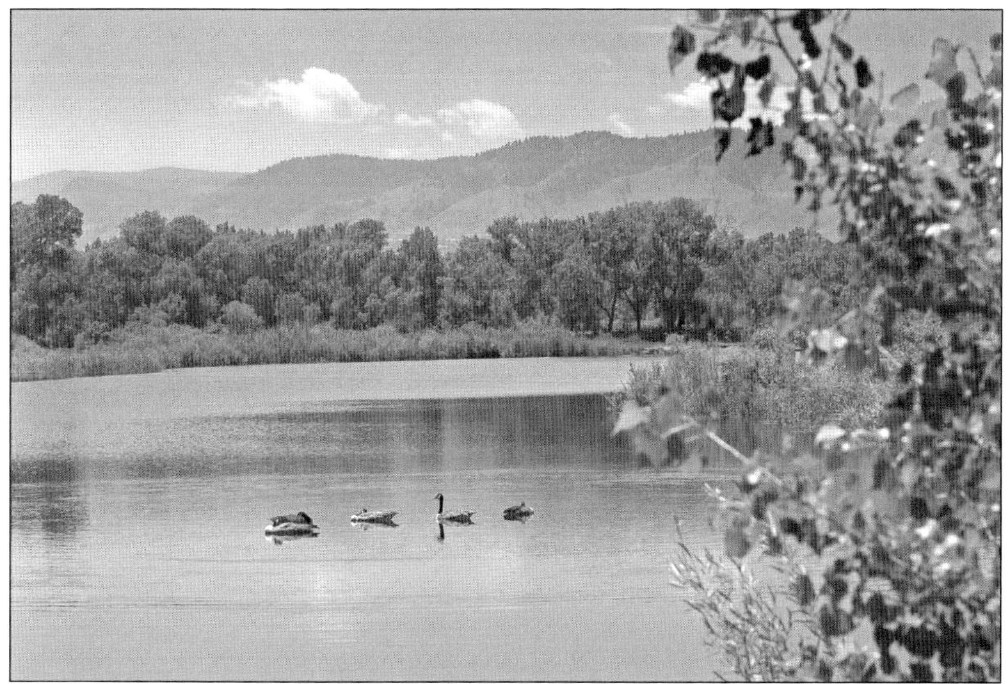

Chilling Out. Geese spend a leisurely day on a calm pond within Chatfield State Park. Pike National Forest is visible to the west. (Tom Olkowski.)

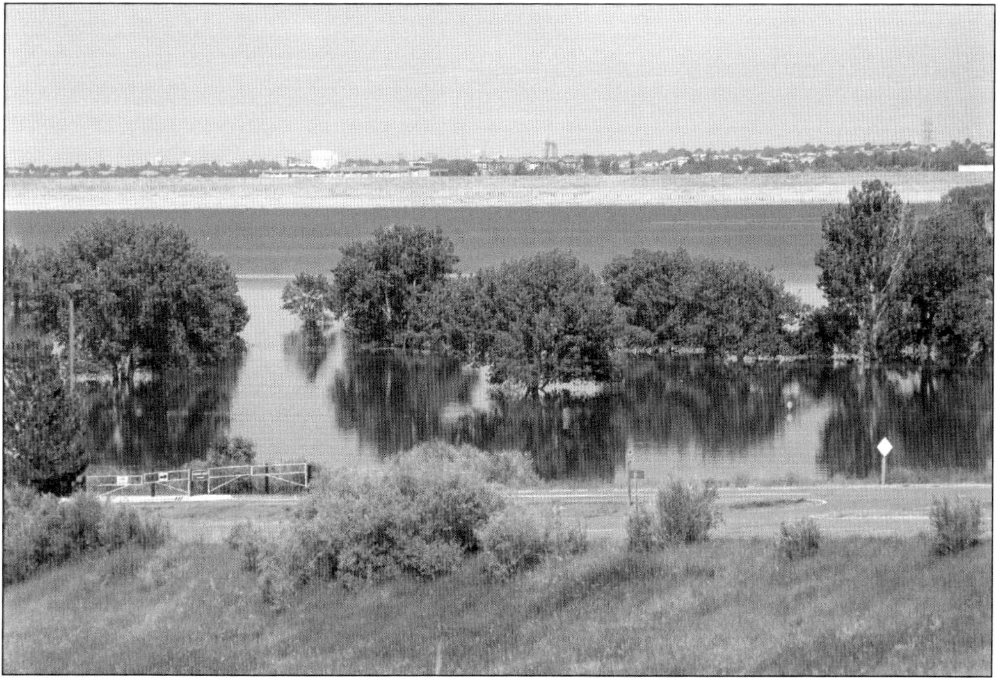

Chatfield Dam and Reservoir. The reservoir and dam were built as a result of the devastating and historic 1965 flood that raged through Castle Rock, Sedalia, Littleton, Englewood, and Denver. This 2015 photograph was taken after weeks of rain. Eventually, the swollen creeks and the South Platte River were contained. (Tom Olkowski.)

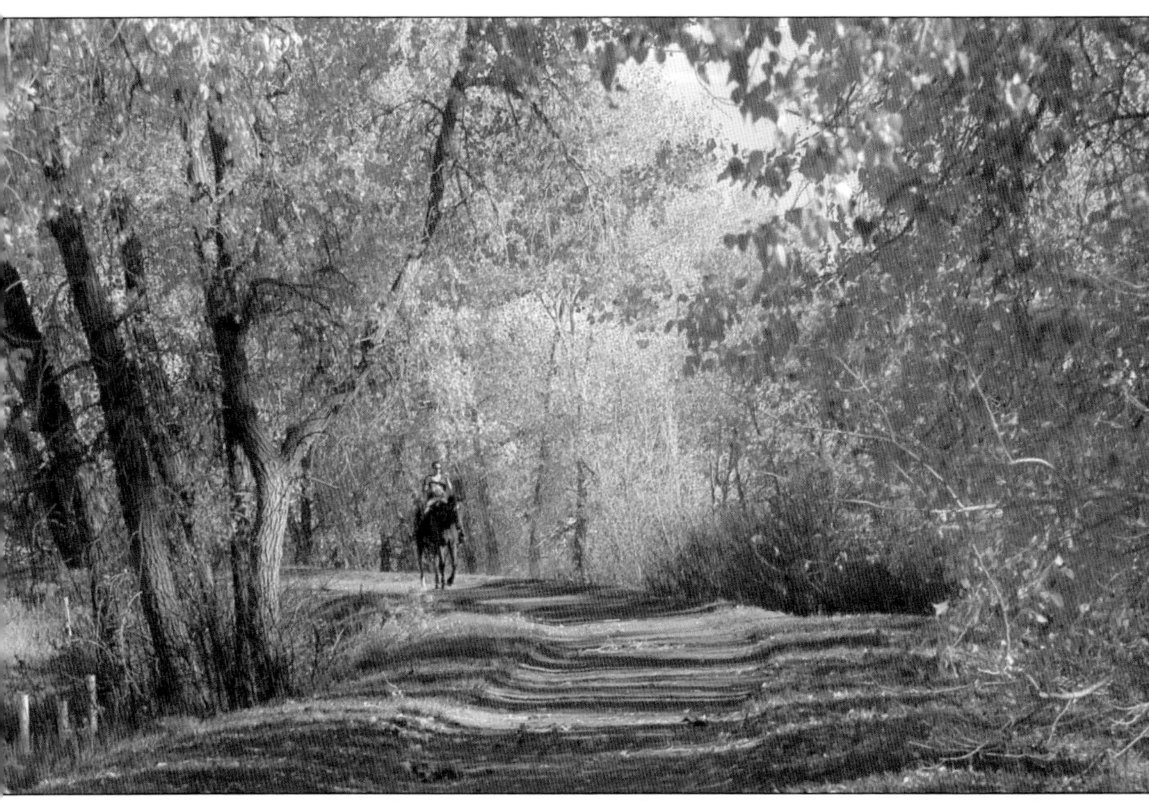

HIGH LINE CANAL. The High Line Canal was completed in 1883 and at that time was spelled as Highline. It starts at Kassler where the South Platte River rushes onto the plains. Built to deliver irrigation water downstream to farmers and ranchers, the canal was a valuable resource to early settlers. Today, the canal and the trail that runs beside it are known for recreational amenities. Owned and operated by Denver Water, it is maintained by recreation districts along the way. Recognized as a National Landmark Trail, it is a recreational treasure to wildlife viewers, hikers, cyclists, and horseback riders. Traveling north on the trail is a downhill journey all the way to Denver. (Tom Olkowski.)

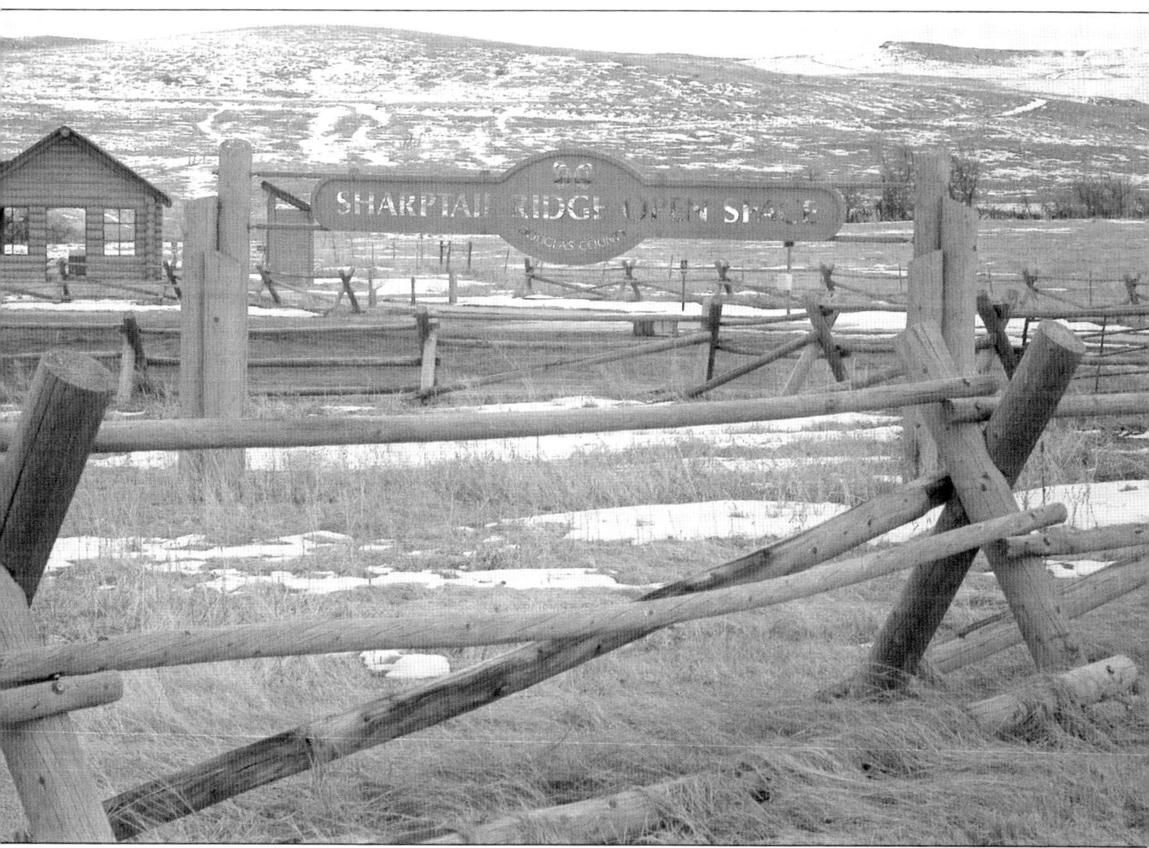

Still Wide-Open Spaces. Open Space funds helped purchase more than 1,000 acres of Sharptail Ridge, which overlooks the open plains and Roxborough State Park. Sharptail Ridge's 4.6 miles of trails lead to other open space trails nearby. Its serene environment is home to a variety of wildlife, including elk herds. Open to hikers and horseback riders most of the year, it is closed to them in the fall when only hunters are allowed on the ridge. Nearby Nelson Ranch and Pike Hill are also areas accessible to hikers and others. All three are managed by Douglas County Open Space and are only minutes and miles from anyone living in Roxborough's 80125 zip code communities. (Tom Olkowski.)

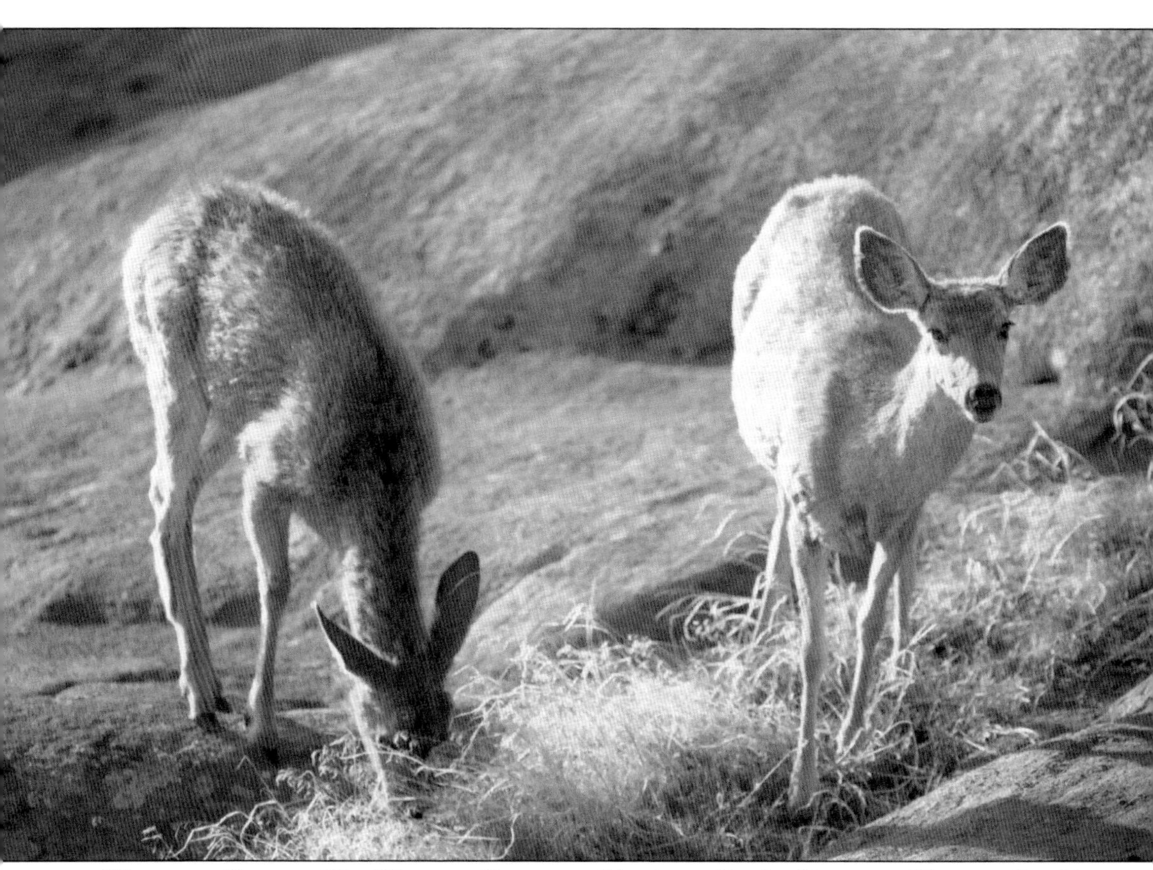

WATERTON CANYON. The Waterton Canyon trail begins at Kassler Center on Waterton Road in Jefferson County, minutes away from the Roxborough Marketplace. The wide trail runs along the South Platte River as it ascends 6.5 miles to Strontia Springs Dam. Bighorn sheep and mule deer (pictured) are commonly seen in the canyon. (Lance W. Moreland.)

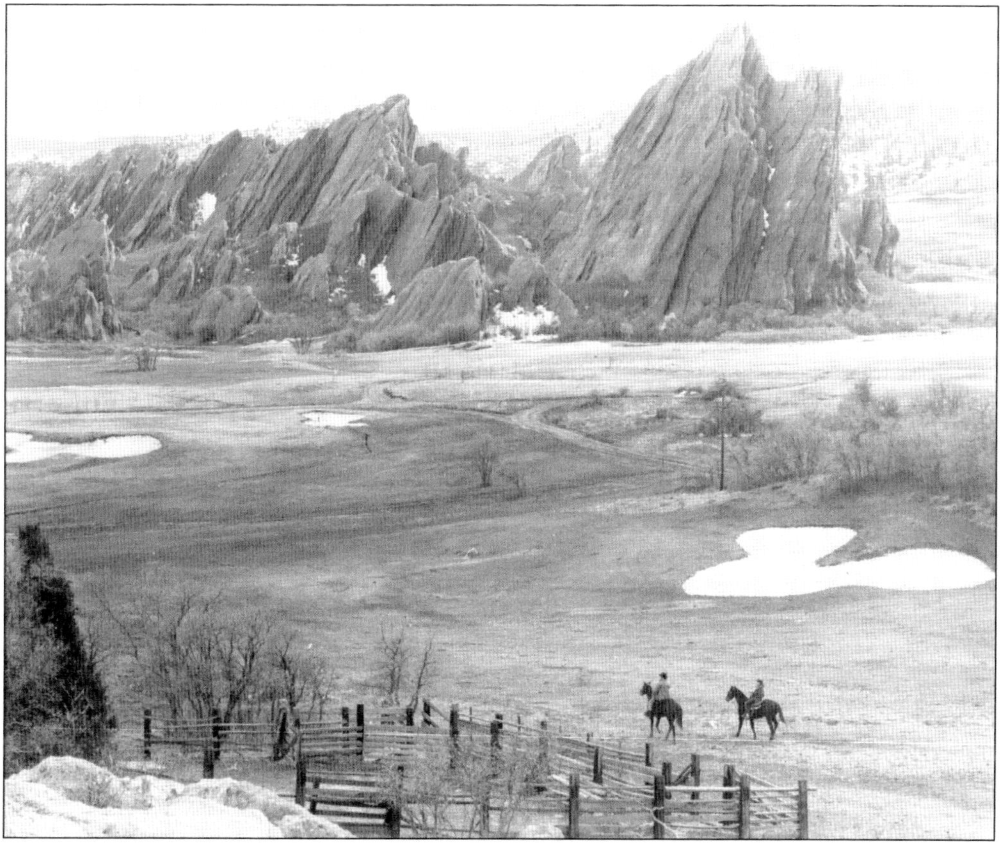

TRANSITIONING FROM 19TH-CENTURY CATTLE RANCH TO 20TH-CENTURY GOLF COURSE. This photograph, taken in the early 1970s, offers a juxtaposition of two periods in Roxborough's life—the Helmer family's ranch corral is still standing as two horseback riders trek across the new Woodmoor golf course designed by Robert Trent Jones Jr. (Ed and Nancy Bathke Collection.)

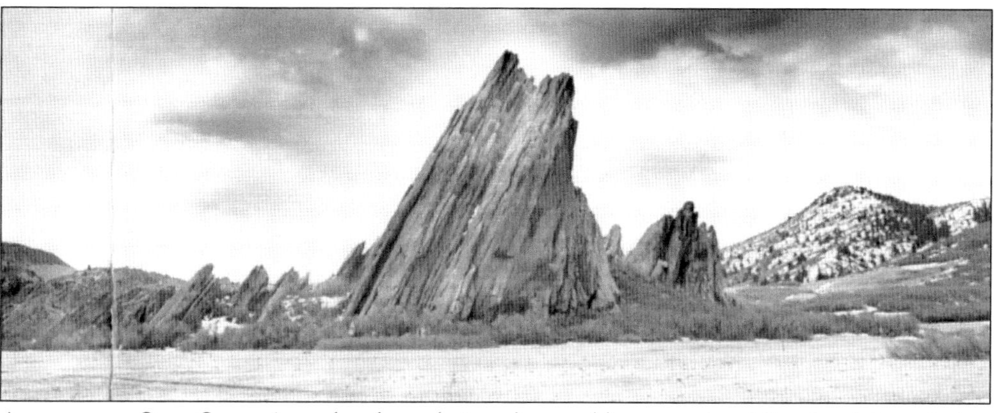

ARROWHEAD GOLF CLUB. Arrowhead was designed as a public course but fell on hard times during the 1970s. By 1977, a full-page article in the *Denver Post* called it "a ghost town golf course." A group of local individuals converted it to a private course in 1986 but was unable to maintain it, and the course failed again. Longtime residents remember when the cattle from a nearby ranch grazed the fairways. (Ed and Nancy Bathke Collection.)

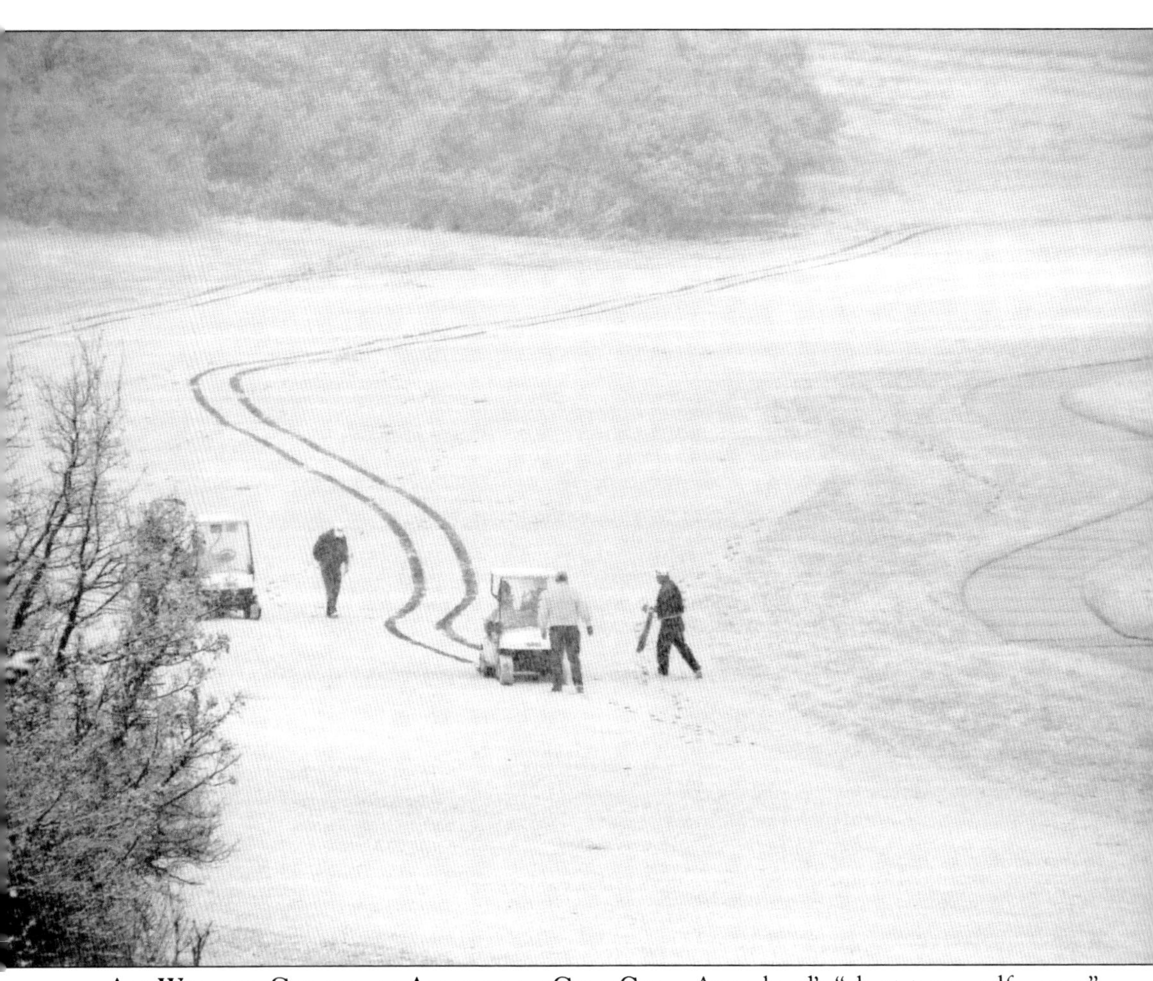

ALL-WEATHER GOLFING AT ARROWHEAD GOLF CLUB. Arrowhead's "ghost town golf course" moniker is no longer remembered. Now, it is not unusual to see golfers playing during inclement weather. In this photograph, three unidentified golfers may be looking for golf balls in the snow. Arrowhead has received dozens of awards for "best golf course," "and "best wedding venue." Social media kudos credit it as one of Colorado's favorite public courses. (Greg Liptak Collection.)

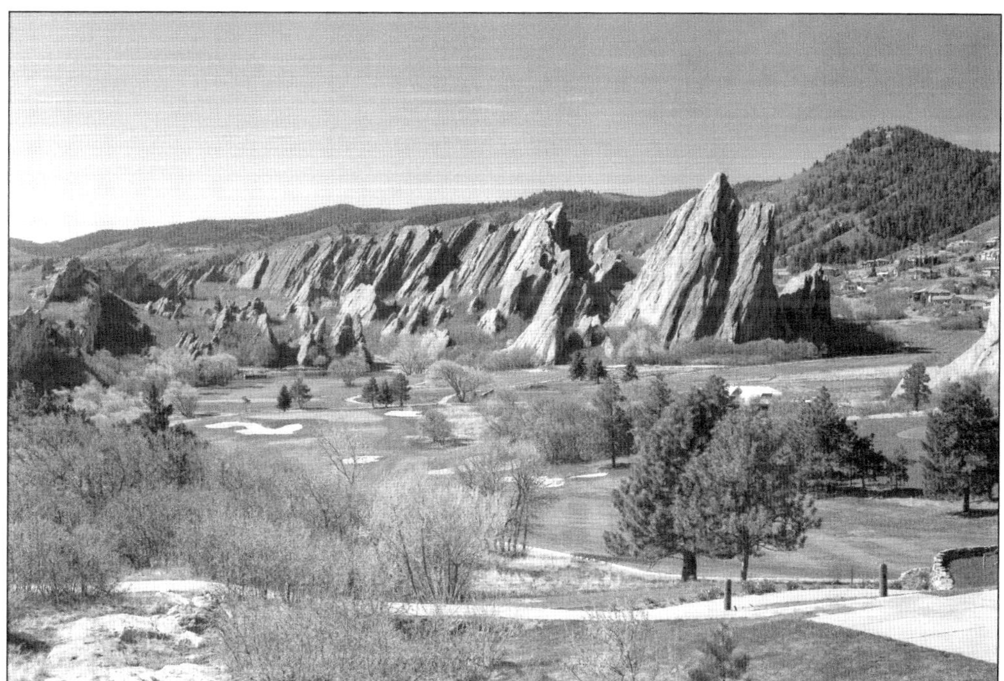

PICTURESQUE ARROWHEAD GOLF CLUB. This photograph was taken from east of Arrowhead's scenic 10th fairway. To the right is a site overlooking the course that has been used for countless weddings. (Lance W. Moreland)

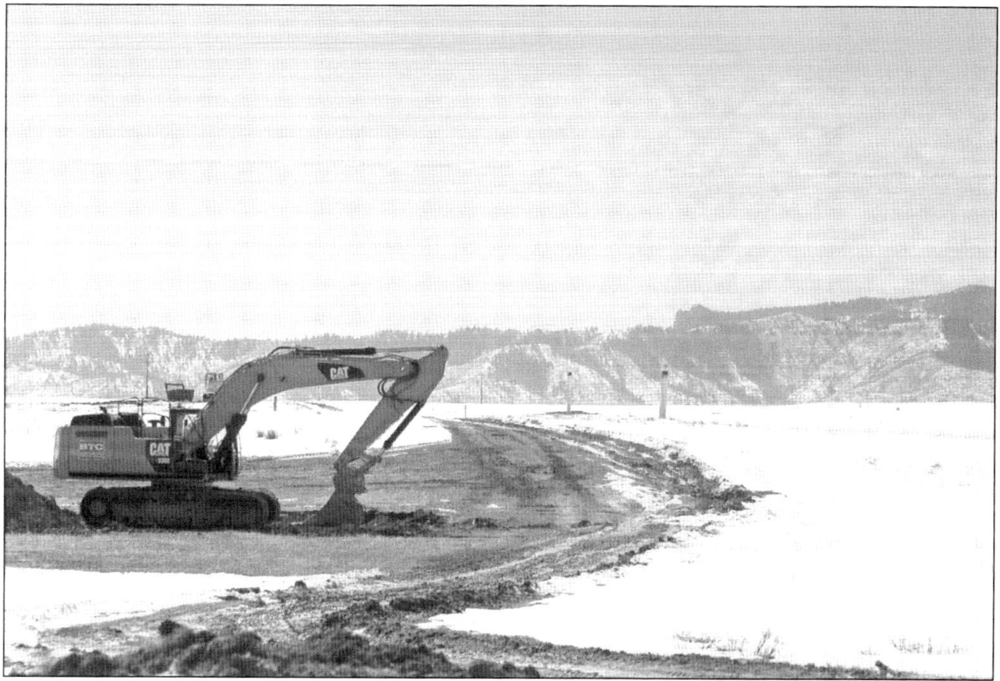

A SMALL SIGN OF A BIG CHANGE. A lone backhoe sits on the high plains on a yet unfinished winding road. Roxborough's hogbacks and Pike National Forest are visible in the background. (Tom Olkowski.)

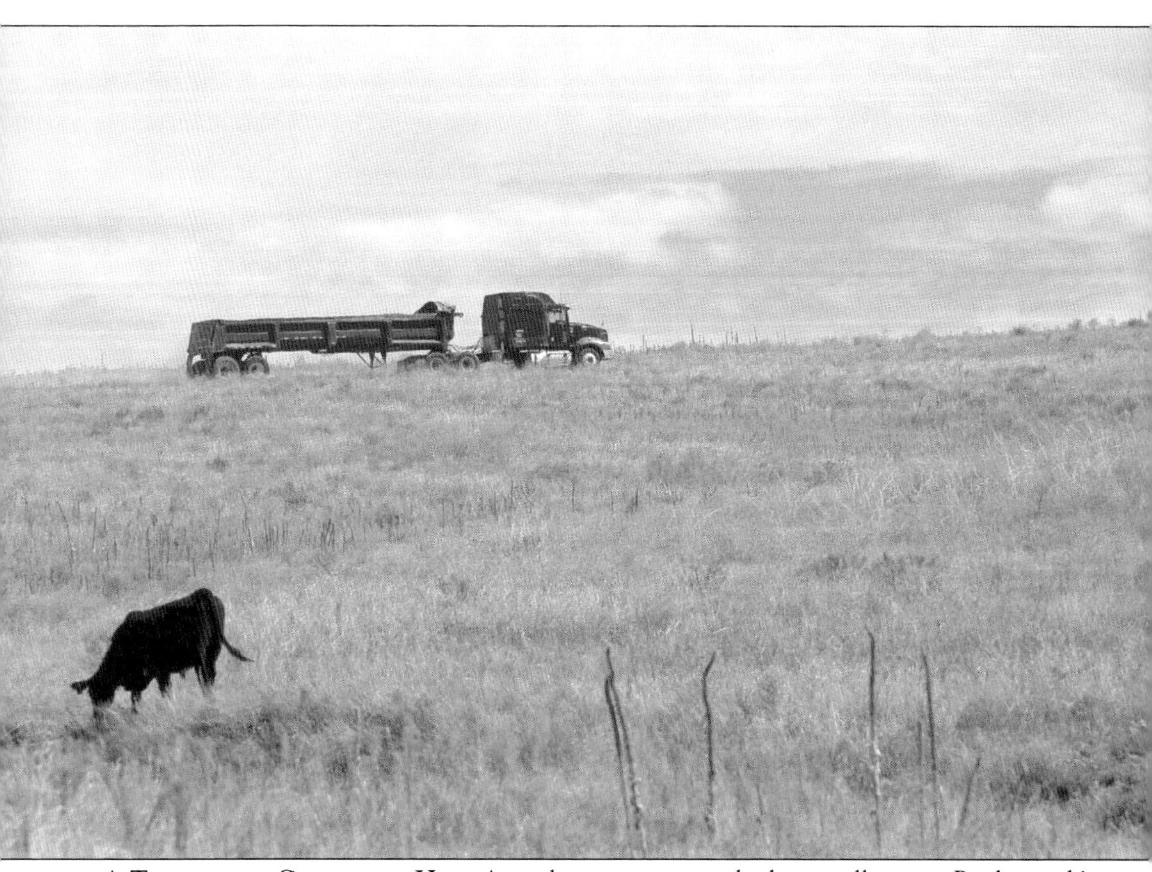

A Truck and a Cow on the Hill. A single cow grazing on high grass illustrates Roxborough's history. Once filled with cattle ranches, the open range is gradually being changed—as evidenced by the truck on the ridge. The high prairie grasslands and rolling hills that reach towards the forest and mountains will soon be home to thousands of new residents. (Tom Olkowski.)

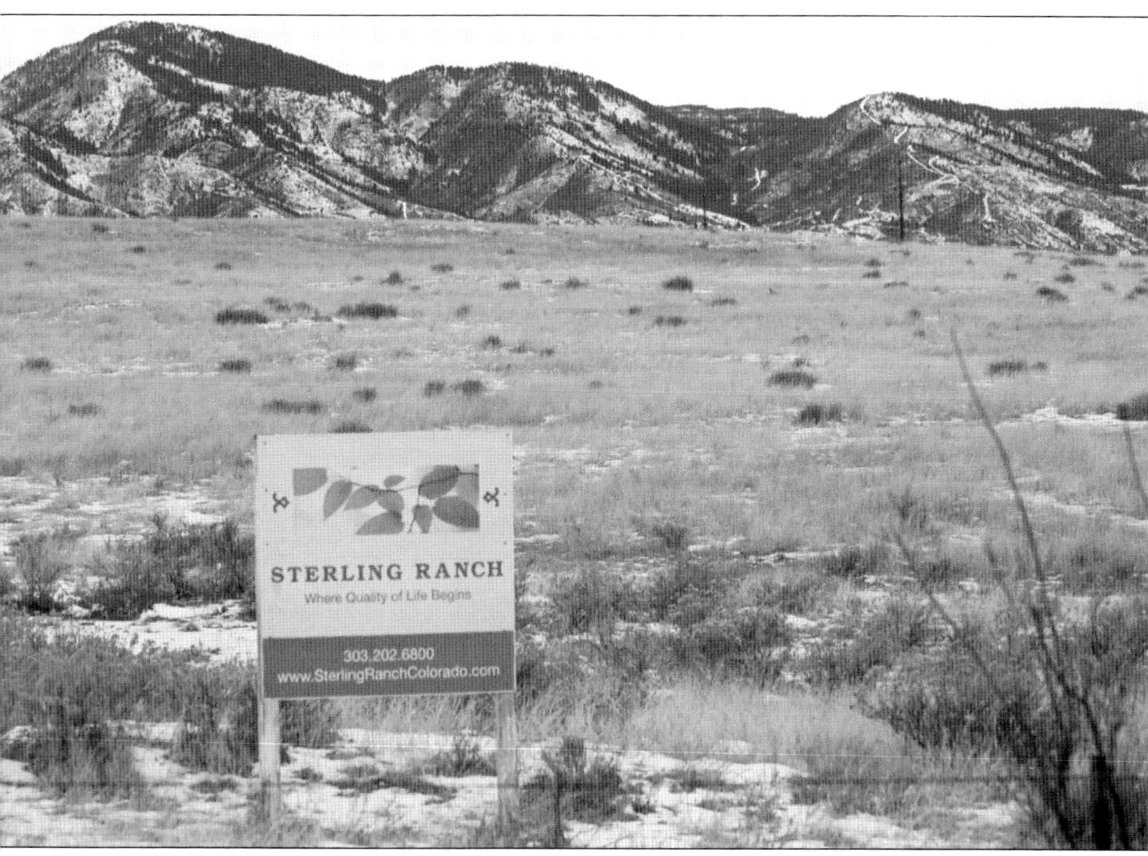

Sterling Ranch's Posted Sign. Late in 2015, it was announced that five homebuilders were selected to develop Providence Village, the first of nine villages to be built on 3,400 acres. Sterling Ranch's master plan calls for 12,000 homes. Projections estimate that these will house 30,000 residents. National builder Shea Homes will develop 1,250 homes on 380 acres south of Chatfield State Park. (Tom Olkowski.)